D1480856

THERE'S NO SUCH THING AS BAD WEATHER

A Scandinavian Mom's Secrets for Raising
Healthy, Resilient, and Confident Kids
(from *Friluftsliv* to *Hygge*)

LINDA ÅKESON McGURK

TOUCHSTONE
New York   London   Toronto   Sydney   New Delhi

Touchstone
An Imprint of Simon & Schuster, Inc.
1230 Avenue of the Americas
New York, NY 10020

First Touchstone hardcover edition October 2017

TOUCHSTONE and colophon are registered trademarks of Simon & Schuster, Inc.

Some names and identifying details have been changed.

For information about special discounts for bulk purchases, please
contact Simon & Schuster Special Sales at 1-866-506-1949
or business@simonandschuster.com.

The Simon & Schuster Speakers Bureau can bring authors to
your live event. For more information or to book an event, contact the
Simon & Schuster Speakers Bureau at 1-866-248-3049 or visit our
website at www.simonspeakers.com.

Interior design by Jill Putorti

Manufactured in the United States of America

10 9 8 7 6 5 4 3 2 1

Library of Congress Cataloging-in-Publication Data is available.

ISBN 978-1-5011-4362-5
ISBN 978-1-5011-4364-9 (ebook)

For Maya and Nora

We have such a brief opportunity to pass on to our children our love for this Earth, and to tell our stories. These are the moments when the world is made whole.

—RICHARD LOUV

CONTENTS

GLOSSARY
OF SCANDINAVIAN TERMS

allemansrätten—The right of public access, a common law that gives the general public in Sweden extensive rights to recreate in nature, including hiking, camping, and foraging for berries and mushrooms on private property. Slightly different versions of the law exist in Norway and Finland.

allmän förskola—Sweden's universal preschool system that offers part-time and full-time care all year-round at heavily subsidized rates.

barnträdgård—The Swedish version of German Friedrich Froebel's original kindergartens. Adopted in Sweden at the end of the nineteenth century and replaced by the universal preschool system in the 1950s.

barnvagn—The type of sturdy pram that is favored by Scandinavian parents and frequently used for letting babies nap outdoors.

educare—A term that is sometimes used to describe the Scandinavian model of simultaneously caring for and educating preschool-age children whose parents work outside the home.

farfar—Paternal grandfather.

farmor—Paternal grandmother.

fika—A casual get-together that usually involves coffee or tea and a pastry. Popular activity for moms and dads on parental leave.

forest school—Preschools/day cares where children spend most of the day playing and learning outdoors, all year-round, regardless of the weather. Also known as forest kindergarten or nature-based preschool in the US.

friluftsliv—Roughly translates to "open-air life" and is used to describe a culture and a way of life that heavily revolve around exploring and enjoying nature in a noncompetitive fashion.

fritids—A subsidized after-school program for school-age children in Sweden, Denmark, and Norway that generally offers arts and crafts, games, physical activity, homework help, and outdoor play.

galonisar—Polyester rain pants that typically come in the form of overalls and are essential for protecting both child and regular clothes during messy outdoor play.

hygge—The Danish way of fighting the long, dark winter by creating a cozy atmosphere and enjoying the good things in life with friends and family. Often involves lighting candles.

inskolning—The process of gradually easing a child into a preschool routine, during which time a parent accompanies the child to the preschool for the entire day or part of the day. Depending on the child, this process can take anywhere between a few days to several weeks.

midsommar—A celebration of the summer solstice in June that involves dancing around a maypole, singing traditional songs, and making flower wreaths. Rivals Christmas as the most popular holiday in Sweden.

morfar—Maternal grandfather.

mormor—Maternal grandmother.

mula—Popular childhood pastime that involves shoving snow in an unsuspecting person's face.

Mulle—An imaginary forest troll that inspires children to care about nature, created by the Swedish Outdoor Association in the 1950s. Can also be used in a generic way to describe somebody who is extremely outdoorsy or "crunchy."

saft—A sweet, typically berry-flavored drink popular with children, especially in the summertime.

school forest—Privately owned woods set aside for use by preschools and schools for outdoor play and learning. Typically permits activities that go beyond *allemansrätten*, such as marking trails and building shelters.

Skogsmulle—(See "*Mulle*")

skolefritidsordning—(Danish. See "*fritids*")

solfattig—"Sun poor." A term frequently used by meteorologists to describe Scandinavian summers.

udeskole—Danish for "outdoor school." A cross-disciplinary approach to teaching in which children between the ages of seven and sixteen learn outside on a regular basis.

uppehållsväder—The Swedish term used to describe a brief pause between two rainy periods.

valborg—An annual Swedish celebration of the spring that occurs on April 30 and usually involves choral singing, racy student parades, and bonfires.

öppna förskolan—Swedish for "open preschool," a free program that offers a meeting place for parents on leave and provides developmentally appropriate activities for babies and children of up to five years.

THERE'S
NO SUCH
THING AS
BAD WEATHER

INTRODUCTION

A Swedish Mother in Rural Indiana

"I don't want to go outside."

My four-year-old daughter Nora is standing in the mudroom, heels dug into the floor, lips pouting, and arms crossed in protest.

Her sister, seven-year-old Maya, chimes in:

"Do we *have* to, Mommy?"

They look like I just asked them to clean their rooms or, worse, offered them a bowl of fermented brussels sprouts.

"I want to watch a movie instead."

"But there's fresh snow on the ground. SNOW! Do you want to build a snowman?" I sing, channeling my inner Anna, betting that their obsession with all things *Frozen* will win them over. I know that if I can only get them outside they will soon start rolling around in the snow and quickly forget all about *Barbie: A Fashion Fairytale*. The hard part is getting there.

"It's cold outside!" Maya moans. "Why do we always have to go outside?"

At this point I'm tempted to tell them all about how we used to play way back when the TV had only two stations (neither of which showed cartoons, except on Saturday mornings), computer games had to be loaded from a cassette tape, and I had to walk three miles to school with snow up to my knees, uphill both ways. Instead, when I open my mouth, my first-grade teacher comes out.

"There's no such thing as bad weather, only bad clothes!" I blurt out a little too cheerily in my attempt to conceal my growing annoyance.

The kids stare at me in utter disbelief. Then Nora screams, "I hate my snow pants!" and throws herself on the floor, kicking off her new insulated pants, inchworm-style.

Deep breaths. Count to ten.

"How about we try going outside for fifteen minutes and see what it's like? Then we can decide whether to stay out a little longer or go back inside."

With this compromise in place, we finally head out the door, into the cold February morning. I'm already sweating from the effort of putting snow pants, boots, a fleece jacket, mittens, a winter jacket, a neck gaiter, and a hat on a squirming child, and slightly exhausted from the heated negotiations. And I can't help but wonder what the heck is wrong with kids these days—why don't they want to play outside?

We drive down to the local city park in the small Midwestern town I call home. The air is brisk, the sky a saturated cobalt blue. We see a couple of squirrels chasing each other up a tree on the way. Aside from that, we might as well be walking on the moon. There are no cars on the streets, no children outside, no sounds. The town is literally shut down. The night before, the weather forecast had called for a chance of one to three inches of snow. In anticipation of being pounded with snow, sleet, and ice, people rushed home from work to fill up their generators and get last-minute staples from the store. By the end of the night, the bread and milk aisles at Walmart looked like a Cold War–era shopping mall in Moscow. The area schools announced that they were going to be on a two-hour delay, and most nonessential activities were canceled preemptively. Come morning, the schools' planned two-hour delay had turned into a full closure—better known as a "snow day"—and the local government had shut down as well.

Everywhere we go, including the park's small sledding hill, the snow is virtually untouched. Initially, Maya and Nora are too excited about the dusting of snow to pay attention to the compact silence. The girls make fresh tracks in the downy powder and throw themselves on the ground to make snow angels, giggling and talking nonstop. Then Maya, who by now has forgotten all about the mudroom drama and her own vocal protests, looks around and notices that something is awry. "Mommy, where are all the other kids?" she asks. "Why aren't they at the park?"

Her question brings me back to a different time and place. I was born and raised in Sweden, in a town that is on roughly the same latitude as the Gulf of Alaska. Growing up, my friends and I spent our free time mostly digging in dirt, climbing trees, collecting slugs, racing our pet rabbits, bruising our legs, and crisscrossing the neighborhood on our bikes. In the winter, we skied, skated, rode sleds down steep tree-lined hills, ate snow from those same hills, built forts of questionable quality, and occasionally entertained ourselves with shoving snow in unsuspecting peers' faces (an act commonly referred to as *mula*).

At preschool, we played for hours outside every day, rain or shine, and at elementary school, indoor recess was only allowed if there was a realistic chance of death by lightning. We knew that whining about it was pointless. We were expected to dress for the weather and endure the elements. And as we headed toward the small woods that bordered our school yard we quickly forgot about the inclement weather as sticks turned into horses, trees became castles, and we immersed ourselves in pretend play.

At the time, research about nature's positive effects on the well-being of children (and adults, for that matter) was in its infancy, but the adults in our lives still instinctively knew the benefits of a walk in the woods. If anybody had asked them why they made us play outside every day, the answer would likely have been as simple as it was obvious: "Because fresh air is good for you."

Scandinavia's nature-centric culture, embodied in the term *friluftsliv* (which loosely translates to "open-air life"), is not just the sum of all outdoor activities people take part in. It's a way of life that to this day is considered key to raising healthy, well-rounded, and eco-conscious children. As research supporting the health benefits of spending time in nature has emerged, more and more schools and nurseries in Scandinavia have been making outdoor time a priority. Recess, most of which is spent outside, already makes up approximately 20 percent of the school day in Sweden. Many schools are moving more of their instructional time outside as well. Forest schools—nurseries where children spend the better part of the day outside, all year-round—are an increasingly popular choice among nature-loving parents.

In Sweden, nature is not an abstract concept that is taught only on Earth Day and through textbooks about bees and butterflies. It's an integral part of everyday life. Daily interaction with nature has helped turn many children, myself included, into passionate advocates for the environment. Not surprisingly, Scandinavia is also a world leader when it comes to renewable energy, recycling, and sustainable living.

Until I moved to the US and had children myself, the concept of playing outside every day was so ordinary to me that I thought it was a universal parenting practice. But as my children grew older and I stood in many more deserted playgrounds, in summer as well as winter, I started to realize that playing outdoors is not the norm here—at least not anymore. Even though most parents and educators recognize the benefits of unstructured outdoor play, research shows that this generation of children plays outside significantly less than their parents did. One cross-sectional study representing four million children in the US showed that roughly half of all preschoolers don't have daily outdoor playtime, even though the American Academy of Pediatrics recommends encouraging "children to play outside as much as possible." Older children don't fare much better, with digital entertainment on average now eating up nearly fifty-three hours of their time every week. By the time they reach their teens, only 10 percent of American children report spending time outside every day, according to the Nature Conservancy.

Meanwhile, many schools are cutting recess to cram more required instruction into a day that hardly had any free time to begin with, not even for the youngest students. Cities are banning sledding out of fear of lawsuits. At home, fear of traffic, abduction, and nature itself, coupled with frenzied extracurricular schedules, is keeping more and more children inside, where they are becoming increasingly dependent on screens for entertainment. Streets and parks that used to teem with children are now empty. Simultaneous with this development, obesity, diabetes, and ADHD and other behavioral problems have become rampant, with American children now being three times more likely to be medicated with stimulants and antidepressants than their European peers.

But what if more toddlers spent their days watching real birds instead of playing Angry Birds on their iPads? What if more kindergartners actually got to grow gardens? What if more schools increased the length of recess instead of the number of standardized tests? And what if more children who *act* out were allowed to *get* out?

INTRODUCTION

Standing at this empty playground in the rural Midwest, I decide that it's time for a fact-finding mission. It's been twelve years since I left Scandinavia and more than twenty-five since I was a child there, so the culture has undoubtedly changed in profound ways since then. Do people over there still know how to raise healthy, nature-loving children in an increasingly high-tech world, and, if so, how do they do it?

Could the Scandinavians in fact be onto a great parenting secret?

1

A RIGHT TO NATURE

The wild is a voice that never stops whispering.
—DANIEL CROCKETT

When I went to Perth, Australia, as an exchange student in college, I really didn't expect to come back with much more than a great tan and a backpack full of good memories. Instead, I returned with a boyfriend from rural Indiana. On one of our first dates, he told me that as a child he used to build dams with debris in the creek in his backyard. In a different creek in Sweden, I used to clear the debris from the stream so that the water could flow freely. We were immediately drawn to each other.

As it turns out, the unlikely union between a Swedish environmentalist and a Midwestern industrialist had more staying power than our families would ever have imagined, and after we graduated we decided to move to Montana, where my husband had spent many of his school holidays skiing with his family. Fresh out of journalism school, I got my first job working for a start-up internet business that might as well have served as the inspiration for the movie *Office Space*, complete with soulless cubicles, mysterious forms, and disgruntled white-collar employees, who were all kept in check by an overzealous supervisor. Still, the move was a smooth transition for me. The mountains reminded me of home, the wildlife was spectacular, and the intensity and length of the winters rivaled those of my homeland.

Bozeman, where we lived, was in the middle of a transition from sleepy ranching community with world-class fly-fishing waters to hipster college town and up-and-coming vacation spot for people from all over the US. This change was not well received by everybody, but with my Scandinavian lineage and experience with harsh weather I fit the mold of a "true" Montanan and was readily accepted by the locals. In contrast, anybody who was the slightest bit hesitant to driving in heavy snow or complained about the cold was jokingly dismissed as a "Californian," whether they were actually from the Golden State or not. Ironically, most of the people who complained about out-of-staters were themselves from somewhere else. Being a Montanan, it turned out, was not so much about the stamp on your birth certificate but more of a state of mind. Success was not measured by how many steps you had climbed on the corporate ladder but rather by how many days you had spent in a tent instead of a cubicle. Wealth was not necessarily measured by the size of your bank account but by how much elk meat you had in your freezer. Skills were assessed not according to what you had learned from a textbook but by how you handled real-life challenges like how to avoid getting buried by an avalanche or attacked by a grizzly bear.

I was clearly not in Sweden anymore. Most of the people I now hung out with put me to shame with their in-depth knowledge of nature and advanced wilderness survival skills. One thing was for sure: If I ever stood face-to-face with the Apocalypse I would grab onto a seasoned Montanan in a heartbeat and not let go.

But I noticed that, parallel with this hard-core outdoor culture, there were forces at work in American society that seemed to create a divide between humans and nature. One of the first lessons I learned in my new homeland was that pretty much all the things I was used to doing either on foot or by using public transportation in Scandinavia could be done without ever exiting your car in Montana. Here, you could go straight from your comfortably heated or air-conditioned house in the morning to your equally comfortable climate-controlled car and drive to work. Actually, this was the only way to get to work unless you lived within walking or biking distance, since public transportation was nonexistent. At lunch, you could go to one of a slew of fast-food restaurants with a drive-through window, idle in line for ten minutes, and then inhale your lunch while running errands in your vehicle. Returning a movie at the video store? There was a drive-by box for that. Mailing a letter? No need to get out of the car. Buying a six-pack? Give your order to the guy at the drive-up window. Even bank errands could be done from the driver's seat. At school, parents waited in their vehicles in a long, winding line until a teacher with a walkie-talkie called on their child to come outside. I had never seen anything like it.

Many roads lacked sidewalks, and just walking across the parking lot at the mall sometimes seemed borderline suicidal. Then again, assuming that I made it, all the stores I could ever need were conveniently located under one roof. I noticed that some people even went to the mall to exercise, walking or jogging down the long corridors. This phenomenon was so well established that they had a name: mall walkers. I was intrigued. I could understand why some older people would want to avoid slippery sidewalks or bumpy trails in the woods, but I saw people of all ages participate in this activity. What were they doing in here when the awe-inspiring Rocky Mountains—and all that they had to offer in terms of outdoor recreation—were just a stone's throw away? I obviously still had some cultural codes to crack.

Since so many people just seemed to be moving from one climate-controlled indoor environment to another, there was no need to dress for the elements, and I found that people often dressed as if they didn't expect to go outside at all, not even putting on a coat in the dead of winter. In one of my columns for a Swedish newspaper, I wrote that, due to the way American society was designed, most people could probably get by with walking less than a thousand feet per day. Now I was starting to think that this was an overly generous estimate.

Back then, I didn't reflect much on what all this might mean if we were to have children. We were too busy enjoying our carefree lives. The biggest decisions we had to make at the time were where to go camping and which peak to hike come the weekend, and we were pretty contented with that. But as I neared my thirties and the idea of having children beckoned, we decided that it was time to move back to my husband's hometown in Indiana to be closer to family. I was yet again about to embark on a cultural journey.

There Is No Such Thing as Bad Weather

In Scandinavia, where I was born and raised, it would be very easy to make excuses for not going outside. The northern part of Scandinavia—which truly comprises Sweden, Denmark, and Norway, but for all practical purposes of this book also will include our eastern neighbor, Finland, which shares much of the same culture—reaches well beyond the Arctic Circle, and the climate in the region is partly subarctic. Heavy snowfall is common in the winter, especially up north, although white Christmases are not guaranteed. The Gulf Stream helps moderate the temperature, especially along the western coasts, making it warmer than is typical of other places on the same latitude. Still, anybody who has spent a winter in Scandinavia knows that it is not for the faint of heart. Temperatures can range from Let's Bring out the Patio Furniture to I Think My Eyelids Just Froze

Shut, but one facet of Scandinavian winters always remains constant: the darkness.

Each year for twenty-seven days, peaking with the winter solstice in late December, the polar nights blanket northern Scandinavia. During that time, the sun doesn't rise over the horizon at all, and life enters the twilight zone. Literally. The south is less unforgiving, offering up to seven hours of precious daylight per day in January. Even then, overcast skies often submerge Scandinavia in a perpetual semi-dusk-like state that has a way of putting people's resilience to the ultimate test. How bad is it? Consider that in 2014 the Swedish capital of Stockholm logged just three hours of sunshine for the whole month of November, a new record. "People on the streets are ready to start eating each other," a friend exasperatedly reported toward the end of the month. "The zombie apocalypse is here."

Every Scandinavian has his or her own way of dealing with the dark winters. The Finnish stay awake by drinking more coffee than people anywhere else in the world. The Swedes build elaborate sunrooms and go on vacations to Thailand. The Danish have *hygge*, one of those unique phenomena that doesn't translate well but evokes images of a family cozying up in front of a fireplace, drinking hot chocolate, and playing board games. The Norwegians eat cod-liver oil to boost their vitamin D levels and seek refuge in their rustic cabins in the woods. Many a Scandinavian has dreamed of calling it quits and moving to warmer, sunnier, and more hospitable latitudes. Some entertain the idea every winter, and a few retirees actually act on it. But more than anything, Scandinavians get through the winter by maintaining a sense of normalcy. Snow happens. Sleet happens. Ice happens. Cold temperatures happen. Life goes on. The trains may not run on time after a big snow dump, but society doesn't shut down either. Weather-related school closures are virtually unheard-of.

In the spring, crocuses and coltsfoots start poking through the ground, the days keep getting longer, and vitamin D stores are finally replenished. In the cities, wool blankets pop up on café patios—a sign as sure as any that the season is about to turn. As the snowmelt starts to drip from the rooftops, survivors of the seemingly everlasting winter flock to the cafés, wrap themselves in blankets, and turn their translucent faces toward the fickle sunshine. The fact that it's forty degrees Fahrenheit outside is irrelevant; by Scandinavian standards it's completely acceptable to enjoy a latte wearing mittens. And by June, when Scandinavians celebrate *midsommar* by making flower wreaths, dancing around a maypole, and worshipping at the altar of the sun that never sets, they are ready to recommit to their homeland, body and light-starved soul.

In the summertime, the weather can be a toss-up, occasionally sunny and warm in the south, where the majority of the population lives, but quite often cool, cloudy, and rainy. More than three days straight of temperatures in the seventies is pretty much considered a heat wave, and it's no coincidence that Swedish supposedly is the only language that boasts the word *uppehållsväder* to describe a break between two periods of intense rainfall. *Solfattig*—"sun poor"—is another commonly used Swedish weather term that speaks for itself. On those few precious summer days when balmy temperatures and cobalt skies converge in perfect harmony, anybody voluntarily staying inside would be declared legally insane. "Whenever the weather is nice, you really feel like you have to take advantage of it. That's what our parents always told us, and that's how I feel with my kids," says Cecilia, a mother of two in Stockholm.

Considering the capricious nature of the Scandinavian climate, it's maybe no wonder that the saying "There is no such thing as bad weather, only bad clothes" originated here. It probably started as a coping strategy, or was perhaps born out of defiance of the weather powers that be. If you were ever a child in Scandinavia, you've heard this phrase more times than you care to count, from teachers, parents, grandparents, and other adults in your life. As a result, Scandinavians grow up with a certain resilience to the weather. The children who once dressed in rain gear from head to toe to go out to recess or play in the woods after school turn into adults who feel a certain urgency about getting outside every day. "If I don't get outside every day, I go crazy. And if I don't have time to take my son out after work I feel guilty about it. I think it's a very Scandinavian thing to feel that way," says Linda, a Swedish friend of mine.

Several researchers have spent much of their careers trying to figure out why Scandinavians are so consumed with the idea of getting their progeny outside every day. One theory is that it is a form of precaution. We believe that outdoor play is good for kids, but we cannot necessarily pinpoint why. We can tell that it's not hurting them, and we worry about what would happen if they didn't have it.

The government is also heavily invested in promoting outdoor recreation for children and adults alike as a preventive health measure. For example, the health care system in Sweden's Skåne region encourages parents to get outside with their children from an early age as a way to prevent obesity and establish a healthy lifestyle from the get-go. "We all know that fresh air and movement benefit both your appetite and sleep," says an informative pamphlet for new parents. "That is true not only for older children and adults, but fresh air every day makes small children feel well too. This also establishes good habits and a desire to exercise."

The idea that fresh air and outdoor play are crucial to good health is so prevalent that it has even found some unlikely champions in the pharmaceutical industry. Kronans Apotek, one of the largest pharmacy chains in Sweden, offers the following advice for flu season on its website: "The first step toward fewer runny noses and less coughing is to let the child spend as much time outside as possible," the company says. "When children are outside, the physical distance between them increases, which reduces the risk for contagion through direct contact or the air. The more time spent outside the better."

Aside from the obvious personal health aspects, having positive outdoor experiences in childhood is seen as a way to build a lifelong relationship with nature. To paraphrase David Sobel, advocate of place-based education and author of *Beyond Ecophobia: Reclaiming the Heart in Nature Education*, if we want children to care about nature, they need to spend time in it first.

"Do You Need a Ride, Hon?"

The sweet corn is just starting to tassel when we move cross-country, into a turn-of-the-century home in rural Indiana. We start the mother of all remodeling jobs, gutting the house room by room. Around the same time, I'm starting to feel the ticktock of the infamous biological clock, which is interesting, since I've always felt awkward around children and didn't realize until I was in my twenties that I wanted to have some of my own. Now it's the only thing I want, aside from a new kitchen.

In between working as a freelance writer and tearing out carpet, I explore my new hometown on foot. With two black Labs in tow, I quickly become an object of curiosity. People that I've never met or talked to come up to me and start chitchatting like they know me, simply because they've seen me walking my dogs. Cars slow and people roll their windows down to shout friendly comments. On Facebook I get questions from strangers about my training methods, and people are constantly awed by how well my dogs walk together. (For the record, this is purely an illusion; in reality, they are constantly tugging in different directions. Barney, the youngest, was once singled out by a trainer during an obedience class as an example of how not to behave.) In Sweden my entourage wouldn't raise any eyebrows, as going for walks is a popular form of outdoor recreation all year-round. Here, I quickly become The Woman Who Walks with Dogs.

At some point in between refinishing the living room floors and painting the guest bedroom, I take a pregnancy test and finally see the two pink lines I coveted. The guest bedroom, it turns out, is going to be a nursery. I keep walking and prepare for the new arrival.

With a tiny life growing inside me, I'm heading into uncharted territory. I was never a natural with children and I know it. As a child I was more interested in listening in on the adults' conversations than in playing with their kids and their Barbies. And the precocious child I once was turned into an adult who gravitates toward predictability and structure. My life runs on a schedule. I'm set in my ways. I make to-do lists and get a kick out of checking things off. The books in my bookcase are, if not alphabetized, then at least neatly organized by category. Given all of this, I realize that I have to approach motherhood from a different, more intellectual angle. I start devouring books about pregnancy, Lamaze, breastfeeding, and child-rearing. It's a brave new world. Not only does this literature represent my first introduction to the many parenting styles I'm expected to choose from, it's also full of intriguing new phrases like "baby wearing," "tummy time," and "elimination communication." Despite the fact that my experience with babies is limited, to say the least, and my ideas of parenting mostly stem from the way my parents raised me, I know exactly what I want for this child. Natural childbirth—check. Cloth diapers in gender-neutral colors—check. Homemade, organic baby food—check.

On a February afternoon nine months into my pregnancy—twelve days before my due date, to be exact—I take the dogs for a walk around the trail that encompasses the town, six miles in total. (Actually, the dogs walk: I waddle like an obese penguin suffering from a bad hernia.) At one point an older guy with a big, dark mustache and an even bigger grin drives by in his pickup truck and honks at this spectacular sight. Toward the end of the walk I can literally feel the baby's head between my legs. Less than twelve hours later my water breaks and we are on our way to the hospital. The next morning, after an epic sunrise and a not-so-epic pushing phase, Maya is born in a tub of water, just as I had planned. Water birth—check.

Had I lived in Sweden, my motherhood experience would have followed a predictable pattern at this point. The Scandinavian countries lead the world in terms of paid parental leave, and Swedish parents get a total of 480 days, with a certain quota reserved for the mother and father, respectively, plus unpaid leave for up to three years. This means the chances of me knowing at least a half dozen people who were on maternal leave at any given time would be pretty good, and I would have devoted my days to doing everything that is expected of a Scandinavian mom. In a simplified breakdown, this would be breastfeeding, napping, and caring for the baby. Sometimes I would get together with other moms for *fika* (generally understood as a coffee break accompanied by a pastry) and take walks in the park or around town, possibly with a stop at an *öppna förskolan*, or "open preschool," a free resource that provides developmentally appropriate activities for babies and children up to five years and, maybe more important, gives parents on leave a chance to socialize and treat cabin fever. Then I would have gone home and napped some more. When my child was around the age of eighteen months, I, like 84 percent of all Swedish parents, would enroll her at a government-subsidized preschool and go back to work. As anybody who has ever cared for an infant knows, it is rarely easy: naturally, Scandinavian moms struggle with the same hormonal roller coasters, sleepless nights, blown-out diapers, and bouts with postpartum depression as their American counterparts. But having a stable income without the pressure of going back to work soon after the birth undoubtedly softens the transition to parenthood and gives Scandinavian parents a chance to bond with their baby at a crucial time of their development.

In the US, I discover that mothers—and fathers, too, for that matter—don't have these luxuries, as labor laws grant very few rights to parents who want to stay home with their baby. Those who do usually have to do it on their own dime, as the US ranks at the bottom of all industrialized nations when it comes to parental leave, guaranteeing only twelve weeks off after the birth of a child. If you work for the government or a private company with more than fifty employees, that is. Only a little more than half of all American moms meet those criteria, and nearly a quarter of American moms go back to work just two weeks after giving birth. Forget about pay, unless you work for an unusually generous employer.

Considering the limitations of maternity leave in the US, it's not a big surprise that I have trouble connecting with other moms after Maya is born. Most of them are probably at work. And those who aren't don't seem to think that late winter is a good time to socialize. At least not outside. I see no other strollers during my daily walks. The park, where I would've expected to find at least a few mothers or babysitters, is deserted and the gate to the main entrance locked. "I wish it was summer so my baby and I could go for walks," a fellow mom tells me when she and her son come over to our house for a visit. "When do you think it would be safe for me to take him outside?" I'm puzzled over the question, since I've never even considered it not safe to take Maya outside in the cold. Slowly, I'm beginning to understand that my perspective on parenting in some ways is vastly different from that of my American peers.

Until this point, I had felt, if not as American as a peanut-butter-and-jelly sandwich, then at least like a pretty well assimilated citizen. To get there I had jumped through all the hoops, filled out all the required forms, taken the tests, and spent countless hours waiting with other hopeful foreigners in drably carpeted government rooms that felt like they had had their already dull life sucked out of them. Then, in 2008, I had finally become sworn in as a naturalized American. Sure, I still mispronounced English words like *porcupine* and *adage* every now and then, and I'd probably never fully grasp the fine print of my American health insurance policy, but overall I had adjusted well to life in my new home country. Even though there were many things I missed about Sweden—seeing my family only about once a year was the hardest part—I was excited about becoming a full citizen, with all the rights and responsibilities that it entailed.

The naturalization certificate should have made me feel more American than ever. Ironically, the opposite happened, because that same year I also became a parent. I think most moms and dads have an idea of what they want for their children, based on their own upbringing. We pass on our ideas, belief systems, and traditions to the next generation to leave our small imprint on the world long after we're gone. Our attitudes about parenting are thoroughly steeped in cultural norms, and our children in a way become an extension of ourselves. We try to re-create the good experiences and eliminate the bad ones, giving our children the best childhoods we can feasibly offer them. This is true of most American as well as Scandinavian parents; we just have different ways of getting there. This soon became obvious to me in many ways.

When Maya is about two months old, I gradually start working from home again. Luckily, she's a good napper. But as she approaches the six-month mark it gets increasingly hard for me to get work done, and I sometimes need to travel for interviews and work-related events. It's time to get a part-time babysitter. As is often the case in small towns, childcare is mainly provided by relatives, churches, or stay-at-home moms who are looking to make a little extra money. There are also a few larger in-home day cares run by older women with grown children. After some searching and asking around, I find a sweet young woman who has a son Maya's age. She and her husband have recently moved to town and she's planning to watch only a few children to make a little extra grocery money. The house that they rent is small but clean, and adjoining it is a large fenced-in backyard where I envision Maya tumbling around with her new little friends. Perfect.

It doesn't take long before I realize that while Scandinavian parents obsess over their kids getting outside to play every day, this is not necessarily the cultural norm here. Maya is not getting out nearly as much as I had hoped; instead, she seems to be spending her days mostly watching TV. When winter rolls around, outdoor playtime grinds to a total halt. Granted, this is not completely the babysitter's fault: A lot of times the other kids in the group arrive in the morning with no jacket and wearing only thin sneakers, which are not really conducive to rolling around in the snow or stomping in mud. The parents clearly had no expectation of them going outside and dressed them accordingly. Playing outside in the winter, I figure, must not be a thing here.

To cure my guilt for Maya's lack of outdoor playtime at day

care, I take her for hikes and walks as often as I can. When she is almost a year old, I'm walking her to the sitter's house on a beautiful but cold winter day when a white SUV pulls up next to us and a woman who looks to be in her fifties rolls down the window and pops out her head. "Do you need a ride, hon? It's really cold out there," she says. I thank her for the offer but politely decline. "We're both well bundled up and I enjoy the fresh air," I tell her. "Are you sure?" she says, looking genuinely alarmed. She drives off with a puzzled look on her face, and I can tell that the idea that I would voluntarily take my daughter for a walk in fifteen-degree weather (−9°C) is beyond her. I'm equally surprised that a complete stranger would offer a ride to me, my baby, a decent-size stroller, and one ginormous diaper bag. Getting that kind of mess into my own car seemed like hard work a lot of the time. As it turns out, this will not be the last time a friendly Midwesterner takes pity on me.

When Maya is three years old and the locals are finally starting to get used to my entourage, her little sister, Nora, is born. Getting around town on foot with a new baby in the mix takes some ingenuity. I order a stroller board—a platform with wheels that attaches to the back of the stroller—which allows Maya to ride behind her sister either standing or sitting while Nora is lying in the stroller. Once again, in Sweden this is not an uncommon way for parents to get around with multiple children, but here it's a surefire way of flying your freak flag. With the two dogs in one hand and the stroller in the other, I don't just cause people to turn their heads. They roll down their car windows and tell me they wish they had their camera. One morning, a woman walking a small dog on the other side of the street actually pulls out her cell phone and snaps a picture of us, as if we were an exotic exhibit at the zoo.

That fall, Maya starts preschool and I get a chance to meet

some more parents. At the school's Thanksgiving party, I'm chatting with some other moms, when the grandmother of one of Maya's classmates approaches me. She's one of the involved grandmothers, one who regularly drops off and picks up her grandson, Alex, from school, keeps tabs on the other kids, and always shows up to every class party. "I've been thinking about you," she says sympathetically. "Really?" I say, puzzled. I can't think of a single reason why this woman, whom I have talked to only a couple of times, would be thinking of me. I haven't been thinking of her. In all honesty, I can't even remember her name. "I've seen you walking in the cold," she says. "I wish I could offer you a ride, but Alex's mother never lets me know until the last minute whether she wants me to take him to school." I still don't know where she's going with this, or why she thinks I would want or need a ride, but I explain that I live only half a mile from the school and don't mind the walk. "Well, I still wish there was something I could do to help," she says. I nod, smile politely, and change the subject. Not until I get home does it dawn on me that she probably thinks I don't own a car and have no choice but to walk in the cold.

The Outdoor Recess That Wasn't

Unstructured nature play is not just key to raising children who will care about nature—it's also essential to their personal health. The World Health Organization calls childhood obesity "one of the most serious public health challenges of the twenty-first century," as it is believed to be a risk factor for diabetes, heart disease, and high blood pressure later in life. It takes only a quick peek into the average American elementary school classroom to understand the proportions of this epidemic. As my daughters' pediatrician, Dr. Sean Sharma, puts it: "A generation ago, there were maybe one or two overweight or obese children in a class of twenty. Today, being overweight is so common that the normal kids sometimes are the ones that stand out. Our expectations have changed: Overweight is the new normal."

Statistics from the Centers for Disease Control and Prevention show that childhood obesity has almost tripled in children and quadrupled in adolescents in the past thirty years. In 1980, approximately 7 percent of American children age six to eleven years were obese; in 2012, that number was nearly 18 percent. Among adolescents age twelve to nineteen years, the obesity rate increased from 5 percent to nearly 21 percent in the same period. When you include figures for those who are simply overweight as well, more than one-third of American children are considered overweight or obese. That means children in the US are nearly six times more likely to be obese and nearly twice as likely to be overweight as children in Sweden. Similarly, approximately 11 percent of American children between the ages of four and seventeen have been diagnosed with ADHD, whereas only 3 to 6 percent of school-age children in Sweden are estimated to meet the criteria for the disorder. Although the number of ADHD diagnoses has increased in Sweden in the past few years, too, the incidence is well below the US trend. When combined with children on the autism spectrum, as many as one in six American children have a developmental disability, representing a 17 percent increase between 1997 and 2008, according to a 2011 study by the Centers for Disease Control and Prevention. Meanwhile, a 2009 study showed that the prevalence of myopia, or nearsightedness, increased from 25 percent in 1971–72 to nearly 42 percent in 1999–2004. The fact that children spend more time indoors is believed to be the main culprit behind this increase. Sensory issues are on the rise as well, with more young children than ever before needing occupational therapy, speech therapy, and physical therapy, even at the preschool level.

Outdoor play can help combat childhood obesity as well as sensory issues and myopia, and many studies have shown that spending time in nature improves ADHD symptoms. Even so, it seemed to me like the deck was stacked against outdoor play in many parts of the US. With no uniform rules guiding outdoor play at day cares and no cultural norms calling for it, I noticed that toddlers and preschoolers were more likely to spend their days watching TV or trying to get to the next level of Candy Crush Saga on their handheld electronic devices than connecting with nature. Over and over, I saw infants strapped into their car seats parked right in front of a TV, their inquisitive gazes and developing minds feeding on an unending string of cartoons and commercials. Older children didn't seem to fare much better, as recess, a source of outdoor play that I had taken for granted, was far from guaranteed in American schools. With this in mind, I'm relieved to hear that Maya will at least get two fifteen-minute recess periods every day when she starts kindergarten, which is a pretty intense, all-day affair in Indiana. At least she'll get them through second grade. And as long as the weather is nice. On paper the students are supposed to have recess outside if the temperature is above twenty degrees ($-6.6°C$) with wind chill. In reality, however, I find that there are many exceptions to the rule and that the arrival of winter is seen less as an invitation to go outside and make snow angels and more as a signal to bring out the iPads. Weather isn't even the only factor affecting recess: I'm surprised to learn that it can also be withheld as a disciplinary tool to penalize individual students or an entire class for things like talking during lunch or not listening to the teacher. Similar offenses can also be punished by making the children spend the first part of recess standing still on a yellow line on the blacktop. The first time it happens I brush it off, thinking that maybe Maya misunderstood the situation. But as it turns out, it won't be the last.

These types of restrictions on outdoor play are far from unique for Maya's school. In fact, recess seems to be under attack across the US. In 1989, according to one survey, 96 percent of all elementary schools in the US offered recess every day, but this has changed drastically over the past twenty-five years as many school districts have cut it or eliminated it altogether. Today only 40 percent of American school systems even have an explicit recess policy, and minorities and children living in poverty are less likely to have recess than white students and those living above the poverty line.

It doesn't take long before Maya starts complaining about not getting outside during the school day. The transition from preschool to full-day kindergarten has been rough anyway, and often she falls apart in the car on the way home, exhausted. Indoor recess is not helping. "I don't like being inside all day. It's boring," she tells me one day. And then, even more crushing, "I hate school."

When I bring up the subject of the lack of recess with a couple of the teachers, I learn that it's hard on some of them too. "We try to get out most days unless it's too cold or rainy," one of them says. "But sometimes we don't go outside for a week and it's awful, because the kids have all this pent-up energy. We don't have any space for them inside, so we usually just end up showing them a movie." Another problem, they tell me, is that children occasionally show up to school without appropriate outdoor clothes. The school tries to provide gloves and hats for those who need them, but sometimes kids show up without even jackets.

To my surprise, the teachers tell me that parents' attitudes toward outdoor recess also seem to have changed over the years. "Parents give the teachers grief if they send the kids out in the cold," one of them says. "We've got some parents lining up on the street to pick up their kids early, and if they see us out on the playground when it's drizzling, they'll call the office and demand that we bring the kids inside. We've had parents call and tell us to bring them inside just because there were dark clouds in the sky."

This parental anxiety in turn fuels schools' fear of lawsuits. What if Johnny slips on the ice or Lisa freezes her fingers while playing on the monkey bars in the cold? Better safe than sorry. And the safest option of all seems to be to keep them inside, playing computer games. I'm not surprised to hear that some children hardly know how to play outside anymore. "They don't even know how to play Red Rover; that's what we used to play all the time," one teacher tells me. "One day I thought I would teach them, but I was pulled aside by somebody else who told me, 'You know they're not supposed to play that anymore, right?' Apparently somebody broke their arm, so now nobody is allowed to do it."

Games that involve balls, snow, or ice are even more likely to be restricted. Forget snowball fights, King of the Mountain, and sliding on frozen puddles of water—these activities have all been banned in the name of safety. This leaves the teachers in a tough spot. "I hate when it snows, because all I have to do is run around and tell the kids what they can't do," says one veteran teacher. When I ask her if the kids are allowed to play on the ice, she laughs, but it's a sarcastic laughter. "Ice? Well, a kid fell on the ice and hit his head. He got a little goose egg and had to go to the nurse. Now the kids can't play on the ice anymore. It's all about safety."

My talks with Maya's school regarding recess go nowhere, so instead I take my effort to promote outdoor play and learning to the Parent Teacher Organization, or PTO. Outdoor classrooms are just starting to become popular, and at one of the meetings I share my vision for a space where the students can learn hands-on in a natural setting. Imagine a butterfly garden! A reading nook! Stepping-stones! A building area! The responses from the other parents range from silence and mild skepticism to implicit opposition. The principal, however, is cautiously supportive, and I do find an ally among the teachers, who loves the idea. Over the next school year, I launch into full gear. I survey the teachers, bring in a designer, and work on cost estimates. The survey shows that a slim majority of the teachers like the idea, but many share the same main concern: How would they possibly fit teaching outdoors into their already packed schedules? "I believe an outdoor classroom would benefit children in all areas," writes one teacher, "but I don't see our requirements getting decreased, so I can't imagine when we would use it."

The principal puts together a committee of three teachers tasked with developing a plan for an outdoor classroom at a grassy lot on the north side of the school. But the idea never gains momentum and eventually the whole project peters out. At one of the last PTO meetings of the year, two parents suggest that, instead of creating an outdoor classroom, the school pave the grassy lot over and turn it into a parking lot. When I run into a fellow PTO member a few weeks later, she tells me that the group ultimately decided to spend that year's funds on electronics. "We ended up buying a set of Chromebooks for the second graders. They will be on a cart, so the first graders and kindergartners will be able to use them too," she says. I must have looked disappointed, because then she shrugs and adds, as if to explain, "These are the times we live in, you know."

DRESS FOR OUTDOOR SUCCESS

A comfortable child can play outside for hours, so high-quality outdoor gear and play clothes are well worth the money. If the clothes are durable, chances are they can also be handed down to younger siblings.

Any advice about dressing children for the outdoors naturally depends on what they will be doing and where. For example, going on a long hike in the mountains or participating in other strenuous activities away from home requires more attention to layering than playing in the backyard. The child's age also matters, since young children move around less and get cold more easily. Keep in mind that weather conditions can change quickly in some areas, and always bring some backup clothes for longer outings.

What to look for in outdoor gear and play clothes for children in general:
* Protects against the elements (wind, sun, moisture, cold temperatures, etc.)
* Stands up to wear and tear
* Easy to put on and take off
* Loose-fitting enough to allow for range of motion while playing

Winter
Layering clothes is key to keeping children warm in cold temperatures.

* The first layer, or the base layer, regulates the child's temperature and keeps him dry. This layer usually fits snugly. Long underwear made from merino wool, synthetic fibers,

or a blend of both works best closest to the body, since these materials move perspiration away from the body. Cotton, on the other hand, soaks up moisture and leaves the child feeling wet and cold.

* The mid-layer insulates the body by trapping body heat in pockets of air in the fabric. This layer can be made of either natural or synthetic fibers and can, for example, consist of a fleece jacket and pants or a sweatshirt and sweatpants.

* The outer layer should be waterproof, windproof, and breathable. This layer also needs to stand up to some wear and tear and is typically made of polyamide or nylon, preferably with reinforced high-impact areas like knees and bottom. For the youngest children, one-piece coveralls are usually the best choice, since they are easy to put on and prevent snow from creeping in. Underfoot straps help keep the coveralls/snow pants in place, and reflective trim or a high-visibility vest are a must for outdoor adventures after dark. Combine with snow boots or fleece-lined rain boots, as well as waterproof mittens with long cuffs, and a hat.

Spring and Fall
The same layering principles apply as for winter, but with lighter or fewer layers.

* For rainy days, the Scandinavian-style heavy-duty rain gear sometimes seen at forest schools in the US is the ultimate outer layer. Typically sold as a set consisting of overalls (bib pants) and a jacket, and made of polyester and polyurethane blends, these garments do a great job of keeping

wind and rain out. Layer them with a fleece jacket in cooler temperatures and combine them with a pair of rugged rain boots for endless fun in puddles of mud.

* For dry days, use regular, breathable shell pants and a windbreaker for the outer layer. Even if the temperature doesn't call for shell pants, they save your child's regular clothes from getting stained and torn.

Summer

Make a mental breakdown of your child's wardrobe into "playclothes" and "school clothes" to avoid stressing over damage wrought by messy outdoor play. Hand-me-downs, yard sale finds, and older clothes with holes or stains that won't come out make excellent candidates for playclothes.

* In cool, wet weather, layer with rain gear as needed.
* In sunny weather, a sun hat with a strap under the chin and thin, long-sleeved UV clothing help protect the child from the sun.
* Shoes are optional!

Friluftsliv—Open-Air Life

The Scandinavian zest for fresh air is maybe best summed up by the word for "outdoor recreation" in Swedish and Norwegian—*friluftsliv*. The term was first used in print by famed Norwegian playwright and poet Henrik Ibsen in 1859, and describes a culture and a way of life that heavily revolve around exploring and enjoying nature. *Friluftsliv* can encompass anything from skiing and hiking to berry picking and fishing, or be as simple as going for a nature walk or bike ride near one's home. In Sweden, *friluftsliv* is generally defined as "physical activity outdoors to get a change of scenery and experience nature, with no pressure to achieve or compete."

To a great extent, *friluftsliv* is made possible by the Swedish common law of *allemansrätten* (the right of public access), which grants anybody the right to walk, ride a bike or horse, ski, pick berries, or camp anywhere on private land, except for the part that immediately surrounds a private dwelling. In short, that means you can pick mushrooms and flowers, as well as light a campfire and pitch a tent, in somebody else's woods, but not right in front of their house unless you have permission. You can also walk through cattle pastures and other farm fields as long as you make sure to close all gates and don't damage any crops. Unlike in the US, where private property rights are king, and land use tends to be ruled by the risk for potential lawsuits and the premise that if something can go wrong it probably will, *allemansrätten* relies on an honor system that can simply be summed up with the phrase "Do not disturb, do not destroy," and trusts that people will use their common sense. What may sound like an impossible free-for-all works amazingly well, with little to no visible littering or destruction in natural areas. The law democratizes outdoor recreation and means generations of Scandinavians have come to view access to nature not only as an inalienable right that is protected by the constitution but also as very much a shared responsibility.

Some even suggest that nature fills the void left by the decline of organized religion in Sweden, which is now one of the most secular countries in the world. "Nature has become the ultimate point of reference," says Carl Reinhold Bråkenhielm, a theology professor at Uppsala University, to *Svenska Dagbladet*, one of the biggest Swedish daily newspapers. "When traditional faith is waning we search for something else to relate to. We need something to create narratives and gather strength from." In what could be interpreted as a move to adapt to the new order, some churches occasionally congregate under the sprawling tree canopies in a forest, with the churchgoers taking in the word of God sitting on blankets on the moss-covered ground.

When the Swedish psychiatrist and author Nils Uddenberg surveyed his countrymen's attitudes toward nature for his 1995 book *Det stora sammanhanget* (which roughly translates to *The Big Connection*), as many as 96 percent of them expressed an actual *need* for being in nature. But when asked why, they often provided vague answers, just referring to nature as "beautiful" or "relaxing." "Asking [Swedes] why they like to be outdoors is like asking them why they want to have children; they are forced to find motivation for something that is so obvious to them that they have never given it a second thought," Uddenberg writes. American researcher Louise Chawla made a similar discovery when she compared the backgrounds of environmental activists in Kentucky and Norway. She found that more of the Americans attributed their activism to positive childhood memories of experiences in the natural world, but only because several of the Norwegians weren't sure whether the outdoor activities they had taken part of as children—skiing and hiking in the woods, for example—really counted. After all, they reasoned, that didn't set them apart from anybody else. They were "just being Norwegian."

Considering the popularity of outdoor recreation in the region, it comes as no surprise that Scandinavians are nearly unanimous in their support for environmental protection. In the 2007 Eurobarometer public opinion survey, a staggering 98 percent of the Swedish respondents—more than in any other country—declared that it is their responsibility to protect the environment, even if it means putting limits on human development. Denmark and Norway were close behind. As a result, Scandinavia is often cited as a world leader when it comes to air and water quality, cuts in greenhouse gas emissions, and overall sustainability. For example, Denmark is a leading producer of renewable energy and environmentally friendly housing; Sweden recycles more than 99 percent of its household waste and is a primary exporter of "green" technology; and Norway was one of the first countries in the world to adopt a carbon tax.

From clean water, zero-waste policies, and green energy the leap to parenting may seem big, but, as Sobel and Chawla have pointed out, it all starts by forming a bond with nature in childhood. And the Scandinavians are experts at it.

A Crime at a Creek

On a hot and sticky Memorial Day afternoon, when Maya is seven and Nora four, I finally make a mistake at a local nature preserve that leaves me wondering if, after twelve years of living in the US, I will ever fit in.

The preserve is just a ten-minute drive from our house, near a small, unincorporated community that, in its heyday from the 1850s until the Great Depression, was a bustling trade hub thanks to its location by the Wabash and Erie Canal. The raucous hotels and taverns that used to accommodate weary travelers on the canal are long gone, and today only a church, a few scattered houses, and a smattering of dilapidated mobile homes remain in the area. If you take a deep enough breath when you drive into town, you'll exit it on your exhale. Unless, of course, you turn onto the dusty gravel road that leads to the nature preserve on the outskirts of the community. The lush woods in the small preserve are home to many of the common Midwestern tree species—hickory, sugar maple, black walnut, oak—as well as some white pines and an abundance of wildflowers. Meandering through it all is a shallow stream that flows to the northwest and eventually feeds into the Wabash River. Over time, the creek has carved deep ravines through the Pennsylvania sandstone that rises from the earth along its banks, creating dramatic ninety-foot drop-offs and jagged talus slopes. In one spot a tributary has whittled an archlike hole through the stratified auburn and ocher rocks by undercutting the sandstone bluff on both sides. The unique rock feature gave the area its name and remains its main attraction. During the canal era what is now a preserve was a popular resort with a park, dances, log cabins, and a dam with a water wheel and dynamo to power it all. A deteriorating concrete base from the dam still stands by the creek, now a giant gray leaf trap that pays quiet homage to busier days.

Among living locals the area is mostly known from the time it was a Boy Scout camp, from 1938 to 1966. Back then, kids would camp, swim, and create some of their most vivid childhood memories here until, tragically, a boy accidentally fell off the cliffs and died. The Boy Scouts eventually sold the property, and it was dedicated a nature preserve in 1972. Today it's owned and managed by the Indiana Department of Natural Resources, Division of Nature Preserves. It's also one of the best-kept secrets of western Indiana. Aside from the presence of some local dog walkers, a few camera-toting out-of-towners, and the occasional college students working on a science project, the preserve is usually quiet. Ten visitors in a day would be considered a crowd. To me, it had been an oasis for nearly a decade, a tiny island of reclaimed wilderness in a verdant ocean of corn and soybean fields. I had come here in the dead cold of winter and the sticky height of summer, on foggy fall days and in the wake of heavy spring rains. I had continued to hike both the north and south trails throughout my first pregnancy; then I'd come back with an infant strapped to my chest. By the time Maya was two she could hike the rugged north loop unaided. The following year her new baby sister, Nora, joined us on the trail, tightly bound to my chest. Here, they slowly evolved from babies and toddlers to pint-size hikers.

On this Memorial Day, only a few other families have signed the logbook before us as we start trekking down toward the arch. When we get to the creek, the girls do what they have done several times before—they strip down to their underwear and jump into the foot-deep, slow-moving water. As I sit down on a log to watch them, the sun breaks through the clouds and a few stray rays dance on the rippling water while the girls giggle and play and get into a few friendly mud fights. After about half an hour they get out and dry off, and we start heading back to the car.

Maya gets back to the parking lot first, since I'm waiting for Nora to climb a rock. When I get there, I see a brown SUV emblazoned with the IDNR logo, and a uniformed officer. Then Maya comes running toward me. "Mom, there's a policeman here who says we can't swim in the creek," she says. "Why, Mommy?" Thinking that she's misunderstood the situation, I walk to my car and get ready to leave. But as it turns out, the officer, a blond guy who looks to be in his mid-twenties, has not only just told my daughter that swimming is not allowed in the creek. He's also decided that we need a lesson.

"I'm going to let you off easy this time. It may not seem like it, but I really am," he says when he comes back from his vehicle with some paperwork. He explains that rather than adding additional citations for all of us for getting off the trail and "disturbing wildlife," he's only going to fine us for violating section 312 IAC 8-2-9 of the Indiana Administrative Code—for "swimming in an unauthorized area."

"The only thing you're allowed to do here is walk on the trail. That's it," he says.

As I'm standing in the preserve's parking lot with my daughters tugging on my shorts, anxiously wondering why I'm being accosted by an officer, my heart sinks as if it were weighted down by a pile of serrated Pennsylvania sandstone. If walking on the trail is the only thing allowed at this preserve, they may as well put up a CHILDREN NOT WELCOME sign at the entrance. It suddenly dawns on me that I've probably unintentionally broken several of the preserve's rules over the years just by allowing my children to play freely here.

"There was another family downstream from you and I'm going to give them a ticket when they come back too," the officer says, as if this is supposed to make us feel better. "We have these rules to keep you safe. There are some loose rocks and the creek is a health hazard. Manure from the farms upstream gets in the creek and the kids can get infected with *E. coli*."

I stare at the pink ticket in disbelief, then buckle up the kids and go home. We have a month to pay our fine of $123.50, and a court date in case we want to fight the charge.

Over the next few weeks, I went through something akin to a mourning process. At first, there was denial. How could this possibly happen to me? After all, I was known as the town's local environmentalist and resident health nut, who had helped start a farmers' market, organized litter pickups, promoted recycling, and done Earth Day presentations at the elementary school. I had grown organic vegetables in our backyard to connect my kids with their food and had tried to persuade my daughter's preschool to switch to eco-friendly cleaning products. My "crunchy"-parent credentials were solid. Yet now I stood accused of the bizarre crime of harming nature by letting my children wade in an agricultural cesspool.

Then came anger. Why this double standard? If the creek was full of agricultural waste, wouldn't it be more productive for the state to track down and stop the source of the contamination instead of treating a hiking family like a weapon of mass environmental destruction? And if the state was truly trying to protect us, wouldn't some sort of information about the contamination and other possible hazards have been more useful than a fine? (The fact that the shallow creek was barely moving and that nobody in our family to date had come down with a case of explosive diarrhea told me that it was probably reasonably safe.)

I bargained. If only I had showed the officer the empty Styrofoam cups and plastic bottles that I had picked up along the trail that day, he would've understood that we were really on the same team. If only he had known about the box turtle that my daughter had helped across the road on our way there, maybe things would have gone in a different direction.

Then I was engulfed in sadness. This was more or less the only public nature area available to us within a forty-minute drive, and I knew that it would never be the same to me again. Frankly, I wasn't sure we'd ever want to come back.

In an attempt to make sense of it all, I wrote about our run-in with the law on my blog. The post quickly went viral and set off a firestorm of comments, shares, and discussions about children's access to nature versus the need to protect it. Clearly, I had struck a nerve. Stories started to trickle in, from both locals and people across the country. "I hope my grandsons will get to see the beauty [of the preserve] before someone decides we can't visit it," wrote Terry, who used to camp there in his youth.

The majority of the locals sided with me and told me they let their children or grandchildren do the same thing. This of course didn't make it legal, but it told me that I wasn't completely off base for thinking that it was. One woman shared her frustration over being fined for having a picnic at the preserve; another told me she wouldn't take her kids back there after learning about my experience. And, unsurprisingly, it didn't take long before I started receiving unsolicited legal advice from complete strangers, encouraging me to sue the IDNR for failing to warn the public of the contamination of the creek and, furthermore, to file a harassment complaint against the officer for basically ruining my day.

Other commenters were less sympathetic.

Of all the things I was accused of (stirring up sediment from the bottom of the creek, potentially destroying a raccoon's nest on our way to the water, endangering my children's health, setting a bad example, having an inflated sense of entitlement, complaining over first-world problems, etc.), what hurt the most was that some people thought that I, through my actions at the preserve that day, had earned myself an honorary membership in the American Association of Bad Parenting.

For some readers, the million-dollar question was whether the swimming ban was posted at the preserve. The answer was more complicated than a simple yes or no. The brown metal sign at the entrance does not say anything about staying out of the creek. It does say to stay on marked trails only, but there are several well-trodden trails leading down to the water and nothing posted on any of them indicating that they are off-limits. Whether we had left the official trail or not didn't even matter, because the minute my daughters' toes hit the water, we had violated a state code that makes it illegal to wade or swim in any public waterway unless it's a "designated swimming beach or pool," or it's done from a boat. Even then, the permission comes with a litany of restrictions. The take-home message of the code seemed to be that unless wading and swimming is explicitly allowed, the presumption is that it is prohibited. Whether this was clear or not, and whether the state should have posted information regarding the alleged contamination of the creek, is something that two overpriced lawyers could probably debate in court until the end of time.

All potential legal wrangling aside, to me the question was not mainly whether the rule was posted or not; I couldn't wrap my mind around why it existed in the first place. The idea that we were damaging or disturbing anything that day wasn't even on my radar. In Sweden, where you can leave the trail, have picnics, pick flowers, forage for mushrooms, and swim your heart out almost anywhere, including at nature preserves, the idea that children playing in a creek would be considered a crime or a threat to the environment is unheard-of. Different place, different rules. I got that. But the Swedish approach also told me that there is more than one way to go about conservation.

As far as the contamination goes, the IDNR's own trail guide describes the creek at the preserve as a "very clean stream, nearly pollution free." But when I called the Division of Nature Preserves I was once again told that it's full of fertilizer runoff and agricultural waste. We will never know for sure, however, since I was also told that the state lacks the funding to test the water, let alone clean it up.

Regardless, what happened that day was more than the story of an overzealous conservation officer and my injured sense of pride. The reactions to my story from across the country made me realize that I wasn't the only one who felt like outdoor play, which research has confirmed is essential to children's physical and mental health, had come under attack. "My son was once yelled at for trying to skip rocks into a river because he 'might harm macroinvertebrates,'" said Laura, one of my readers. Heather from New York chimed in with, "Sadly, something that was once normal is now incredibly regulated, due to liability, or simply as a means to make money."

"Too many parents and people in authority have embraced rules that their own parents would have scoffed at," said Michael Lanza, author of *Before They're Gone: A Family's Year-Long Quest to Explore America's Most Endangered National Parks*, in response to our incident. "Unless we push back against this trend, we risk raising a generation of children who don't value outdoor time or even preserving places like this, where kids can't even play in a creek."

In some ways, our incident at the preserve symbolized a larger, national narrative, first depicted by Richard Louv in his best-selling book *Last Child in the Woods: Saving Our Children from Nature-Deficit Disorder*. It's a story that I've heard many times from Americans who are my age or older. The time and settings vary, but it always goes something like this: "When we were little we were out in the woods all the time, setting up forts, splashing in the water, using our imaginations. Mom kicked us out in the morning and we wouldn't go back inside until the streetlights came on."

There has been a shift from a time when playing outside at school and at home was the norm and young children, like the Boy Scouts who used to camp at this preserve, still learned valuable outdoor skills, to a time when many children's only contact with the wild is through guided tours at air-conditioned nature centers. Any meaningful interactions with nature in many public parks and preserves are now forbidden—look, don't touch!—and most private landowners would probably rather invite a leper for dinner than have unsupervised children playing on their property. Causing this shift were the usual suspects: electronic-media bingeing, frivolous litigation, overscheduling, standardized testing, and parents' fear of strangers, traffic, and nature itself.

The last phase of mourning is acceptance. For a while I considered fighting the charge, but then I decided to let it go and pay the fine. The rules are the rules are the rules, and I had unwittingly broken them. When I talked to John Bacone, director of the IDNR's Division of Nature Preserves, about my experience, to my surprise I found that we essentially agreed on the problem. "Kids don't play outside like they used to," he lamented. "We need to get them out there again so they don't just stay inside and play video games."

But how? For seven years I had fought to keep my daughters as connected to nature as possible in a culture that didn't seem to value outdoor play. The creek incident was just the straw that finally broke the possum's back. I was starting to question whether it was at all possible for my daughters to have a childhood anything like my own.

Unless I took them to my native Sweden.

Scandinavian Parenting Tip #1

Prioritize daily outdoor time from when your child is a baby to make it a natural part of your routine from the get-go. Remember that not every nature experience must entail a grand adventure to a scenic national park—watching a caterpillar make its way across a sidewalk or simply lying in the grass and watching the clouds go by in the backyard can be a great adventure to a small child. Celebrate these everyday nature experiences together, and come back to the same places often to make sure your child forms a bond with your community and its natural areas.

Suggested reading: *Last Child in the Woods: Saving Our Children from Nature-Deficit Disorder,* by Richard Louv. Algonquin Books, 2008.

2

FRESH AIR IS GOOD FOR YOU

*Fresh air affects children's constitutions, particularly in early years.
It enters every pore of a soft and tender skin, it has a powerful effect
on their young bodies. Its effects can never be destroyed.*
—JEAN-JACQUES ROUSSEAU

There is another, more pressing reason why I'm yearning to go back to Sweden. About a month after our creek debacle, my dad experiences severe stomach cramps and is rushed to the hospital by his wife. Emergency surgery reveals a ruptured, cancerous tumor in his large intestine, and after suffering complications from the procedure, he is literally fighting for his life. If moving to the US had seemed like a grand romantic adventure when I was fresh out of college, it's an understatement to say that being over four thousand miles away from my aging parents at this point in life isn't exactly ideal. With my dad now facing a tough recovery from surgery, followed by six weeks of chemotherapy and radiation, then another surgery to remove the tumor and possibly more chemo after that, I start planning for an extended stay in Sweden. I schedule a flight for early January 2016, which means that the girls and I will arrive on the heels of my dad's second surgery. We are to return in June, giving us nearly six months in Sweden. My husband, although not thrilled about being left behind, is understanding given the circumstances.

The news of our extended overseas stay spreads quickly in our hometown in Indiana, and although most people seem excited on our behalf, others express different variations of one of the biggest American parental fears of all: that my taking the girls to Sweden for nearly six months will cause Maya to Fall Behind. I have some reservations myself. I worry that both kids are going to miss their dad, friends, and extended family in the US, and I worry that Maya will have a hard time adjusting to a new school. The fact that she's going to miss a semester of second-grade Common Core math, however, hasn't really registered as a concern of mine. She will be going to a public school in Sweden for one semester, she's already bilingual, and I feel like this could be a once-in-a-lifetime opportunity for her to immerse herself in her Swedish heritage. In my opinion, she's already ahead.

Shortly before we leave, I meet with Maya's teacher to discuss our upcoming trip and what I can do to help her stay on track academically while we're gone. The teacher is warm and caring, and genuinely concerned. "I don't want to overwhelm you—I just want third grade to be easy for her," she says apologetically after going over all our options for keeping up with the math, reading, and writing curricula while in Sweden. "As a second-grade teacher you feel pressure because you want the kids to be prepared for the testing in third grade—otherwise you'll cause problems for the third-grade teacher."

As I somewhat exasperatedly look at the stack of books and worksheets in front of me I recall a conversation I'd had with a grandmother of one of Maya's classmates the previous week. Her older grandchild was in third grade, that crucial year when students in our state start taking the Indiana Statewide Testing for Educational Progress (ISTEP), as required by No Child Left Behind. "Wait until she gets to third grade," the grandmother had told me in an ominous voice, referring to Maya. "There's a drastic difference compared with second grade. The kids get much more homework, and then you have all the extra-credit projects on top of that." She shrugged and laughed. "I don't know who we're competing with—China, I guess. But I don't think it's working, because by the time they get to high school they're already burned out."

The conversation with Maya's teacher leaves me feeling deflated, but I dutifully pack the folder with math worksheets in our already bulging suitcases. I'm starting to wonder if I should be more worried that my failure to keep up with the weekly spelling lists and periodic math assessments will not only determine Maya's ability to pass the standardized tests in third grade but potentially forever destroy her chances of getting into Harvard. Oh well. There are plenty of ways to get ahead in life without an Ivy League education.

When we arrive in Sweden, the plane touches down in a wintry landscape and my mom picks us up in the tidy but somewhat tired old Saab station wagon that will be our ride for the coming months. As we drive toward Borås, the city of nearly seventy thousand people where I went to high school, the girls curiously watch the landscape go by from the backseat. They've seen this scenery every summer when we've visited my family in the past, but it looks a lot different this time of the year. Long swaths of pine trees and wildlife fences eventually give way to signs of civilization, industrial parks mixed with towns just big enough to sport a gas station, a school, a soccer field, and a pizzeria run by Turkish immigrants. Then, just as you start to think that you've left the forest behind, it reappears and swallows you whole until it spits you out in the next little town.

You can't go to Sweden and not notice the forest. There are more than eighty-seven billion trees in Sweden—the equivalent of three and a half soccer fields of woods for every man, woman, and child in the country. Maya notices it as well. "I know what the most common tree in Sweden is, Mommy," she observes from the backseat. "It's the pine tree. There are just too many pine trees here." I'm not paying much attention to the endless stands of coniferous forests that look like they were splattered with whipped egg whites in the last winter storm. I'm looking for people. It's been years since I spent the winter in Sweden, and part of me wonders if I've been wrong to assume that people here still enjoy the outdoors like they used to. After all, the last time I lived in Sweden the iPad had yet to be invented and fiber was something in your diet that helped you stay regular, not a gigabyte highway that connected every apartment, house, and cottage in the country to the internet. There's a lot of new bandwidth and gadgets to compete with Scandinavia's traditional *friluftsliv*.

But I quickly realize that I don't need to worry. As soon as we get off the main highway and approach the small town of Äspered, where we will be staying, I see people on foot. A man walking three large Saint Bernards. An octogenarian getting her mail supported by her hiking poles. A couple of kids pulling sleds. Teenagers walking to the bus. And, of course, a small army of men and women pushing strollers down slushy sidewalks, snowsuit-clad toddlers in tow. On a frozen lake nearby, some kids are playing hockey, and by the lodge a few miles down the road the parking lot is packed with families who are getting ready to hit the cross-country tracks.

"The house looks fantastic," my mom exclaims giddily as we approach the rural red-and-white nineteenth-century homestead that I will be renting. "I thought the décor was a bit dark, so I've redecorated it for you. There was a lot of black and white, but I thought you should have a little more color." She's right—it is a different place than when I first checked it out during our last summer vacation in Sweden. It's been gutted and remodeled, and old and new elements now fuse effortlessly in the one-bedroom, five-hundred-square-foot cottage. A beautiful antique ceiling lamp hangs over the dinner table next to the glossy white IKEA kitchen with its state-of-the-art induction cooktop. The crumbling old vinyl floors have been replaced by a stylish wood laminate, which my mom has all but covered in mismatching rag rugs. In the only bedroom, a bunk bed made of traditional lacquered pine sits in front of an accent wall featuring a modern black-and-white tree-print wallpaper. The composting toilet in the bathroom has been torn out and replaced by a modern water-saving model that resembles and operates like a large airplane toilet. The girls marvel at the novel sound effects and elaborate flushing procedure. I'm apprehensive and slightly skeptical. The waste pipe in this toilet is smaller than normal, and each flush contains only half a quart of water, which is great for the environment but places an awful lot of faith in the power of suction. Going number two is initially surrounded by a certain element of suspense, but to my surprise—and great relief—our airplane toilet delivers every time.

However, the place does have some issues. "The floors are a bit cold," my mom says, pulling out a gift box from her purse. "It's a belated Christmas present. I thought they would come in handy." It's a pair of gray knitted wool socks with a traditional Swedish pattern. I waste no time putting them on right on top of the wool socks that I'm already wearing, and I still feel like I'm walking barefoot in a meat freezer.

The bathroom also holds a washer that looks like it came from a yard sale at the Seven Dwarfs' cottage, and the kitchen features an equally small dishwasher. If I run both at the same time, the landlord has warned my mom, I'll blow a fuse. Then there is the shower, which has only two settings: Mountain Stream Cold and Angry Moose Fending Off Mob of Overzealous German Tourists Hot. When I first turn it on, the water almost scalds me. Then, when I'm all lathered up and getting ready to rinse off, the hot water abruptly runs out. As time goes on I learn that the water heater has approximately four minutes and thirty-five seconds' worth of hot water, just enough time for me to quickly apply and rinse out shampoo and conditioner, but not long enough for shaving one's legs. Fortunately, it will be at least four months before my legs will see the sunshine again.

The cottage is heated by a few scattered radiators and a wall-mounted heat pump that quickly loses its mojo when temperatures start dropping down to zero degrees Fahrenheit. One bitter-cold night just a few days into our trip I go to bed wearing my new wool socks, long thermal underwear, and my knitted beanie, and still shiver under the thick duvet. I have three TV channels and no internet, at least not for another week. All the clothes that I'll be wearing for the next five months fit in two small dresser drawers. I have everything I need but not much more. I affectionately name our new home the Shack.

When you've grown up in a place but have been gone for a long time, it sometimes strikes you as strange and strangely familiar at the same time. The past is constantly present and will find you, whether you seek it out or not. At the grocery store in nearby Borås, the big city where I went to high school, the cashier turns out to be an old classmate who grew up in another small town near the Shack.

"You live out there now?" she asks me incredulously when I tell her my story in a forty-five-second sound bite, to avoid holding up the line. "Well, welcome to the end of the world! I'm glad I got out of there and moved to the city."

Twenty years ago, when I was in high school, I probably would have said the same thing. Being away for so long has made me see everything in a new light. True, the grocery store by the gas station in Äspered was shuttered years ago. More recently, the buses stopped coming through here as well, and what used to be two Christian congregations have merged into one. A devout crowd still meets for worship every Sunday, and for the rest of the villagers the nineteenth-century church on the hill remains a popular venue for some of life's major milestones: christenings, commencement ceremonies, confirmations, weddings, and funerals. But, like in many other small towns in Sweden, the heart of the community is really the brown-and-white clubhouse half a mile outside of town. From these headquarters, the local sports association organizes an impressive smorgasbord of family-oriented activities: cross-country skiing school for kids, soccer leagues for both children and adults, weekly bike-riding meet-ups for families, gymnastics, land hockey tournaments, a running club, and various noncompetitive outdoor family outings. Just months before our arrival, volunteers completed a new outdoor gym with tires and monkey bars and boot-camp style climbing structures. All in a community of fewer than a thousand residents.

The Shack is located about half a mile from the clubhouse, nestled between a narrow blacktop road with little traffic and a large lake with water that is remarkably clean but as cold as a supersize trough of ice. A few hundred yards down the road is a small nature preserve with mostly deciduous forest and a trail system that probably dates back to the time when walking was most people's main mode of transportation. To the west, the town is flanked by a bog, and to the north and south, it's surrounded by pine forests so thick that even on sunny days only slivers of light can reach the soft, bright green moss that covers the ground. No matter in which direction I turn my face, I am completely immersed in the natural world. Here, I will be able to bring life down to its bare nuts and bolts and focus solely on connecting with nature, my daughters, my family, and myself. If this is the end of the world, I'm more than happy to face it.

*　　　*　　　*

A couple of days after we arrive, we visit my dad, who has just been released from the hospital. He's tired but in good spirits. And he can't wait to get back outside. "Two weeks in the hospital with no fresh air," he mutters and shakes his head. "You can't have that. Our bodies need fresh air." Considering that my dad was a smoker for over forty-five years and just recently quit, he may not be the best judge of what constitutes fresh air in the literal sense. But although he didn't always make the healthiest choices in life, he, like most Swedes, has always had an innate longing for nature. Last summer and fall, while recuperating from the difficult emergency surgery, he had prepared for his radiation and chemotherapy sessions by going for daily walks in the woods behind his and his wife's house, my childhood home. Some days, the walks were short, as complications from the surgery left him tired and winded. Other days he would walk one, two, even four miles. But he walked with his neighbor Bernt every day at 11 a.m. sharp, rain or shine. And every day he felt a little bit stronger.

While reacquainting myself with Sweden, I soon make another observation—most people around me are in annoyingly good shape. I have always been a fairly healthy eater and exercised on a regular basis, mainly, in all honesty, so that I can keep eating chocolate without having to buy bigger clothes. But I clearly have nothing on the clusters of Middle-Aged Men in Lycra (known locally simply by the acronym MAMILs) who fly by the Shack on their expensive bikes as soon as the road is cleared of snow. A quick check with some of my old friends confirms that the interest in *friluftsliv*, health, and fitness seems to have reached a new all-time high. One friend's husband has, in a slightly intoxicated moment, been persuaded by his friends to do the Swedish Classic Circuit, a four-race event over twelve months that involves 56 miles of cross-country skiing, 186 miles of bike riding, 1.8 miles of open-water swimming, and 18.6 miles of running. Another friend's husband has, out of the blue, come up with a plan to ascend Kebnekaise, which at 6,882 feet is the tallest peak in Sweden, with a couple of his workout buddies. A third friend has registered herself and her boyfriend for a twenty-mile trail run in Norway as his birthday present, and now they are both hard at work training for it.

Apparently I have arrived in the middle of a great health awakening.

Sleeping Baby—Outdoors

There's an old Danish proverb that claims that "fresh air impoverishes the doctor." Ironically, the Scandinavian penchant for fresh air can be traced back to a time when outdoor air was not necessarily very fresh, at least not in the cities. At the start of the twentieth century, children played outside a lot, but poor sanitation, disease, and smoke from coal and woodstoves made for an unhealthy cocktail. Tuberculosis was rampant, and one of the few treatment options was to send children as well as adults to so-called sanatoriums in the countryside, where they were encouraged to eat healthy and rest outside. Although this was not an entirely effective treatment for tuberculosis, people discovered that nature had other healing qualities. Soon the wealthy started flocking to the countryside to get their beneficial dose of nature, whether they were sick or not, and children from poor families were sent to summer camps or on extended stays with families in rural areas.

Elin Wägner, a prominent Swedish journalist and author during the first half of the twentieth century, argued that spending time in nature on an everyday basis is key to both our personal health and our spirituality, as well as to the health of the planet, long before these ideas had become widely accepted. The cultural and academic elites started to promote the idea that the Swedish people were one with nature, and in 1940 a government report for the first time recommended that public spaces in the cities be set aside for outdoor recreation. In the same report, the term *allemansrätten*, the right of public access, was used for the first time, even though the custom had been in place since the Middle Ages.

After World War II, urbanization and industrialization increased, and Swedes had more leisure time and money than ever before. Nature became a source of joy rather than simply a necessity for survival, as well as a symbol of national identity, just like the flag, the national anthem, and the Swedish language. The outdoors was also depicted as a democratic meeting place where everybody was equal, rich and poor. The Swedish Tourist Association, the education system, and other institutions reinforced this new, positive view of nature by encouraging people to enjoy *friluftsliv* and educating children about wildlife and the environment. National parks and nature preserves were created to protect unique landscapes, and by the middle of the twentieth century fresh air had been established as a pillar of public health, which it remains today.

In Scandinavia the belief that fresh air is good for you applies to people of all ages, not least infants. Daily fresh air is seen as essential for babies, ranking just behind food, sleep, and the nurturing love of a parent. And the most common way for them to get their fresh air is from the comfort of a pram. Scandinavian prams are a different animal than most American strollers and travel systems, which are mainly designed for portability and seamless transfers in and out of a car. If the travel systems are the baby equipment equivalent of a Prius—lightweight, small, and easy to maneuver in crowded mall parking lots—most traditional Scandinavian prams feature a heavy chassis and drive more like a sturdy Volvo on a rough mountain road. Forget about multiple cup holders and mandatory snack compartments—when Scandinavian parents shop for prams they look for big wheels, fat tires with good traction, and superior suspension that will help them conquer sleet, mud, and snow on cobblestone roads and dirt tracks alike. More important, this type of stroller, called *barnvagn* ("child carriage") in Swedish, allows the baby to sleep flat on its back. This is key, since prams aren't just used for walks around town. With their characteristic flat bottoms, they double as outdoor cribs on wheels.

The Scandinavian practice of parking prams with young babies outside all year-round dates back at least a century. At the time, the infant mortality rate was high and indoor air quality poor, and many children suffered from rickets and other diseases. In Finland, a well-known pediatrician named Arvo Ylppö, who is sometimes referred to as that country's Dr. Benjamin Spock, set out to change all that. In the 1920s, he started to distribute childcare guidelines to new mothers, to improve the health and survival rates among infants. Among his many recommendations was to expose children to sunlight as well as fresh and cold air regularly to create "sound blood" and prevent diseases. Specifically, cold air was believed to increase immunity against bacteria by improving blood circulation in the linings of the nose and mouth. When Ylppö died in 1992, the infant mortality rate in Finland had fallen from 10 percent in 1920 to 0.6 percent, making it among the lowest rates in the world (as of 2015, it stood at 0.2 percent).

Ylppö is widely credited for contributing to this decline and his legacy lives on to this day, as the Finnish government still promotes outdoor napping. For example, all new parents receive an educational pamphlet titled "Having Children in Finland," which explicitly recommends the practice: "Irrespective of the season, many children have their evening naps outside in prams. Many babies sleep better outdoors in the fresh air than in the bedroom. Sleeping outdoors is not dangerous for a baby."

When Maya and Nora were born, this was also one of the first Scandinavian parenting traditions that I put into practice. Just like generations of Swedes had done before me, I intuitively lined our stroller with lamb's wool and a bunting bag, bundled the girls up in layers, and walked them around until they fell asleep. Then I would park the stroller by the wall on our back porch, turn on the baby monitor, and go back inside. The Woman Who Walks with Dogs had become the Woman Who Leaves Her Napping Baby Outside. Since I couldn't quite shake the fear that somebody would call Child Protective Services on me, I didn't advertise this napping regimen to anybody but close friends and family. Meanwhile in Sweden my friends were lauded for being good, caring parents for doing exactly the same thing. A friend in Stockholm, Cecilia, a feisty redhead with a contagious smile, says that she felt like exposing her two daughters to fresh air every day was among the most basic of her parenting responsibilities.

"I was raised to think that it's important to get fresh air every day, and that's how I raise my daughters too," she says. "I was under the impression that if I didn't get my babies outside every day, people would almost think that I was a bad parent."

When Cecilia's oldest daughter, Matilde, was born the temperature was hovering around five degrees (−15°C), and the prospect of taking her firstborn outside in the cold seemed a bit daunting at first. But as soon as she was comfortable in her new role as mother and it warmed up to around seventeen degrees (−8°C), she regularly started taking her baby daughter for walks in freezing temperatures and then, instead of waking her up when they returned, left the pram on the porch behind the house while she went back inside. In the winter she left a baby monitor by the pram, and in the summertime she left the door to the porch cracked.

"Of course you check on them just like you would if they slept inside," she says. "If it was below minus ten degrees [Celsius; fourteen degrees Fahrenheit] I didn't put them outside by themselves, but I would still take them for walks. And if it rained I just put a rain cover on the pram and went outside anyway. You can't let that stop you."

Cecilia's daughters always took longer, deeper naps outside, and many Scandinavian parents will second that notion. "In my experience, they sleep better outside, since they get fresh air, and they also get used to sleeping with normal background noise," says my younger cousin Josephine, whose one-year-old daughter, Valerie, has slept outdoors for up to three hours per day since she was two months old. "I also think that they stay healthier this way. At least they look healthy when they come in from their power nap in the pram with rosy cheeks, and they feel much more alert and energetic after napping outside rather than inside."

Of course, not all Scandinavians have a back porch on which to park a pram, or even live in an area where it would be safe to do so, but they still go to great lengths to provide their young children with a daily dose of fresh air. Those who can't safely leave their child outside on their own can often be seen pushing a stroller around for hours, sometimes in groups, or "stroller mobs," as Cecilia jokingly calls them. Apartment dwellers are sometimes known to park the stroller or bassinet attachment on a balcony. As it turns out, their babies too get so used to sleeping outdoors that they wouldn't have it any other way.

"A lot of children who are used to sleeping outside don't want to go to sleep unless they're in their pram," Cecilia says. "I think they feel better both physically and mentally from being outside a lot."

Surprisingly little research exists about outdoor napping, but a Finnish study from 2008 did confirm that children take longer naps when they sleep outside. The study was based in the city of Oulu, Finland, where 95 percent of the parents let their babies nap outside, generally starting from when they are a couple of weeks old. The study also showed that the ideal napping temperature was perceived as twenty-one degrees (−6°C), although many parents reported that they let their charges stay outside in temperatures as low as five degrees (−15°C) or even colder. A majority of the parents also said that their children were "more active" and ate better after napping outside in the cold. A whopping 94 percent of the parents felt like napping outdoors was "healthy because of the fresh air."

I, too, had always been under the impression that outdoor napping is healthier than sleeping indoors. But is it? According to Roland Sennerstam, a pediatric specialist in Sweden, the practice makes perfect sense from a germ-management standpoint, and he recommends that both babies and older children go outside both in the morning and in the afternoon. "As a rule of thumb, you can let babies sleep outside in temperatures down to minus ten degrees [Celsius; fourteen degrees Fahrenheit]. It's a misconception that cold temperatures make us sick," he says. "We get sick because we contract viruses and bacteria when we spend too much time inside, stand too close to each other on the subway, and so on. The risk of getting infected is especially high at day cares, where you might have twenty children spending the whole day inside in a virtual cloud of germs."

Sure enough, a 1990 study of Sweden's preschools (which essentially function like day cares) by the National Board of Health and Welfare showed that children who spent five or fewer hours outside per week at day care were sick more often than those who spent six to nine hours outside per week. In 1997, another study that compared traditional preschools with so-called forest schools, where the children spend most of the day outside, confirmed that outdoor kids generally have fewer sick days.

Outdoor experiences in a stimulating environment can also be a boon to the brain, which develops rapidly in the first three years of a child's life, according to a study from the University of Missouri, Kansas City. Listening to the sound of an airplane, grasping a leaf, smelling the ocean, observing colors and shapes in nature, crawling on a rough surface, and experiencing different types of weather all help form neural pathways in a baby's brain, which essentially paves the way for learning later in life. "A baby's brain absorbs a lot more then [sic] we realize as they try to make sense of the world through soaking up noises, sights and experiences around them," the authors note. "Outdoor play gives an infant the opportunity to develop their senses" and "introduces the environment . . . they live in."

All guiding documents for preschools in Sweden guarantee children's right to spend time outside, and even at traditional preschools in Scandinavia it's extremely popular to let the youngest children sleep outside. Come nap time, it's common to see a long line of prams with napping babies lined up against a wall outside, and in Denmark some preschools even have a special sheltered area with stationary pram-like bassinets where the youngest children sleep. And preschools that skimp on outdoor nap or playtime can quickly draw the ire of parents, who expect them to provide it.

Nurses working in Sweden's universal health care system also recommend that parents take their children outside for fresh air every day. "Some people are afraid to go outside if the weather is bad or if the child is sick," says Lotta Bohlin, one of the country's many nurse-midwives who provide free health checkups from when a baby is born until he or she starts school. "But unless the child is really sick we still recommend some fresh air. As long as they're protected in the pram, it's no problem for them to be outside with a low-grade fever. It's important to get a little daylight every day."

The practice of napping and playing outdoors in almost any weather is not only common in Scandinavia—it's viewed as key to good health and a surefire sign of sound parenting. But some things inevitably get lost in cultural translation.

The practice of letting babies nap outdoors got a bad rap in the US with the notorious case of a Danish tourist who left her fourteen-month-old daughter in a stroller outside a restaurant in New York on a cool Saturday night in May 1997. The tourist, Anette Sørensen, and her boyfriend were having drinks at a Dallas BBQ in New York's East Village while keeping an eye on their sleeping daughter through a window, when officers from the NYPD showed up and arrested both parents. Somebody— whether it was a waiter, a patron, or one of various passersby is not entirely clear from news reports—had noticed the girl, Liv, on the curb and notified the authorities because they were concerned about her safety. Sørensen was dumbfounded, and her attempts to explain to the police officers that letting babies nap outside is standard practice and considered healthy in her homeland went nowhere.

After being taken to the police station, where they were strip-searched and placed in custody over the weekend, both parents were charged with child endangerment. Meanwhile, Liv was examined for signs of potential neglect and sexual abuse, and placed in temporary foster care. The charges were later dropped and Liv and her mother were reunited after four days, but the case set off a fiery debate about parenting cultures on both sides of the Atlantic.

Parents and columnists alike weighed in on the custom of leaving babies outside shops and restaurants. Most people interviewed by the *New York Times* in Manhattan believed that the couple had been negligent, though some didn't think their intent was malicious. Then-mayor Rudy Giuliani even spoke out about the case and defended the policemen's actions, saying that they "did the right thing." *New York Times* writer Clyde Haberman wryly noted that "weather reports said it was quite cold in Copenhagen yesterday, with temperatures near freezing and snow on the way. To follow Anette Sørensen's logic, it was a grand opportunity for Danish mothers to bundle up their babies, put them in strollers and leave them outside to enjoy the bracing air while the moms stayed toasty indoors."

In Denmark, however, many were shocked by the treatment that Sørensen and her daughter had been subjected to. There, as Sørensen had tried to explain to the New York police officers, it's commonplace to see babies alone in strollers outside cafés and restaurants, and the temperature on the night of Sørensen's arrest—reportedly in the mid-fifties—was pretty tame by Scandinavian standards. Granted, weather was not the only thing at issue in the Sørensen case. Copenhagen, a low-crime city of 1.3 million mostly friendly people, is a long way from New York City. Though Sørensen's defense lawyers described 132 Second Avenue, where the restaurant was located, as a safe tourist area, others portrayed it as rife with drugs and crime. Night was falling and it was starting to get dark while little Liv was soundly asleep outside in her stroller.

Was it naïve of Sørensen to act the way she did, considering the circumstances? Most definitely. Irresponsible? Maybe. But criminal? By Scandinavian standards—not by a long shot. And to get hauled off by the police, have to spend two nights in jail, and get charged with child endangerment while your child is taken away from you for four days at a crucial point of her development was from a Scandinavian perspective far more shocking than the act of leaving a child outside a restaurant and watching her through the window.

Apparently not all Scandinavians took note of the Sørensen case. In 2011, a Swedish woman in her thirties left her sleeping one-year-old child outside a Mexican restaurant in Amherst, Massachusetts, while she went inside to order a taco. According to the Swedish daily *Aftonbladet*, she was gone for about ten minutes and kept an eye on her baby through a window.

In Scandinavia, this likely wouldn't have caused any concern. But in Amherst somebody saw fit to call the cops. And even though the baby was found in good spirits and the mother was right there, the case was turned over to Child Protective Services, which planned to "investigate whether the child was in good hands"—i.e., whether the Swedish woman would pass muster as a good mother. Her defense echoed that of Sørensen's: "This is common in Sweden and not strange at all," she reportedly told the police when they showed up at the restaurant.

Even though I probably wouldn't have acted the same way Sørensen or the other woman did in that particular context, their stories are interesting because they in a way represent a microcosm of two vastly different parenting cultures, one that is slightly fanatical about getting fresh air on a daily basis, and one that is equally obsessed with safety. Eleven years after Sørensen was detained in jail in New York, I had found myself at the confluence of the same two parenting cultures as I gave birth to Maya and was preparing to raise her in the US.

OUTDOOR NAPPING 101

The secret of outdoor napping is to dress for the weather, as it's not good for the baby to be too hot or too cold. Dress the baby the way you would dress yourself, and don't double up on everything just because you're dressing a child. Lastly, use good judgment when determining whether the weather permits outdoor napping.

These tips can help get you started:

* Very young babies should sleep on their backs in a stroller that has a flat bottom or a bassinet attachment.
* Place the stroller near a wall and out of the wind, and make sure that the baby is protected against rain.
* In the summer, make sure that the sun is not shining directly into the stroller.
* Use a mosquito net to protect the baby from bugs, stray animals, and debris that may blow into the stroller.
* In the winter, dress the baby in warm layers (preferably starting with woolen long underwear in very cold temperatures) and use a bunting bag. Lining the stroller with lamb's wool helps insulate it.
* Avoid over-bundling, since this can restrict airflow around the child's face and increase the risk of sudden infant death syndrome.
* Place a baby monitor by the stroller or crack a window, and check on the child regularly.

An American Kid in a Swedish School

In Sweden, most children start something called "preschool class" the year they turn six, although this is not mandatory. (I would compare it to American kindergarten if it were not so completely different. Judging by what some older teachers in the US have told me, I imagine that it is a lot like kindergarten

was thirty years ago.) Formal, mandatory schooling starts the following year, when the children turn seven and start first grade.
Since Maya had essentially had formal schooling from age five,
when she started all-day kindergarten in Indiana, she was a year
ahead of her Swedish peers and would therefore join her older
cousin Oliver in second grade.

The night before Maya's first day of school we get several
inches of snow, and for about a millisecond I wonder if school
will be closed, or at least on a two-hour delay. For the past five
years, since Maya started preschool, this had been the norm. No
wonder my brain was doing a double take. Then I remember that
snow tires are mandatory during the winter months in Sweden,
and that both schools and workplaces will be open as usual. I'm
barely able to maneuver out of the Shack's microscopic parking
space, and then take a wrong turn, but finally we get on the
right track. As we get closer to the school, we see kids on foot,
some accompanied by parents and younger siblings, others by
themselves. All, including the adults, are wearing the kind of
bright yellow high-visibility vests that most Americans probably
associate with hunting. Here, they are a practical, cheap ticket
to survival for pedestrians on the road: At close to eight o'clock
in the morning the school is still draped in a predawn veil of
semi-darkness.

We walk into the school building just as Maya's classmates
are lining up and getting ready to go into the classroom. After
passing a couple of industrial-size drying cabinets on our right,
we leave our snowy boots in the hallway and put on some slip-
pers for wearing in the classroom, as is customary in schools in
Sweden. Maya's teacher, Suzanne, a tall lady with short dark
hair, greets us with a warm smile. "Welcome, Maya! We've been
looking forward to meeting you."

Maya swiftly hides behind my back as fifteen brand-new

classmates pierce her with curious looks. I squeeze her hand and remind her that I'll stay with her the entire day, since this is her first day in a new school. "Today I want you to write about your Christmas break," Suzanne says after the class finishes its morning routines. "It's okay if you don't finish before recess; you can keep working after you get back inside."

At nine thirty, an hour and a half into the day, it's time for a twenty-minute recess. The kids quickly jump into their insulated, waterproof coveralls and snow boots and run outside. About a dozen so-called snow racers, basically fast-running sleds on skis, lean against the wall of the school. "They're welcome to bring their own sleds to school, but they do need to wear a helmet in order to ride them," Suzanne explains. "We also have some toboggans and helmets that they can borrow."

The hilly school yard fills up with children, who immediately get busy in the snow. Those who are not sledding are either climbing up a big pile of snow and finding creative ways of getting down, or making things out of the snow, which is just wet enough for building. Maya, who is shy and sometimes takes a while to warm up to new people, starts to roll a big snowball with some of the girls from her new class. At the far end of the school yard, six boys are working together to break the unofficial record for "the biggest snowman ever built at the school," according to one of the boys. "Suzanne, we need your help putting the head on!" another boy shouts. (In Sweden, pretty much everybody but members of the royal family goes by their first name.) "It's too heavy for us." Suzanne excuses herself to go assist with the giant snowman and I watch as Maya flies down the hill on a small toboggan.

At the bottom of the sledding hill is a small soccer field that is partly covered with ice. "Our wonderful PTO is making an ice-skating rink," Suzanne explains after ensuring that the record-breaking snowman has all its parts. "It's not quite done yet, but as long as it stays cold they'll finish it any day now. We're hoping to ice-skate for PE class on Thursday."

I almost can't believe it. Thirteen years in the US have conditioned me to always weigh a situation from a legal standpoint. I was used to signing one liability waiver before going to yoga, another one for letting my daughter go on a field trip, and a third one for leaving my Labrador at a kennel, to confirm that she knew how to swim and wasn't likely to drown in a dog pool with six inches of water. I knew that for a certain type of personal injury lawyer the combination of a slick, hard surface, sharp skates, speed, and young children would be like blood in the water to a shark. Yet there were no liability waivers in sight, not even a sign stating the rules, and definitely no mention of any lawyers. How did the school handle the responsibility? The risk? The injuries? After all, getting out on the icy blacktop had been strictly verboten at Maya's school back home. But in Sweden, ice-skating was apparently not only allowed at recess, it was encouraged as part of the curriculum.

"It's very rare for somebody to get injured. We have our rules and the kids are really good about following them," Suzanne says, as if she were reading my mind. "We nag them about wearing helmets a lot, and they know that they're not allowed to start sledding or ice-skating until there is an adult outside."

"But what if something were to happen?" I insist.

"All the students have casualty insurance coverage through the county. But, really, nothing serious ever happens."

And that was the end of that.

After recess, the students do individual work, depending on what they need to catch up on. Some students read; others write in their journals. Just like when I was in second grade some thirty years ago, a lot of the work is project based and the children are fostered by the teachers to plan out and take responsibility for

their own work. There is also a new focus on integrating movement and physical activity into traditional academic lessons—for
example, by using math cards with prompts to bounce a ball so
many times or count the number of steps required to walk to the
other side of the room. "We try to keep the schedule varied so
that the children don't have to sit all day," Suzanne says.

Sometimes, regular classes like art, science, and physical
education are taught outdoors. In the woods, the children learn
while moving around, something that is especially important to
the youngest students. Chatrine, who is in charge of the school's
environmental education, believes that nature makes subjects
like math and physics come alive in a way they never will in a
classroom. "With the six-year-olds we've looked for sticks and
compared length, which ones were shorter and longer," she says.
"In science class, with the older children, we've used the sledding hill to learn about friction by comparing different ways of
getting down—for example, with a wax cloth, a plastic sled,
shoes with grooved soles, and so on. There really isn't anything
you can do inside that you can't do outside."

All the changes in Sweden have not necessarily been for
the better. Years of plummeting results in the Programme for
International Student Assessment (PISA), an evaluation of
fifteen-year-olds' skills in math, reading, and science in different
countries, has caused outrage and led to some erratic experi-
mentation with the Swedish education system. Inevitably, it has
also increased the focus on testing. Whereas I didn't have to
take a single national standardized test until eighth grade, these
are now given out in third, sixth, and ninth grades. "I think the
tests steal a lot of time from teaching, and we know where the
children are at anyway," Suzanne says, echoing a sentiment that
I'd heard from many American teachers. "But we don't teach to
the test—we continue to follow our curriculum as usual."

At eleven o'clock, the class breaks for lunch. The next class starts at noon, effectively giving the students another thirty to forty minutes of outdoor recess, depending on when they get done eating. "Do the kids always go outside for recess?" I ask Suzanne as we once again watch the children bounce around in the fluffy white stuff covering the school yard. She seems a bit surprised at the question. "Why, yes. They're always outside, unless it's storming so badly that it would be too dangerous."

During the lunch break, more sleeting snow starts to come down from overcast skies and some of the cold, humid air seeps in through the crack between my snow pants and my puffy coat. Had we been in Indiana on a day like this, it's a stretch to think that Maya's school would even have been open. It's even less likely that the kids would have been outside for recess, since that might have caused them to get wet or cold, or to slip on the blacktop. These were the kinds of conditions that would cause people to curse winter, announce the coming of the next snow-pocalypse, stay at home from work, and hibernate. But in this small town in Sweden, the first- and second-grade teachers saw it as a reason to move the last class period of the day outside as well, giving the kids a rather cushy start to the new semester. When I, slightly skeptical, ask Suzanne if the students' schedule really allows for more sledding today, she says, "Well, yes. We're required to have a certain number of hours for instruction, and we have our academic goals that we must meet." Then she adds, without so much as a trace of sarcasm, "But today we felt like we had to take advantage of this lovely weather. I'm so happy that we have snow; I really hope it'll stick around."

After lunch, during the last class period of the day, the sledding picks back up. Maya and three boys find a creative way to go down the hill all crammed on the same sled, recalling the dangerously overcrowded *tuk-tuk*s that I had often seen people drive around in Southeast Asia. To further increase the challenge, the older kids have built a big bump in the middle of the hill, which these first and second graders are now trying to hit. As they go down the hill they fall off one by one, squealing with a mix of delight and terror. Not once do they all make it down to the bottom still sitting or standing on the sled. And not once do I see an adult trying to stop their risky games.

I can't help but think about the poor teacher back in Indiana who told me that all she did during recess in the winter was tell the children what they were not allowed to do, and how different the approach of teachers seemed here in Sweden. "I actually believe that you have to let them take some risks," says Lisa, one of the older staff members on recess duty as she watches Maya and her new friends at the top of the hill. "That's how children learn. It's a form of trial and error—they try one thing and if that doesn't work they'll try something different. It's hard to watch sometimes, because as an adult you're wired to intervene. But even though it looks chaotic, they do a really good job of looking out for each other."

"Sometimes I think that it's better for the adults to take a step back, observe, and not interfere," one of the younger staff members chimes in. Watching the organized chaos on the sledding hill, she jokes, "Sometimes it's better to just look the other way."

At 1 p.m., Maya's first school day is over. The anxiety from the morning has all but vanished and been replaced with a big smile and flushed cheeks. She looks healthy and happy. During her five-hour day she has been outside for two hours. Granted, this is not a typical schedule, because the teachers wanted the children to enjoy the newly fallen snow, but even on a regular day outdoor recess will make up about an hour, or 20 percent, of the school day. This is pretty standard for the Scandinavian countries, where students have recess through high school. In

Finland, a country envied by educators worldwide as the only non-Asian country to consistently rank in the top ten on the PISA test, students typically get a fifteen-minute break after each lesson, averaging seventy-five minutes of recess every day. They also have fewer instructional hours than students in any other country in the developed world, and little homework, leaving the children with more time to play outside. This is a drastically different approach to education than what is normally found in Asian countries, where many students rack up twelve hours or more per day hunched over their textbooks. Obviously, many other factors go into the Finnish success story. But one thing is for sure: The fresh air that teachers and parents in Scandinavia insist that children get every day is not just good for them—it's actually essential to their health and well-being.

According to the rules of survival, we can go about three weeks without food and three days without water, but only three minutes without breathing. Every single cell in our body needs oxygen to live and produce energy. Fresh air helps oxygenate our cells, which in turn makes us feel more energetic and alive. If that fresh air is combined with exercise, like sledding or climbing up a pile of snow, even better.

In some American elementary schools, cutting recess has become a popular way for administrators to gain instructional time and pad the schedule with subjects that are most easily assessed with standardized tests—reading, writing, and math. But the research is not on their side. A 2011 Swiss study of five-year-olds showed that aerobic fitness improves children's attention span, and that better motor skills, like balance, result in improved working memory. Both are crucial to academic success. Many other studies have shown that movement and regular breaks from the routine help children's ability to learn and pay attention, and that recess makes hyperactive children less fidgety and more capable of concentrating. A meta-analysis of two hundred studies showed that physical activity during the school day resulted in increased fitness, better attitudes, and a slight improvement in test scores. Moreover, recess is often the only time of the school day that students have a chance to socialize and play in an unstructured setting. This is when they make up their own games, negotiate rules, and resolve conflicts, honing their social skills in the process. And the effects of recess are most tangible when it is held outdoors. Children may view watching movies or playing computer games in a classroom during "indoor recess" as a welcome break from routine, but it gives them none of the benefits that are associated with outdoor recess: fresh air, exercise, and a chance to develop social skills.

Even if indoor recess is held in a gym, it is less effective from an exercise point of view. A 2011 study of urban public school children in Missouri showed that both boys and girls take more steps and work up a higher heart rate when recess is held outdoors, compared with recess in a gym or classroom. Experimental research has also shown that children who are physically active during recess at school are more likely to stay active after school, according to Olga S. Jarrett, a professor of early childhood education and science education at Georgia State University, who is nationally renowned for her research on recess. Conversely, children who have no recess or PE during the school day tend not to compensate after school but are instead more likely to get stuck on the couch. Finally, several studies have showed that outdoor recess can help prevent myopia, or nearsightedness, in elementary school children, since children's eyes need bright, natural light in order to develop normally.

Calling for research-based decisions on recess policy in elementary schools, Jarrett writes, "The available research suggests that recess can play an important role in the learning, social development, and health of elementary school children. While there are arguments against recess, *no research clearly supports not having recess.*" (Italics added.)

Then there is the anecdotal evidence. Parents who complain that their children are depressed because they have no recess and are inside all day long. Teachers who struggle to make school fun for the youngest children when recess is sacrificed on the altar of standardized testing. Children who act out in the classroom but whose characteristic signs of ADHD improve significantly after they spend more time outside.

Rebecca Lowen, a history teacher at Metropolitan State University in St. Paul, Minnesota, experienced a radical change in her nine-year-old son's behavior after the family moved to Norway for six months and she decided to leave his ADHD medication behind. Back in Minnesota he had needed the medication to cope with school, but now she wanted to give him a break from the side effects. Besides, her expectations for what her son would learn while the family was abroad were limited anyway. Amazingly, her son stopped fidgeting in the classroom and all of a sudden found joy in his schoolwork, even though he was unmedicated and taught in Norwegian, a language that was new to him.

"Incredibly, he cannot wait to get to school each day," Lowen writes in the *Minneapolis StarTribune*. "He is rapidly learning Norwegian. He is happy to do homework and, in fact, sometimes works ahead or asks his sister to make up math problems for him to solve. At night, he readily reads before falling asleep, something he would never do back home."

What accounted for this dramatic change, according to Lowen, was neither an altered diet nor reduction in screen time, two factors that are sometimes believed to improve ADHD symptoms. Rather, she credited his school experience for the turnaround. "He has three recesses here, rather than just one, as in Minnesota. The school day is about an hour shorter than at home, giving him extra time to play before doing homework. He enjoys nearly two hours of unstructured, outdoor play every day here, four times more than in the United States."

ADHD is a recognized condition in Norway, and 3 to 5 percent of Norwegian children and adolescents are estimated to have it. That figure is consistent with the American Psychiatric Association's *Diagnostic and Statistical Manual of Mental Disorders* (*DSM-5*), which estimates that 5 percent of children in the US have ADHD. Yet 11 percent of all American children are currently diagnosed with the disorder, a figure that has been rising steadily for at least two decades. Of these, more than half receive medication for it, and among preschoolers who are diagnosed, the number is over 75 percent. Researchers are still scrambling to explain the recent ADHD epidemic, and the debate about how to treat it goes on. Outdoor play is certainly no cure-all for ADHD, but in Lowen's case it was a game changer. Her son's behavior no longer fit the diagnosis, nor did his Norwegian teacher see any evidence of it.

The Sledding Party

Maya quickly adapts to her new school and new routine. So quickly, in fact, that I'm baffled by the change in her behavior. Unlike Lowen's son, Maya didn't have ADHD or problems with acting out in class. On the contrary, she was quiet, generally kept to herself, and did her work diligently and well. Her teacher back home had called her smart and, as the admittedly biased parent I was, I would have to agree. The problem was that, even though she had so many things going for her, Maya didn't seem to enjoy school much. In kindergarten she had struggled with the long school days and complained that she wanted to go back to preschool. She was moody and tired after school, and things didn't get any better as the homework load started to build up in first and second grade. Her standard five-syllable response whenever anybody asked her something about school was "I don't remember," and unless a classmate had a birthday (which meant there was a reasonably good chance of scoring a cupcake), I rarely saw her excited about anything that had to do with school. It was difficult for me to relate. I had always loved school, at least until I was faced with incomprehensible algebra sometime in eighth or ninth grade. Then again, having grown up in Sweden thirty-some years ago, I had a school experience that was very different from hers.

After Maya's first day at her new school, she confidently announces, "Tomorrow I want to go by myself," politely declining my mom's offer to go with her. When she comes back in the afternoon she is again bubbling with stories about class, the food she has eaten, and the new friends that she has made. During the week that follows I get bombarded with reports: "Guess what we did for PE class today! We went sledding and I went with Oliver and Hannes and Nellie down the hill and we went soooo fast, over a bump, and then we ended up in a big pile! For lunch we got fish; I didn't like that much but the potatoes were pretty good. Then we had social science and we talked about different professions. Hey, by the way, did you sing this song when you were little?" she rattles off, and starts singing a song that, sure enough, I sang in music class when I was in second grade. For the first time in her soon-to-be-eight-year-old life I could tell that she was genuinely excited about school. She was no longer just "Ready to Learn" as that behavior chart with the wooden clothespins on the wall in her classroom back home had often noted. She was *motivated* to learn.

After two weeks at her new school, Maya receives an invitation to a birthday party from one of her classmates. "Sledding Party," the invite says. "Bring a helmet and something to ride on!" I'm intrigued. I had always tried to incorporate outdoor treasure hunts for Maya's birthday in February and thankfully her friends' parents were good sports who never complained about getting their kids back muddy. But the concept of holding an entire party outside in January was new to me.

On the day of the party we load up the car with some borrowed snow racers and toboggans, including some sort of plastic stand-up board contraption that looks like it may have caused a few hairline fractures back in the '80s. Maya's classmate Hannes lives outside of town on a small farm with some egg-laying hens, a few sheep, and arguably one of the best sledding hills in the county. His mother, Anette, is an energetic and straightforward woman who smiles almost as much as she talks. When we arrive she's busy cooking hot dogs and heating *saft*, a sweet drink popular with kids, over an open fire. She's surrounded by sixteen snowsuit-clad children, sitting on blankets and cushions laid out on seats dug out of some big piles of snow, and a couple of old benches. The kids are champing at the bit to get down to business on the long, steep, and slightly curved hill by the house, and don't even bother taking their helmets off as they inhale carrots and hot dogs by the dozens.

"We did a sledding party last year, too, and the kids wanted to do it again," Anette says when I ask her why they decided to do an outdoor birthday party. "They really like it." She tosses a few hot dogs on the grill and implores one of the boys to please finish chewing his carrots before getting on his sled. "We always have our birthday parties outside," she continues. "One year we had a disco in a teepee, disco ball and all. I like having the parties outside. Honestly, we do it partly because we're lazy. Can you

71

imagine having sixteen kids in the house? No, thank you! That's going to turn into chaos really fast. It's a lot easier to clean up after an outdoor party."

As I suspected, Anette and her husband and three kids spend a great deal of time outside in general, not only during birthday parties. On the weekends, the family often cooks lunch over the fire pit rather than going inside. Getting outside on a daily basis has been a priority since the kids were little. "You have to get them out now, not when they're thirteen, regardless of how torturous it can be sometimes. I don't know how many times we've bundled them up to go ice-skating, and then they get tired of it after fifteen minutes. But now we're reaping the benefits from taking the kids outside a lot since they were little. Now we can go down to the lake and ice-skate together as a family."

On the sledding hill, the kids are packing down the snow with their snow racers, and the track seems to get a little faster with each run. One after one the kids come flying down the hill, one blond girl screaming with terror as she quickly approaches a tall barrier of snow at the bottom of the slope. "Veer to the right!" Anette yells, but the girl's hands appear frozen to the steering wheel, and she crashes straight into the embankment. "I couldn't steer!" she cries, tears flowing down her bright pink cheeks. Anette wraps her arms around her and comforts her. "You're okay. Nothing happened. You just need to steer away from the snowbank next time."

"Don't you worry that somebody will get hurt?" I ask Anette when things are back under control. It's the little liability voices in my head that are talking.

"In the beginning I did, but no, not anymore," she says. "It's dangerous to be inside, too, you know. What if a ceiling lamp falls down on your head?"

She's joking, of course, but there is a serious undertone. As a nurse, she's all too familiar with the health consequences of sitting on the couch (obesity, heart disease, diabetes, rickets, and myopia, just to name a few), and she was damned if she was going to let her family fall into that trap.

"It's so important to our health that we stay active. I think we're going to face a public health crisis if we don't use our bones when we're young," she says. "We like our *fika* and we like baking together. But if we have something sweet we also go outside and move around. If the kids don't want to do that I tell them they can eat some carrots instead."

After a while, it's time to break for hot chocolate and homemade brownies that are individually decorated with the Swedish flag—a yellow cross against a blue backdrop. It's a simple dessert but no less appreciated by the kids, who wolf down the chocolaty treats and move on to do a treasure hunt in the snow, led by Anette's husband. Then more sledding until the parents start showing up to pick up their charges. A few parents can't resist the call of the hill. "Sledding is underrated," one mom hollers as she comes to a stop at the bottom. Maya and Nora are the last stragglers on the sledding hill, high on hot chocolate and their own speed.

"I'm sorry, I feel like we've overstayed our welcome," I tell Anette as night starts to fall around us, an hour after the official end of the party. "I'll call the last run now."

"Oh, no, not at all. Don't you just love it when the kids want to stay outside and play in the fresh air?"

We bond over that statement and decide to get the kids together again sometime.

On our way back to the Shack we see about a dozen teenagers out on the lake, ice-skating and singing at the top of their lungs. The light from their headlamps is bouncing back and forth on the ice, making the ice skaters look like the cast in an impromptu and unchoreographed stage show.

At this point, I was no longer worried about Maya not finding any friends at school or getting homesick, and I had all but forgotten about the weekly spelling lists and math reviews that I was supposed to have her work on. I had a much bigger issue on my mind: What if she wouldn't want to go back to the US when our time in Sweden was up?

Scandinavian Parenting Tip #2

If it is safe and practical where you live, let your baby nap outside when the weather permits, and seek out opportunities to spend as much time outside as possible. As your child gets older, choose outdoor activities that the whole family enjoys and be sure to adjust your expectations to your child's pace and day-to-day form. Plan well for longer outings, and remember that you can never bring too many emergency snacks!

Suggested reading: *Balanced and Barefoot: How Unrestricted Outdoor Play Makes for Strong, Confident, and Capable Children*, by Angela Hanscom. New Harbinger, 2016.

3

JUST LET THEM PLAY

Most of what children need to learn during their early
childhood years cannot be taught; it's discovered through play.

—RUTH WILSON

One night, I get a phone call from my friend Sue back in the
States. She tells me that she started having trouble getting her
oldest son out of the car in the drop-off line at preschool. "I
asked him why he doesn't want to go to school and he said he's
bored. He's four! How does he even know what 'bored' means?"
she laments. "I think it's some combination of him not connecting with any of the kids and having to sit still at a desk for the
first time in his life and do papers when he's a kid who loves to
move around."

She had sent her son to preschool with the same idea a lot
of parents have when they send their kids to preschool: that he
would play and socialize with other kids. Now she was feeling
defeated and was in disbelief about the whole thing. "I don't
even want to send him to preschool again next year, and I don't
want to send his little brother at all, but when I tell people that,
they tell me they're going to fall behind," she says.

Sue herself didn't go to preschool at all, and kindergarten
only lasted for a mostly play-filled half day back then. She still
managed to make it through school with top grades, put herself
through college and law school, and today runs a successful law
firm. Her gut instinct told her that her sons, too, would be fine,

but she wasn't getting a whole lot of support. "There's a lot of pressure. What if I ruin their chances of getting into college and they end up in the gutter living off the government because I didn't make the right decision about preschool?" She's only half-joking—and thanking her lucky stars that her youngest son has a September birthday, so he'll miss all the cutoffs. If she and her husband do end up sending him to preschool, he'll be almost five by the time he starts.

The preschool that her older son goes to is a parent cooperative that has a play-based approach to learning, with plenty of field trips, sensory bins, and hands-on experiments mixed in with traditional academics. At least it tries to. Lately, the teachers had come under pressure from the public school to adapt to the ever-increasing requirements of kindergarten. Parents, too, feared that socializing, playing, singing, and learning how to be a good friend didn't do enough to prepare their prodigies for what was to come. Some even felt like they had no choice but to move their children to other preschools that focused more on academics.

"It was nothing against the teachers, I just heard so much about all the testing that is done now, and I felt like he wasn't making much progress," said one mom who was disappointed that her three-year-old son wasn't learning how to write fast enough. "Finally we decided to move him, and this school is completely different. Now he brings home little worksheets for tracing letters every week."

Meanwhile, the teachers seemed exasperated from the pressure. "I even felt guilty for letting the three-year-olds play for an hour yesterday," one of them divulged. "I had to tell them to get back to their book work."

Bowing to the pressure from the school district and from disgruntled parents, the teachers at the parent cooperative recently started handing out weekly homework assignments to the four-year-olds. This was by no means unique for this preschool, just a symptom of a national trend of putting more and more pressure on three- and four-year-olds to learn academic facts. If kindergarten was the new first grade, as some educators claimed, it certainly seemed like preschool had become the new kindergarten.

Talking to Sue made me think of the time when Maya had gone to preschool, four years ago. In the fall of her last year, with just under two semesters to go, some of the other parents had gotten stressed-out and antsy about their children's progress. They complained that the children spent too much time playing and doing crafts and experiments. I was puzzled. Most of the kids were only four years old; what did they expect them to be doing? Like Sue, I had sent Maya to preschool thinking that it would be good for her to socialize and play with children other than the ones she saw at the babysitter's house. She was still learning to tie her shoes and stand in line for the bathroom and make great mud pies. Her vocabulary had grown immensely since she started preschool, and academically I couldn't think of much to worry about at this age. Then again, I was still blissfully ignorant of the rigors of American kindergarten.

"When we went to preschool, it used to be all about playing and sitting in a circle and singing songs," one mom, an elementary school teacher, told me. "Parents still think they're sending their kids to kindergarten so they can learn how to share and take turns, but that's just not how it is anymore."

"These hands-on activities are great fun and all that, but I just don't see how that's going to get them ready for kindergarten," another mother said, voicing her concern about the direction of the preschool. And then, ominously, "I guess we'll find out at kindergarten screening."

These parents had gotten the message from the US Department of Education, and it was crystal clear. Kids these days need to spend less time molding Play-Doh and more time preparing for their corporate careers.

Until that time, I hadn't even known what kindergarten screening was. I had simply trusted that Maya would learn what she needed to learn in her own time, and it hadn't struck me that she might flunk some cryptic entry test to elementary school—in fact, I didn't even know those existed. Now it sounded like this was a real threat, something that I hadn't worried nearly enough about.

When I asked a kindergarten teacher about the screening process, she assured me that it was not a high-stakes test that would make or break my daughter's future, but rather an assessment tool that was used to determine whether a child was developmentally ready for kindergarten, and whether he or she might need extra assistance in the classroom. The teacher also told me she thought preschool should be about having fun and doing "all the things that we don't have time for in kindergarten, like playing, painting, singing, reading stories, and playing games."

That took care of my concern about kindergarten screening, but the more I learned about actual kindergarten, the more I fretted about enrolling Maya.

Playing Is Learning

Before we left the US, Nora had gone to the same preschool as Maya, and now that she was about to enroll in a preschool in Sweden, we were in for a radical change. Preschools in Scandinavia are different from those in the US since they generally offer full-time or part-time care all year-round for children who are as young as one year old. The model is sometimes called "educare," because the purpose of the preschools here is to simultaneously educate and care for children whose parents work outside the home. Since that is most parents, a vast majority of Scandinavian children (as many as 84 percent in Sweden) between the ages of one and five are enrolled in preschool.

Another big difference is that preschool in the Scandinavian countries is more or less universal, as the fees are heavily subsidized by the government. To a lot of Americans, having the government in charge of your child's day care probably sounds as wise as giving the fox a VIP pass to the chicken coop. But Scandinavian parents don't see it this way. When the parents of 108,000 preschool-age children in Sweden were asked what they thought about their child's day care, 95 percent of them responded that they were happy with it. This is pretty remarkable considering that it can sometimes be hard to get that many people to agree that snow is white, and that any opinions relating to raising children have a tendency to trigger tribal warfare.

Although preschools in Sweden are funded by the central government, they can be owned and operated directly by local municipalities, private businesses, or parent cooperatives. Regardless, they are required to have a certified preschool teacher in charge, and they all follow the same national curriculum. Part of the reason why parents in Sweden are so contented with the preschool system is probably that this national curriculum very much reflects Swedes' general idea of what early childhood should be about. And tracing letters is not it.

The national curriculum for the Swedish preschool is twenty pages long and goes on at length about things like fostering respect for one another, human rights, and democratic values, as well as a lifelong desire to learn. The document's word choices are a pretty good clue to what Swedish society wants and expects from toddlers and preschoolers. The curriculum features the word *play* thirteen times, *language* twelve times, *nature* six times, and *math* five times. But there is not a single mention of *literacy* or *writing*. Instead, two of the most frequently used words are *learning* (with forty-eight appearances) and *development* (forty-seven).

The other Scandinavian countries have similar early child-hood education traditions. In Finland, formal teaching of reading doesn't start until the child begins first grade, at age seven, and in the Finnish equivalent of kindergarten, which children enroll in the year they turn six, teachers will only teach reading if a child is showing an interest in it. Despite this lack of emphasis on early lit-eracy, Finland is considered the most literate country in the world, with Norway coming in second, and Iceland, Denmark, and Swe-den rounding out the top five, according to a 2016 study by Cen-tral Connecticut State University. John Miller, who conducted the study, noted that the five Nordic countries scored so well because "their monolithic culture values reading." They have something else in common: their commitment to play in the early years.

There is no unanimous, internationally recognized definition of *play*, but the British organization Play England calls it a "pro-cess that is freely chosen, personally directed and intrinsically motivated," noting that "all children and young people need to play. The impulse to play is innate. Play is a biological, psycho-logical and social necessity, and is fundamental to the healthy development and well-being of individuals and communities."

The curriculum for the Swedish preschool doesn't just pro-mote play in all its activities—it also establishes children's legal right to play and learn outside, both in planned environments, like the school yard, and natural environments, like the forest. This applies to preschools in the country as well as in the city. Urban preschools that lack natural environments in the school yard meet this requirement by simply taking the children to a public green space, like a park or nearby woods, on foot or via public transportation. "All of our children live in town, so they're used to traffic. Even the one- and two-year-olds learn quickly to hold on to a buddy and walk," says Cecilia Ramning, who runs the preschool Fyra Elementen in Stockholm. Although some of the parks are within a five-minute walk of the preschool, occasionally the children walk up to forty-five minutes to get to their destination, with the youngest ones taking turns using the preschool's two double strollers. "Some people think that spending time at the park is the most important thing, but a lot of things can happen on the way. Sometimes we find acorns, chestnuts, or a really interesting beetle. The way to the park is an important part of the experience," Ramning says.

A survey of a hundred preschools in Stockholm showed that the average time spent outside was one and a half hours per day—on a bad-weather day in the winter. On a nice day in the summer, the average was nearly six hours. I was particularly excited about this outdoor play guarantee. Nora's new preschool was an ordinary municipal preschool, much like the one I myself had gone to many years ago. It didn't cast itself as a nature preschool and was not a forest school by any means, but at least I knew that at a very minimum nature would be part of the curriculum and she would be able to play outside every day.

When we show up for Nora's first day, the fenced yard outside the preschool is covered in well-trodden snow. Her spirit is still high from seeing three moose lazily cross the road so close to our car that I literally could have reached out of the window and poked them with one of the cross-country skis that I had sitting in the back.

A low hill on our right bears evidence of heavy sledding, and straight ahead we see a little snowman whose mouth is made of small clumps of mud. He is leaning ominously but still standing. There is a big plastic culvert in the snow-covered grass, some bushes with bright red branches, a small hillside slide, and a large sand play area with some benches, a mud kitchen, and a table. A woodshop and a playhouse are locked up for the winter, but a third building is unlocked and chock-full of outdoor toys that are used all year.

I'm carrying a plastic bag with supplies, and they look nothing like the things I used to bring to preschool every fall back in the States (one box of Kleenex, one box of jumbo-size crayons, one roll of paper towels, a bottle of hand sanitizer, one box of markers, and about twelve hundred glue sticks). In Sweden all the supplies needed for activities and daily operations are provided by the school. They don't need more markers—what they want is children who can play outside in all types of weather. Which prompts this list of recommended supplies for winter:

* Thick mittens (two pairs)
* Woolen socks
* Winter coveralls
* Thick sweater/fleece
* Warm hat
* Rain gear
* Rain boots
* Complete change of clothes for indoor use

And, at the end, a cheery reminder: "We go outside rain or shine!"

Just like at Maya's school, two industrial-size drying cabinets in the mudroom are humming quietly across from a whole wall full of colorful polyester rain clothes (*galonisar*) as we enter the building. We take our shoes off and go into the main hallway, where winter gear is stacked high in each child's cubby space.

"Welcome!" says one of the lead teachers whom I have previously talked to over the phone. Like most Swedish preschool teachers I've met, she takes great care to get down to eye level with Nora and speaks directly to her. "My name is Ellen."

Ellen gives us the rundown of this section of the preschool. There are twenty-three children (most of whom are between the ages of four and five, plus a couple of three-year-olds) and five staff, but not everybody is there at the same time. The first children show up at six thirty in the morning. Breakfast is served around eight, then the kids play until ten, when everybody gathers for circle time and a morning snack (universally referred to as "fruit time," since fresh fruit is the go-to snack for Swedish preschools). After that, it's time for outdoor play until lunch. This is followed by rest or naps for the youngest children, and story time for the older ones. The afternoon is mostly devoted to unstructured play—during the warmer months, usually outside again—or projects in smaller groups, broken up by a snack at two thirty. The last child leaves the facility at five in the evening.

Nora is taking it all in, curiously watching the kids around her. Some are busy playing a board game with a teacher; others are building a fort out of cushions in the reading room. There is an art room and a corner for pretend play, with dolls and a miniature kitchen. The walls are decorated with pictures and posters documenting projects that highlight different areas in the national curriculum: nature and technology, math, language development, creativity, and social skills. "Diversity—We are similar but still different," one poster says, underneath a row of flags from different countries that the children have colored. A photo of four children wearing orange high-visibility vests in the forest is captioned, "We look for treasures in nature and check what is hiding underneath the leaves." Another picture shows three boys building a house out of a cardboard box. "Collaboration," the caption reads. "Helpfulness," says another caption, next to a photo of a boy helping a girl slice a sausage. As we sit down on the floor for fruit time, I make another observation: None of the children in the room are overweight.

"We want our children to learn in a fun way," Ellen explains later. "We don't sit and teach the children to count to ten, but we use math constantly. For example, when we have circle time, they take turns counting how many children are here. We also incorporate science through simple experiments. Sometimes we bring in natural objects like rocks and sticks and test which ones float in a bucket of water. If we have snow, we might bring some inside and see what happens when it melts and we pour the water through a coffee filter. And of course they use physics every time they build something."

"So how do you work with literacy skills?" I ask Ellen while Nora decides to join a group of older kids listening to a teacher reading a book.

"We don't schedule time for the children to work on writing, if that's what you mean," she says, "and we don't have specific lessons when we teach them the alphabet. But we work a lot on reading comprehension during story time, and the children further their language development immensely through creative and imaginative play."

"Nora already knows how to write her name. She even uses the correct capitalization," I volunteer a little too enthusiastically. Since I myself didn't stop writing my name in all caps until I was about seven years old and Nora mastered this feat at her American preschool at age three, I of course think that she borders on genius.

Ellen raises her eyebrows behind her dark-rimmed glasses. "Wow," she says, looking more surprised than impressed. "Well, we usually notice when the children become interested in writing and then we give them little notebooks that they can use. The idea is that it will come naturally when they're ready for it. It's a lot easier for them to learn when they have that intrinsic motivation."

The idea that children learn through play is far from new. Plato said that "the most effective kind of education is that a child should play amongst lovely things." Much later, in the 1700s, Swiss-born Renaissance philosopher Jean-Jacques Rousseau championed the idea that all education of children should be based on play in his groundbreaking treatise *Émile, or On Education*. "Do I dare set forth here the most important, the most useful rule of all education? It is not to save time, but to squander it," he famously wrote, in support of children's innate ability to learn through their own experiences. Then, in the 1830s, a German teacher and staunch nature lover named Friedrich Froebel picked up on the idea that play is key to children's physical, moral, and spiritual development. He was so convinced of this idea that he decided to create an early childhood education program that revolved around singing, dancing, gardening, self-directed play, and experiencing nature with all senses. Froebel viewed children as plants who would flower if they were allowed to learn at their own pace, nourished and guided by a teacher. He called his concept "kindergarten"—literally, a child's garden.

In the second half of the nineteenth century, Froebel's play-based, child-centered philosophy caught on in Sweden, and until the 1950s preschools here were called *barnträdgårdar*, or "children's gardens." Froebel remains one of the most influential figures in early childhood education in Sweden, along with the Russian developmental psychologist Lev Vygotsky and Swiss psychologist Jean Piaget, both of whom advocated for a child-centered approach to learning. In a classroom setting, Piaget believed the learning process was more important than the end product, and that children can learn problem-solving skills only through active discovery. Vygotsky held that children's cognitive development is heavily influenced by their culture and that they learn primarily by playing and interacting with older and more skilled children and adults.

He is mostly known for his theory about the zone of proximal development, according to which one should respect each child's individual space and readiness to learn a new concept. Parents and preschool teachers can do this by providing the "scaffolding" for development and giving the child just enough help to build his or her confidence to climb to the next level, without pushing or carrying. By giving children this space, adults allow them to develop self-esteem and learn to solve their own problems.

Anette Eskilsson, a Swedish early childhood educator who often speaks about stimulating children's desire to learn, explains the Scandinavian attitude toward play and learning this way: "It's two completely different ways of looking at it. You either view children as empty containers, waiting to be filled by adults through teaching, or you believe that they have the innate capability to learn together with others. In Sweden we have faith in the child's own curiosity and desire to learn. We call this concept 'the competent child.'"

Later, as I'm standing outside in the snow with another of Nora's preschool teachers, Barbro, watching a dozen kids negotiate their way up and down the tiny sledding hill, she talks along similar lines. She strongly believes children learn more from direct experiences and play than when they are just asked to memorize information that is passed down to them by a teacher.

"Some children become interested in writing early, and when that's the case we encourage them. It may be that they're involved with pretend play and want to make tickets for something. In that case, the writing has a purpose. Otherwise they may just end up drawing lines that have no meaning to them," she says.

"I know there are different philosophies out there. Some people think that you should focus on literacy, but I don't like it when everything we do is just a straight line pointing toward school. This is preschool. Why can't we let the children be in the here and now?"

Go Outside and Play

Parents and early childhood educators in Scandinavia seem to agree that if you want to raise healthy, capable learners, letting them play as much as possible is key. So why, if active play and learning are inseparable, are they so often pitted against each other on the other side of the Atlantic? How did it get to a point where an American preschool teacher feels guilty about letting a group of three-year-olds play, when this is exactly what three-year-olds are supposed to be doing?

Part of the explanation can likely be found in education reforms that have increased the academic requirements for kindergarten beginning in the 1980s and further exacerbated by No Child Left Behind, Race to the Top, and, most recently, the Common Core State Standards, according to the advocacy group Alliance for Childhood. Although child-centered early education models can be found in the US through the Montessori, Waldorf, and Reggio Emilia approaches, "teacher-led instruction in kindergartens has almost entirely replaced the active, play-based, experiential learning that we know children need from decades of research in cognitive and developmental psychology and neuroscience," the group notes. And now pre-K is suffering from the ripple effects.

Maureen Vandermaas-Peeler, a petite, fast-speaking professor of psychology at Elon University in North Carolina, doesn't believe this change has been for the better. After spending a great deal of time researching early childhood learning, and teaching as a visiting scholar in Copenhagen, Denmark, she feels like the US could take some pointers from Scandinavia when it comes to attitudes about play-based learning. "Most people are unaware of the need in early childhood for play," she says. "I think the teachers themselves want the children to learn through play, so they have to explain to the parents how important it is. When people are clamoring for more academics, I don't think most of them want their kids to sit down all day. Unfortunately, by kindergarten they are expected to do that."

Playing comes naturally to a child, regardless of what materials he or she may have on hand. A stick can become a doll, a sword, a horse, or a magic wand. A cardboard box can become a rocket ship, a cave, or a car. Kids can play for hours with extremely simple means. In fact, researchers have found that children play even more creatively when they don't have ready-made toys at hand. Play is about as universal as it comes—it crosses all cultural and socioeconomic boundaries. What differs, Vandermaas-Peeler has found, is the value that various cultures place on play. American parents value play highly and often play with their young children. They are also extremely concerned about academics. Just do a quick Google search for "educational activities for two-year-olds" and find yourself sifting through nearly half a billion results. Likewise, Pinterest is ablaze with preschool printables and color-sorting activities and 101 ways to make geometric shapes out of a toilet-paper tube. Marketers naturally feed on parents' anxiety about their children's education too. "While your baby is beginning to explore, it's never too soon to spark a love for subjects like art, music and language," says the company behind the supposedly educational Baby Einstein videos that researchers actually found had no value to and may even hamper language development. "Take advantage of it by trying some expert-approved activities and products for a 'cultured' baby," the company goes on, reinforcing parents' fears that their children will be left behind sorting shapes while their peers are busy writing symphonies by the end of preschool.

While it is possible to integrate learning activities in the early years rather subtly and successfully, Vandermaas-Peeler points out that some people tend to get overzealous and unintentionally interrupt children's play in their attempts to make it more "educational." "I think parents become very nervous very early that their children will not become as successful as the next person if they can't read or do addition and subtraction when they come to kindergarten," she says. "In Denmark, play is valued for its own sake, whereas for many American parents it's more about building skills and how it will help us later. That's just how we're culturally oriented, unfortunately. There are probably some good things and bad things about all of this, but there are so many opportunities for children in Denmark that are different. More freedom to choose, less structure. You choose and we help you figure it out."

Whereas many American parents see no choice but to jump on the early-academics bandwagon, Scandinavian parents seem remarkably unconcerned about formal instruction for preschoolers. They are confident that their children will learn what they need to learn when they are ready to learn it, and are happy to "just" let their preschoolers play. Preferably outside. Daniel, a Danish father of a kindergartner, explains it this way: "We see childhood as an important part of a human's life and not as a race to adulthood. We believe and respect the fact that children have the right to a happy childhood."

When I ask Kristoffer, a Swedish father of two young children, what he expects his children to learn between now and when they start formal schooling at age six, his answer is swift and affirmative. "I expect them to be children," he says. "Soon enough they'll be in school and they'll get the rest there. All children are so different too. Some are interested in doing math and reading and writing early; others are not."

Sure, children can be trained to learn how to read and write earlier through drilling and direct instruction. But why the rush?

Alliance for Childhood notes that many children are not ready to read in kindergarten and that pushing them to live up to unrealistic academic goals can lead to inappropriate classroom practices. Plus, there is no scientific evidence that teaching children to read early will help them be better readers in the long run. A study that compared two groups of children in New Zealand who started their formal literacy lessons at ages five and seven, respectively, showed no significant difference in reading ability by the time they were eleven years old. But the children who had started at five had developed a less positive attitude to reading and had worse text comprehension than the children who had started when they were seven. Other studies have shown no significant association between the age a child starts school and his or her reading ability.

Those baby flash cards and the word walls so often seen in preschool classrooms may seem harmless enough, but putting pressure on young children to read early can actually limit other aspects of their learning that may be more important, like spontaneous exploration and discovery. Testing creativity and problem-solving skills is arguably harder than testing factual knowledge, but the results of two separate studies conducted by MIT and the University of California, Berkeley, show that teaching children too much too early can backfire. At MIT, the researchers gave a group of four-year-olds exactly the same toy, and only varied the method with which they introduced it to the children. In one group, the researcher acted naïve and clueless when she demonstrated one of the functions of the toy, whereas the other group was given direct instruction by the researcher on how to use it. When left alone with the toy, all the children in the study were able to replicate what the "teacher" had done—pull on one of the toy's tubes to make it squeak—but the children in the first group played with the toy longer and discovered more of its functions. They were simply more curious and more likely to discover new information than the children who had been told by the teacher how to use the toy. The study at UC Berkeley had similar results: When the children with the "clueless" researcher were left with the toy, they discovered a smarter way to get it to play music, whereas the children who were taught how to use it only replicated what the teacher had done.

Of course, there is a time and place for academics and direct instruction. But Vandermaas-Peeler doesn't believe this teaching style behooves the preschool years. Instead, she thinks education in the early years should focus on supporting children's curiosity and sense of wonder, and getting them excited about the world around them. As luck would have it, there is a perfect place for this: nature.

"Play in and of itself has a therapeutic effect on children," says environmental psychologist Fredrika Mårtensson at the Swedish University of Agricultural Sciences at Alnarp. "And they play differently outside. The games are more open and flexible, and it's easier for them to organize the situation in a way that's beneficial to them physically, socially, and psychologically."

Some of the cognitive skills that are honed through play are decision making, problem solving, and abstract thinking. They can happen in any environment, but more so in nature, where children tend to engage in a lot of fantasy play. Researchers believe these critical thinking skills are crucial not just to early childhood, but for children to succeed academically later in life. As a parent, a great way to support them is simply to spend a lot of time outside, ask open-ended questions, and encourage your child's innate curiosity and willingness to investigate.

"Outside children are constantly moving, they are active. Active children learn better and more," writes Ylva Ellneby, a veteran preschool teacher and author in Sweden, in one of her popular books about early childhood. "Children need to use their imagination and nature gives them the freedom and inspiration that is required to make it happen. . . . The woods and fields offer many adventures and magical experiences."

There's another reason why hands-on, meaningful play experiences in nature are so conducive to learning. Nature activates all the senses, but without being overwhelming. When children play in nature, they tend to be calm yet alert. "When their senses are engaged, they are strengthening their sensory skills. And strong sensory integration results in a higher incidence of learning," says Angela Hanscom, a pediatric occupational therapist and author of *Balanced and Barefoot: How Unrestricted Outdoor Play Makes for Strong, Confident, and Capable Children*. Conversely, Hanscom believes the rise in sensory issues in children is directly linked to the fact that children play less outside. Hanscom recommends as much as five to eight hours of active play every day, preferably outdoors, for toddlers and preschoolers, and four to five hours of physical activity and outdoor play for school-age children up to the age of thirteen. She notes that children need movement and frequent breaks throughout the day in order to learn effectively or they will start to fidget and lose focus. "In order for children to learn, they must be able to pay attention. And in order to pay attention, children need to move," she says.

Ruth Wilson, professor emeritus in the Department of Special Education at Bowling Green State University in Ohio, also sees a natural connection—a "goodness of fit"—between children and nature. "Nature invites authentic play—the best kind of play for young children. Authentic play is fun, open-ended, self-directed and freely chosen. Authentic play occurs naturally when children and nature are brought together," she writes in her book *Nature and Young Children: Encouraging Creative Play and Learning in Natural Environments*.

Wilson claims many parents are caught up in the "waste no time" syndrome out of fear that their children will fall behind in our achievement-oriented society. To prevent academic failure, parents feel the need to carefully engineer every aspect of their children's lives, from introducing early academics and scheduling enrichment activities like music and science classes, to pushing children in competitive sports and pressuring them to excel in school, where from an early age they are subjected to high-stakes testing and the stress of getting good grades. Or, as one American mother explained it to me: "When my daughter was little I wanted her to be involved in everything. She was in Girl Scouts, ballet, gymnastics, swim club—everything. I wanted her to *be something*, not just, you know, *be!*"

I felt like asking her when she thought her daughter would ever get a chance to "just be" again, but I shut my mouth. For most people the answer to that question is "when they retire." Of course, by that time, the irresistible urge to jump in muddy puddles just to see how filthy you can get is probably long gone. (Not to mention that the window for when this is considered socially acceptable will have closed.) Unfortunately, she was just one example of the prevailing idea that children are the sum of their weekly activities, and that busiest schedule by third grade wins.

It's Okay to Be Bored

After two days of me tagging along to her new preschool to make sure that she is adjusting well (a process which is called *inskolning* and is mandatory for all new children), Nora is ready for me to move on. "You can go home now, Mommy," she declares as we walk into the preschool on the third morning. "I want to go by myself. I'll be fine."

With this, we settle into our new routine, with Maya at school and Nora at preschool while I stay at the Shack and write. Since Maya's school day ends already at one o'clock, we decide that she will stay at the school's *fritids* until four most days of the week. In Sweden, *fritids* is a subsidized childcare service that is available for students ranging from six to thirteen years old, and its mission is twofold: to give kids something meaningful to do after school, and help cover the childcare gaps for working parents. Our local *fritids* is open from six to eight in the morning and then again from one in the afternoon to six in the evening, and it's a popular alternative for kids who either aren't old enough to be latchkey or simply prefer to stay after school to hang out with friends. At Maya's *fritids*, which typically focuses on active play and creative arts, the kids are outside from one to two thirty, when they come in for a snack or, on nice days, sometimes eat outside. The rest of the time is usually spent playing or crafting, either inside or outside. Soon, Maya starts to bring home muddy pants, a gazillion bead crafts, and—in a particularly proud moment—a pink hat for her little sister that she knitted herself.

Aside from solving parents' childcare woes, *fritids* makes it easier for the kids to get to know each other outside of school, and it doesn't take long before Maya, who has always been a bit of a loner, has a throng of new friends. A logical extension of all this is that *fritids* becomes an important hub for initiating casual playdates. In a few short weeks, Maya has exchanged phone numbers and—with my permission—made plans with several other girls to play after school. The parents are just the facilitators and overseers of this process, the ones who will generally say yes if they don't have anything else going on that day and no if the family already has other plans. Several times a week I find myself either bringing home an extra child or two from *fritids* or picking Maya up from a friend's house in the evening. Not that playing after school is all that revolutionary; kids have been doing that forever. What strikes me is that so many of them seem to have so much free time after school and that the children are largely in control of it. Some of this can of course be explained by the fact that the school day is short and homework is only given once a week, which makes it easier for families to plan around it. But there also seems to be less pressure to enroll kids in organized after-school activities. And the parents are not the least embarrassed about this lack of adult-led enrichment.

"We've chosen not to have a lot of structured activities after school," says Sara, whose daughter Liv is in Maya's class and is one of her first playdates. Sara, a teacher whose unruly Scandinavian-blond curls are cut in a short bob that is often tucked behind her ears, reveals that Liv, who is nine, and her little brother Noa, who is five, only have a play-based gym class once a week for a few months in the spring and a few months in the fall. Sometimes they take a swim class or, in Liv's case, a weekly dance class.

"I think that's enough," Sara says. As a teacher and herself a high achiever in school, she clearly cares about her children's education and future. But she also likes to give them the time and space to play. "I personally don't like having things scheduled after work and I think that having too many activities after school stresses the kids out too. When I get back at four thirty I just want to kick back and be with my family."

Sofia, a nutritionist who lives in Borås with her husband and two sons, who are six and three years old, is on the same track: "I guess I've been pretty lazy about signing my kids up for activities," she says. "I think it's pretty nice that they don't have that much going on, at least until they themselves ask for it. I think it's healthy for their development to be able to influence their free time as well."

Occasional trips to the zoo, the pool, and story time at the library, sure. But before age six, when Swedish kids start formal schooling, they generally don't have a whole lot of organized activities. For babies and toddlers who stay home with a parent, the activities are more about treating the parents' cabin fever than about keeping the kids busy or giving them an edge over their peers. Once or twice a week, these children are most likely found at *öppna förskolan*. For the adults, *öppna förskolan* is a popular place to meet peers, drink coffee, and trade battle stories from everyday life in the parenting trenches. And the children? They just play.

I decide to visit our local *öppna förskolan* over Easter break, where I meet Maggan, who is home from work with her youngest son, Manne. He is teething and not feeling well enough to go to preschool for a full day, so Maggan brought him here just to get out of the house for a couple of hours. She is soon joined by Kristoffer, who is on a six-month-long paternity leave with his one-year-old son, John, and his two-year-old daughter, Ellen.

Kristoffer's children haven't taken part in any organized activities yet, but he says that eventually they'll probably go to swim class. Having grown up in the country himself, Kristoffer spends a lot of his paternity leave outside with the kids. "Now that the weather is better we go outside for a while in the morning and then again in the afternoon. I definitely feel a need to go outside every day; the more the better."

Maggan's children have been to a baby swim class and currently go to a play-based gymnastics class once a week. She, too, feels like swimming and learning to be safe around water is important, as the family spends a lot of time on a lake. Maggan and Kristoffer both say they would like their children to take up some sort of organized sport eventually, as another way to stay active beyond everyday play. But they don't seem to care too much what that activity is.

"If my son wants to play soccer he can, but I'll never make him. It has to come from him, and it will when he's ready for it," Maggan says. "Not everybody likes team sports, and if he doesn't, we'll have to find something that's a better fit."

Since Maggan is single and works full-time, her boys spend most of the week at preschool, where they play outside for three to four hours per day. On the weekends she usually takes them to the playground or, once the weather gets warmer, spends time with them on the big deck in their backyard. "My kids love to bounce around, run, and crawl under things, so I usually make obstacle courses on the deck to keep them busy," she says.

As I start to look into extracurricular activities for my girls, I soon find that our options are limited. For Nora, there is a weekly play-based gymnastics class. That's it. I could drive twenty minutes to Borås for a weekly swim class for preschoolers, but other than that, there is not a whole lot going on for kids her age. Maya has a few more options. Besides the gymnastics class, there is choir on Tuesdays, and a jazz dance class is supposed to start in the spring. For those in third grade and up, there is Scouts on Wednesdays. (In line with Sweden's tradition of equal treatment of the genders, Girl Scout and Boy Scout organizations here merged in the 1960s and '70s, with the result that all troops are coed.) And then there is, of course, soccer, the cherished national sport, which, unlike just about any winter sport, gives Sweden a rare chance to outshine its neighbor to the west, Norway. It's the one sport that can drive grown men to tears and fist-fights, the sport that you will find Swedish kids playing in every one-stoplight town—or, in this case, a no-stoplight town.

Despite soccer's status as a national obsession, Swedish parents seem to be in no rush to hothouse the next Zlatan Ibrahimović, the country's most famous and admired soccer player of all time. In general, Swedish children don't start playing soccer until they are around six or seven years old, and regular, weekly games usually start even later. Zlatan himself got his first cleats when he was five but didn't start playing on a team until he was seven. And he says that he learned most of his tricks and refined his technique while playing casual pickup games on a rough gravel lot between the high-rises of Rosengård, a poor suburb on the outskirts of Malmö. "When I played soccer for fun in Rosengård, that's where all my ideas came from. I brought that with me to the big arenas," he told the daily newspaper *Dagens Nyheter* in an interview.

My nine-year-old, soccer-crazed nephew, Oliver, is a big fan of Zlatan. And, like many other Swedish mothers, my sister Susanne is utterly uninterested in soccer. "You know me, I'm definitely no 'soccer mom,' and I can't say I enjoy going to these tournaments," she tells me when I ask her about it, "but I do love that he has a hobby and something that he's passionate about."

By American youth sports standards, my nephew doesn't even have a very busy schedule. In the winter he has practice once a week, and up until now he hasn't had any regular games, just four or five tournaments per year. Now that he's nine, he will have practice on Thursdays and usually a game or practice again on Sunday. Plus, that's his only after-school activity, unless you count building with Legos in his bedroom. In the summer, aside from the occasional soccer day camp there's no organized soccer at all—or any other organized activities, for that matter—since Swedish parents are extremely protective of their vacations. And typically they spend at least a few of those five to seven weeks of annual time off in a camper van or cabin near the ocean, or sunbathing in a place with a more consistent supply of sunshine than Sweden.

"What I really like about soccer is that the kids are not dependent on us parents to play. They keep playing whether they have practices or not. As soon as the snow melts in the spring, they play during recess at school. In the summer, they all gather by the soccer fields and play all day," Susanne muses. "It's just in their blood."

Some teams have a tougher practice regimen than my nephew, and far from all parents are as relaxed about the sport as my sister. Nonetheless, the Swedish soccer federation seems determined to uphold a playful atmosphere among its youth teams. In 2017, the organization went as far as banning the practice of crowning overall winners of soccer series and tournaments for children age twelve and younger. This was not an uncontroversial decision, as many parents felt like learning how to lose is an important part of life and helps build resilience. Youth leaders, however, welcomed the rule, as it helped pacify the small subset of aggravated parents who used to cause problems for referees and the opposing team during high-stakes games.

Naturally, there are many benefits of participating in organized sports. It can teach kids a lot about hard work, social skills, self-discipline, sportsmanship, and other desirable traits. But too much too early means there is very little downtime for kids to "just" play outside; additionally, it reduces parents to frazzled, grumpy chauffeurs. Of those who start too early, many are burned-out and lose interest by the time they are twelve, according to Hansi Hinic, a researcher at Halmstad University in Sweden, who specializes in the psychological effects of organized sports on children.

"Parents book up their kids' schedules and push them because they care. But if they're not receptive to their children's signals, they may be missing them," he tells the Swedish daily *Upsala Nya Tidning*. "The well-being of the child is the parent's responsibility, and they are the ones who need to make sure that the kids don't have too much going on." A former soccer coach, Hinic believes children in general start organized sports too early, and that most children of preschool and early elementary school age benefit more from playing outside. "Kids shouldn't get enrolled in organized sports until they want to themselves," he says. "Sometimes you've got to wonder if it isn't the parent that wants the child to start playing soccer, more than the child himself."

One of the reasons why many American parents like to enroll their children in as many sports as possible is that they don't want them to become sedentary, gaming-addicted couch surfers. This is well-intended and, in the age of record childhood obesity rates and gloomy slogans like "Sitting is the new smoking," completely understandable. But according to a review of current research on youth sports from the American College of Sports Medicine, it's not possible to establish that playing sports actually prevents obesity. (Part of the problem seems to be that whatever calories the kids burn playing sports, they make up for by eating more junk food and drinking more sugary drinks, racking up more total calories than their non-sporty peers.)

Exercise is of course beneficial to a child whether he or she is overweight or not, but if little Johnny doesn't want to play soccer or T-ball or peewee football, it may be comforting to know that he is just as well off (and less likely to get injured) if he simply spends time playing outside. A study by the University of Copenhagen showed that children actually got more exercise while playing freely outdoors than when they participated in organized sports. Glen Nielsen, a sports researcher who led the study, put accelerometers on five hundred children in Denmark and five hundred children in New Zealand, then tracked their activity over three days. Unexpectedly, he found that the children got most of their exercise at recess or recreation centers, or from simply playing in the neighborhood, while organized sports made only a small contribution to the overall level of activity.

But not all outdoor free play is created equal. The more versatile and varied the outdoor environment is, the longer children will stay outside, and the more physically active they will be. This can in turn contribute to slimmer waistlines. When a research team in Sweden compared children at nine different preschools, they discovered that the longer the children played in high-quality outdoor environments—meaning places with plenty of trees, shrubs, rocks, and hills—the more likely they were to have a normal body mass index and the less likely they were to be overweight. Moreover, when Ingunn Fjørtoft, a professor at Telemark University in Porsgrunn, Norway, compared five- to seven-year-olds at three different kindergartens in Norway, she found that those who played in the forest daily had significantly better balance and coordination than children who only played on a traditional playground. Once again, the reason is believed to be that children are faced with more complex physical challenges in nature, and that this boosts their motor skills and overall fitness.

"Children who spend a lot of time in nature have stronger hands, arms, and legs and significantly better balance than children who rarely get to move freely in natural areas. In nature children use and exercise all the different muscle groups," Ellneby, the preschool teacher, notes. "Children will themselves choose to exercise their joints and muscles, if only given the opportunity."

Another advantage of having less structured and more child-led activities is that it can improve children's executive functioning. Essentially, this makes them better able to delay gratification, show self-control, and set and reach their own goals. Overscheduling children, whether it is with organized sports, clubs, or other adult-led activities, also means that they are missing out on the benefits of being bored. Too many stimuli means little time for the mind to rest and recover. And, frankly, little time for kids to figure out who they are and what they want. In the US, this busyness begins already in the early years, but it doesn't end there. Rather, the wheels of after-school activities seem to spin even faster—on top of an increasing homework load—the closer the students get to college.

Jesper Juul, a renowned Danish family therapist and the author of *Your Competent Child: Toward New Basic Values for the Family*, who has challenged many traditional parenting tenets, claims that boredom is key to achieving better balance within yourself, regardless of age. Boredom can even foster creativity, and not just the type that you would normally find in an art class. "Creative periods are full of reflective, almost meditative, pauses . . . that offer peace and recuperation," Juul writes. "This makes [children] more independent and leads to greater social competence."

So what is Juul's advice to parents who feel pressured to constantly entertain their children and provide them with an endless buffet of activities? "When your child comes to you and says he's so 'booored,' give him a hug and tell him, 'Good luck, my friend! I look forward to seeing what you get up to.'"

The End of Winter

In the US, Maya had been active in Girl Scouts, and both girls had periodically gone to swim class and ridden horses, but neither one had expressed any interest in organized sports. We didn't watch TV during the workweek, and aside from homework, their schedules were pretty open. Our backyard had picturesque deciduous woods with a small creek running through them, and several nature play areas where I had helped the girls build forts out of sticks and little houses for fairies and other imaginary forest critters.

But providing them with the perfect conditions for outdoor play and all the boons for healthy development that came with it was one thing. Getting them to actually go outside and play was something else.

Before I became a mother, I had a somewhat romanticized idea that my children would spend their afternoons playing freely outside until they got called in for dinner at nightfall, much as I had done when I was little. Before we went to Sweden, this had happened exactly once. Usually they were back inside long before the pot was boiling.

Considering my daughters' not-so-stellar track records when it comes to independent outdoor play, I'm curious to see how Nora in particular is going to handle the routine at her new pre-school. Is she going to start screaming at the teachers that she hates her snow pants? Sink down into a writhing ball on the floor when it's time to play outside? Demand to be carried when her class walks to places outside the school yard? After a couple of weeks, I pull Barbro, one of the preschool teachers, aside and ask her how things are going—specifically, how Nora is coping with all the outdoor play. "I haven't noticed her complaining," Barbro says. "Then again, all the kids go outside, so it's not really up for discussion."

This is great news, but at home I initially don't notice much change. Nora still prefers to stay inside on the weekends, and getting her to go outside requires considerable effort on my part. Walking places is a gamble, which on more than one occasion ends with her dramatically claiming a sudden ailment and me copping out by giving her a piggyback ride to the car or house. Unless there is a game, a visit to the playground, or the promise of hot chocolate involved, Nora is simply not all that interested in outdoor recreation. But since we're in Sweden I think I may just have the right fix for that.

In France, children are steeped in a culture of haute cuisine and learn to devour delicacies like blue cheese and escargots from an early age. In Scandinavia, they're instead immersed in outdoor activities, both at school and at home. From skiing and ice-skating in the winter to hiking and riding bikes in the summer, knowing how to get around outdoors is considered an essential part of a well-rounded education. Parents have many reasons for instilling this spirit of *friluftsliv* in their children, maybe primarily because it's a fun way to stay healthy and do things together as a family. For many Scandinavians it's also the highest form of appreciation of nature, and it can only be passed down to the next generation through firsthand experience.

I don't remember the first time I stood on a pair of Nordic skis, but I'm pretty sure a love for nature was not the first thing that came to mind. Cross-country and downhill skiing both require their fair share of stamina, athleticism, and balance, but although Nordic skiing is easier to master, it lacks the kind of primal thrill that only standing at the top of a wind-battered mountain seconds before you drop in on a black-diamond run can evoke. And then there is the fact that there is no lift to help you get over the hills. If downhill skiing is a given kid-pleaser—full of adrenaline and instant rewards—its cross-country cousin is more of an acquired taste that may or may not grow on you over time.

I hadn't cross-country skied for close to two decades, but when in Sweden, you do as the Swedes do. And they were out in the woods hitting the cross-country tracks. As winter was starting to come to an end, I figured it was high time for Maya and Nora to go through this rite of passage as well. I dug out my old gear from my sister's shed and borrowed two sets of skis for

Maya and Nora. They had learned how to downhill ski in Michigan and Montana at the ages of five and three, respectively, but I'd never had the opportunity to teach them how to cross-country ski. I wasn't sure what they would think—at this point they had already ditched the alpine skis for snowboards, since these were "much cooler" than regular skis. Cross-country skiing can be a lot of things, but *cool* is not an adjective that is normally associated with it. By introducing them to downhill skiing so early in life, I wondered if I had forever killed their desire to even try cross-country skiing. I also knew that although outdoor sports can be a wonderful way to bring your family together, this usually cannot be said about the initial learning phase, which admittedly could push even the strongest relationships to the brink of rupture.

I bide my time until, one afternoon after school, the conditions are perfect. The snow is just deep enough and the sun is soaking the tracks by the clubhouse near the Shack, making them glisten as if somebody had sprinkled them with a billion tiny precious diamonds. It's time to launch Operation Cross-Country Skiing.

The kids are anything but thrilled.

"I don't like cross-country skiing," Maya whines.

"How do you know?" I retort. "You've never even tried it!"

"It's boring."

Nora is quick to chime in.

"Nooooo! I don't want to go skiing!"

Somehow I once again successfully work through the protests, and as soon as we reach the tracks, excitement starts to build.

"I want to go fast!" Maya says.

"You need to learn the right technique first, honey. Look at Mommy! Right arm and left leg forward, then left arm and right leg forward. Let's practice together and do some laps around this soccer field first."

Maya pretends she didn't hear me and takes off toward the woods.

"Nora, will you look at Mommy, please? This is your right arm and this—"

She cuts me off.

"I got this, Mom! I already know how to cross-country ski."

"That's great, but I still think we should stay here on the soccer field. It's going to get dark soon."

Nora, too, ignores me and instead starts following her sister toward the two-mile-long track that points to the woods. As they reach the first small descent at the end of the soccer field, the narrow, tall skis throw them off balance and they both fall down in hapless piles, causing Maya's left binding to come loose. Nora uses the commotion to get in front of her big sister, and everything goes surprisingly well until Nora falls again and loses her lead. While I'm trying to prevent the already distressed situation from deteriorating into an epic tantrum, Maya keeps going to secure her lead position. If *friluftsliv* was supposed to be outdoor recreation "with no pressure to achieve or compete," my kids clearly haven't gotten the memo.

By the time I've gotten Nora calmed down and ready to get back up, Maya is nowhere in sight. We follow the tracks deeper into the woods, calling Maya's name, but get no response. Then, out of nowhere, I hear her voice from the left. She has left the tracks and somehow managed to get to the top of the biggest hill in the area.

"Mommy, I'm up here! I'm finally going skiing!" she yells, excited.

At that moment, I realize that you can take a child out of the mountains, but you can never take the thrills of downhill skiing out of the child, and before I have as much as finished that train of thought, she has plunged forward with her skinny Nordic skis in a wobbly "pizza" position. She doesn't get far before she accidentally crosses the tips and falls headfirst into the snow. This turn of events effectively paves the way for tantrum number two, just from a different child this time.

"Stop whining!" Nora yells unsympathetically to her sister, having already forgotten all about her own meltdown not too long ago.

This only adds fuel to the fire. With at least another half mile left of the trail and darkness quickly embracing the surrounding woods, I almost wish I'd left cross-country skiing where it was for more than twenty years—a quaint childhood memory in a dusty filing cabinet in a rarely used part of my brain. Just as I think the situation can't get any worse, another skier quickly approaches us on the trail. She's slightly older than me and, judging by the looks of her gear, she's a regular on the track. I do my best to look unfazed while awaiting her silent judgment. She slows down, her eyes wandering from the furious eight-year-old on the hill to the smug five-year-old on the track, then back to me, the exasperated mom. "It's not easy," she says, and shakes her head sympathetically. I feel like crying and pouring my heart out to this complete stranger, but I don't. Instead I repeat her words like a mantra in my mind and squeeze out my last drops of energy to help get Maya back up on her skis. Somehow we manage to finish our inaugural cross-country ski trip without any further interruptions.

Back in the car, I'm ready to write off cross-country skiing with kids for the foreseeable future. But, to my surprise, the girls' moods have suddenly shifted.

"That was awesome!" Maya says.

"I want to go again," Nora says.

I'm secretly smiling on the inside. It wasn't glamorous, it wasn't easy, and it most definitely wasn't cool, but I don't care. I'm silently checking off my first win for *friluftsliv*.

Scandinavian Parenting Tip #3
Simplify childhood and resist the urge to try to keep up with the Joneses' kids. Remember that a preschooler needs very few things besides ample time to play freely, and that filling his or her schedule with a litany of "enriching" activities can do more harm than good. And if you think that your child's preschool is too focused on academics, try to find other options that offer more child-led play and nature experiences.

Suggested reading: *Under Pressure: Rescuing Our Children from the Culture of Hyper-Parenting*, by Carl Honoré. Harper-One, 2009.

4

WE MUST ALL TAKE
CARE OF NATURE

*If you can help children love nature,
they will take care of nature, because you cherish things you love.*
—MULLE

In late February, a high-pressure system moves in with warmer air, and the remaining snow melts faster than a glob of coconut oil on my new induction stovetop, turning the yard outside the Shack into a slushy quagmire. The sky is fifty shades of depressing, and with no snow left on the ground, daylight is elusive. And it rains. Not hard, just a steady downpour that slowly corrodes any motivation to recreate in nature. For a day I stay inside and stare at my computer screen. Then I talk to my dad. He's had a good couple of days.

"We walked around the lake yesterday," he says. "Bernt was expecting me to call and cancel because of the weather, but of course I didn't. You don't want to be the guy who bails. You've just got to bite the bullet." He sounds upbeat and happy, even though his last consultation with the oncology team at the hospital was a mixed bag. The good news is that the doctors got everything they needed to get during the surgery, and that it doesn't look like the tumor has metastasized. The bad news is that they still want him to go through six months of preventive chemo. "My Runkeeper says I'm at 570 kilometers since September. I think that's more than I've walked my entire life," he says, and adds, almost sheepishly, "I never thought I would say this, but I think I've become addicted to my daily walks."

Meanwhile, I feel like I've walked 570 kilometers since last week. If I was struggling to find places to walk in the US, that's definitely not a problem here. In fact, it seems like every time I've come to visit in the summer, another street in Borås has been shut down for traffic and made into a pedestrian-only area, or at the very least turned into a dead end to prevent through traffic. Parking spaces have been replaced by bike racks, streets transformed into pocket parks crowned with obscure contemporary sculptures and riverside pathways. Mind you, this is a popular strategy among local politicians in Sweden who want to reduce pollution in the cities and improve the people-to-car ratio in downtown areas: If you make it inconvenient or expensive enough to drive— or "inspire environmentally friendly modes of travel," as the city prefers to call it—people will eventually choose to walk, bike, or take the bus. Not stopping at that, the city runs most of its own vehicles on biogas and is aiming to make the entire city fleet, including buses, completely fossil fuel–free by 2030.

When the streets were first closed to car traffic, decades ago, some of the shop owners in downtown Borås feared that they would go out of business if their customers couldn't park outside, or at least relatively close by. As the years went by, these fears turned out to be unfounded. Downtown thrived and became even more of a hub of activity than before, with an urbane café culture, weekly concerts on the town square in the summer, unique hole-in-the-wall boutiques side by side with several busy department stores, and, smack in the middle of the city, a new, large, and whimsical playground that has become a favorite hangout for families with young children.

Today you'd be hard-pressed to find anybody who wants the cars back in downtown. I don't either. In fact, this city is doing exactly what I would love for all cities to do—setting an ambitious agenda to reduce greenhouse gas emissions and create a truly sustainable community, of which decreasing traffic in downtown is just a small part. But one day, as I'm circling around the main library in my Saab, trying to find a parking space that is at least within half a mile of the building, I do feel a little bit inconvenienced—and ripped off, as I had already paid the equivalent of twenty dollars in parking fees while running a few errands across town.

Later, I make the mistake of complaining mildly about these circumstances to my sixty-nine-year-old mom, who has come over to the Shack to see the kids. She's not sympathetic. At all. She has that disapproving frown between her eyebrows and the tight-lipped smile that's meant to be disarming, but in reality is a good indicator that she's about to get confrontational.

"You've become Americanized," she says, in a way that makes it abundantly clear that this is not meant as a compliment. "You should've parked over by the railway station. It's the cheapest place in town."

"Well, yes, but I was going three different places and none of them were anywhere near the railway station," I respond, feeling myself involuntarily getting defensive.

"It's not that far to walk from the railway station. You're close to everything from there."

"Yeah, but I was carrying my laptop and another bag, so I had a bit of a heavy load, and I was trying to be efficient," I say, and point out that the distance I would have had to travel on foot to get to all my destinations would have been almost two miles total.

"That's not that far. You usually like walking and getting some fresh air. What's the problem?"

"Okay, as I mentioned, I was carrying some stuff. And I was dressed for a meeting, not a hike. I don't mind walking at all, but it was kind of cold without shell pants on."

"So you expect to be able to park exactly where you're going? You've gotten way too comfortable."

We agree to disagree on my purported laziness and move on to a less charged topic. But after she leaves I start to wonder if my perspective hasn't changed after all. Although I'd never admit it to my mom, it's entirely possible that I've gotten a little too comfortable with that drive-up window at the bank and the ability to drive pretty much anywhere I please back home.

The transformation that my hometown has gone through is far from unique—all over Scandinavia cities and governments are vying to reduce their carbon footprint and create sustainable communities. It seems to be working. In 2014, the *Global Green Economy Index* ranked Sweden as the greenest economy in the world, followed by Norway in second place and Denmark in fifth. Copenhagen, the capital of Denmark, where 45 percent of the residents bike to work and school every day, was ranked as the greenest city, while Stockholm came in third. The air and water quality in Scandinavia is among the highest in the world, and the countries are leaders in renewable energy as well as sustainable building practices. Swedes are so diligent about recycling that the country now has to import trash from its European neighbors in order to fuel its incineration plants, which in turn generate heat and electricity for hundreds of thousands of households. Home composting is facilitated by the government, and in a majority of the municipalities household waste is collected and composted in a central location, where it generates either soil or biogas. In Sweden there's a recycling center within three hundred yards of every residential area, provided by the packaging industry, according to the "polluter pays principle." Separating your household waste is considered a basic civic duty, and when all is said and done, over 99 percent of the waste in Sweden is reused, recycled, composted, or incinerated to generate energy, leaving less than 1 percent to be deposited in landfills.

When incandescent lightbulbs were banned in the EU a few years ago, people switched them out for LED bulbs without much ado, and many happily pay a little extra for products to offset their carbon footprint. Many businesses are all-in as well, rarely missing an opportunity to tout their green credentials. Max, a popular Swedish burger chain, recently introduced five new vegetarian dishes to reduce their carbon footprint, and instead of calorie counts, the restaurant labels each item on the menu with the CO_2 emissions generated. (A Grand Deluxe Cheese 'n' Bacon Burger will saddle the climate with 3.1 kilos of CO_2, whereas a fish burger comes in at a bargain 0.2 kilos.) Sales of organic foods in Sweden increased by nearly 40 percent in 2014, causing shortages for some products. As many as half of women of all ages and people under forty say that they often or always buy organic, and two out of three are willing to pay more for locally produced food. Interestingly, the trend transcends class, as low-income earners are just as likely to spend a little extra for organic food as the wealthy. At the grocery store, there's no longer just a choice between conventionally grown or organic snap peas but a choice of organic, ethically sourced, fair trade snap peas, the proceeds from which also help pay for watering systems for impoverished Maya Indians in Guatemala.

Although many factors likely contributed to this green ethos, it doesn't take a great leap of the imagination to assume that a significant part of it stems from Scandinavians' close relationship with nature. Many cultures in the industrialized world are dominated by an anthropocentric view of nature. They see nature almost as a detached entity, something that is mainly there for humans to master and extract resources from. Other cultures subscribe to the idea that humans are stewards of nature and all other living beings, and in some cases that this responsibility is bestowed on us by a divine creator.

In Scandinavia, however, a third narrative prevails, as here most people see themselves as inseparable from nature. Nils Uddenberg, the Swedish psychiatrist and author, notes that Swedes even tend to value other living beings as highly as they value humans. "This attitude is generally motivated by the fact that all living beings—including humans—are dependent on the ecological context of which they are a part, and fill a function in these." Following this logic, if you harm nature, in the end you also harm yourself. Helle Nebelong, a Danish landscape architect who is passionate about designing natural play spaces for children, puts it this way: "Us humans are a part of nature and we have a need to be in nature. I think this need will grow with the global development. We need to be in nature on a regular basis to achieve balance and harmony. In the long run, we can't deny that we are biological organisms."

Many parents pass down this ethos to their children through *friluftsliv*. Andreas, whom I meet during an outing with a family nature group, says that he started bringing his son Arvid to the woods partly because he enjoys the outdoors himself and wanted them to have something to do together. "But of course I also hope that it'll lead him to become aware of environmental issues," Andreas says. "At this age we mostly just talk about not littering and destroying nature. You don't have to become an activist, but at the very least you need to know that."

Parents are not alone in this quest. In Sweden, nature conservation, which involves making sure children "acquire a caring attitude to nature and the environment," is considered so important that it's one of the main tenets of the national curriculum for the preschool. On top of making sure that children have an opportunity to play in natural environments, the preschool is tasked with helping them understand how they can contribute to a better environment, both now and in the future.

This doesn't mean children at Swedish preschools spend their days talking about burning rain forests, climate change, and species extinction, something that David Sobel believes can actually cause them to fear nature. Instead, a young child's first simple act of environmental stewardship may very well be putting his apple core in the black composting bag after snack time. At Nora's preschool, composting is one of the first "green" behaviors that is usually learned. There's good reason for this: I know from personal experience that once you've gotten used to separating out your food waste from the trash, it becomes very hard to knowingly send a banana peel to the landfill when you get older.

At most preschools, environmental education is part of the daily routine, but sometimes it's also highlighted through special events. At Nora's preschool, the annual litter pickup in the neighborhood around the school is one of them.

"Today I want you to put on your special glasses, because today we're going to look for trash that people have thrown away," says Ellen, one of the preschool teachers, when preparing her group before leaving the school grounds. "When we see it, we're going to pick it up so that it doesn't destroy nature."

Nora, who is used to picking trash from going on litter sweeps with me back home in Indiana, quickly grabs one of the white trash bags and takes charge. The other kids know the drill too, since many of them have done it before both at the school and at home.

"Trash! Trash! Trash!" they yell in unison as they scatter across the small grassy field behind the school, then continue their search behind the indoor tennis arena nearby. Cans, plastic bottles, a metal wire, some candy wrappers, and a couple of pieces of a broken hose all end up in Nora's bag. I've never seen children so elated about finding discarded bottle caps before. They might as well have been hunting for Easter eggs full of candy.

"Why do you think some people throw trash on the ground?" I ask Kerstin, Nora's best friend at preschool, while she's trying to reach a plastic cup that has blown into some bushes.

"Because they don't know where the trash cans are," she responds assertively.

After they're done with their assigned area, the kids get to go down to the basement and see where all the trash from the preschool is sorted into recycling bins. Cardboard, glass, light bulbs, batteries, plastic, compost, and nonrecyclables all have separate bins. The trash that the children have picked up, too, will be sorted at a special recycling event with several other preschools the following week.

Even though the preschool is obliged by law to provide the children with environmental education, it's obvious that the teachers are excited about it. "The kids think this is a lot of fun; they learn it quickly. Sometimes children tell us that their family doesn't recycle at home. If that's the case, we just tell them, 'Well, now you've learned how to do it here, so maybe you can show Mommy and Daddy how to do it,'" says Barbro. "I think the parents are positive, too, because all of this is so widely accepted today."

She's right. All the parents I talk to think that it's a good thing that children learn environmentally friendly behaviors early. "At my son's preschool, they've worked a lot with composting, and I think it's great that they learn how long it takes for things to decompose," says Veronica, a mother of three boys under the age of ten. "Sometimes I don't feel like it makes a difference if I throw my cans in the right bin or not, but I know we all have to do our part if we want to keep living on this planet. Recycling is something we've been drilled with since we were little too."

Come spring, the children at Nora's preschool also start to visit their "school forest," about a fifteen-minute walk from the preschool, on a more regular basis. School forests are sections of woods that can be used by schools and preschools for outdoor play and environmental education, and in Sweden there are over one thousand of them. The concept was developed in the 1980s as a collaboration between private landowners and schools to increase children's knowledge of forests and the forestry industry. Typically, the agreement with the landowner allows the school to alter the environment beyond what's permitted through *allemansrätten*— for example, by marking trails, making fire pits, building shelters, putting up signs, and, in some cases, even cutting down trees.

Outdoor learning is an old tradition in this part of the world. Swedish physician and biologist Carl Linnaeus, who's mostly known for organizing all living beings into families and classes, a system that's still used internationally today, championed the idea in the eighteenth century. "If you do not know the names of things, the knowledge of them is lost, too," he famously wrote. Even if his goal to map out all of nature proved overwhelming (by the time Linnaeus died, in 1770, approximately 20,000 species had been classified; today the number is close to 1.5 million, with more being discovered every year), his spirit of nature exploration and education lives on.

As late as a hundred years ago it was mandatory for Swedish schoolteachers to take their classes tree planting for a day, and forest excursions were a common component of the biology curriculum. Today, many teachers in Scandinavia use the school yard and nearby nature areas to teach math, science, history, and other subjects on a regular basis. The concept of teaching students outside of the classroom is called *udeskole*, or "outdoor school" in Danish, and isn't just a hands-on, cross-disciplinary approach to learning traditional academic subjects. It's also seen as a way for students to build a relationship with their environment and get in contact with nature during the school day. "Studies show that if you alternate outdoor and indoor learning, and the teacher is prepared, you get good results," says Anders Szczepanski, director of the National Center for Environmental and Outdoor Education at Linköping University, Sweden. "There are certain parts of the brain that are stimulated when we move around and have fun in a varied environment. We turn on our intuition when we go outside—and we need to do it more often."

The school forest that Nora's preschool uses is located in a typical Swedish pine forest, where the hilly ground is dominated by boulders, blueberry bushes, mosses, ferns, and a few fallen trees. When I accompany her class to the forest one day, the children gather on logs around the fire pit for a quick sandwich and fruit; then, after a game and some songs, they disperse for free play. Nora immediately claims the only suitable climbing tree and quickly scurries up the branches until she is about eight feet off the ground. Several other girls gather in a circle by the fire pit to take a closer look at a beetle that is dragging another, seemingly dead, beetle around on a rock. Nearby, a group of four or five children climb up on a boulder and pretend to be pirates on a big ship, swinging sticks like gangly swords.

"Are you going to a different country?" Marit, one of the preschool teachers, asks them.

"No, we're going to the store!" one of the boys on the rock yells excitedly.

"Here comes the mayor!" shouts another boy, whose imagination sees no problem with the combination of Jack Sparrow and a local government official buying groceries together.

One thing that strikes me is that these children all seem completely comfortable and at home in the woods. In fact, when Barbro points out that we can see the lake glimmering through the trees below the hill, Julia, a four-year-old girl, exclaims, "That's my lake!" Julia lives right by the water not too far from the street where I grew up, and I know exactly what she means. Children in Sweden have a deep sense that nature belongs to them and they belong in nature, a feeling that follows them into adulthood.

Many thinkers in the children-and-nature movement believe that in order to develop this type of affinity for nature, children need to engage with it hands-on, using all their senses. And when they do, they don't always comply with the leading American outdoor code of ethics: Leave No Trace. Leave No Trace was originally developed as a guide for recreating responsibly in the backcountry and has been crucial to protecting heavily used and particularly vulnerable areas from getting loved to death. But when the principles are interpreted literally and applied indiscriminately, they also have some unintended consequences for children, who are typically experts at leaving traces everywhere, from muddy footprints on newly cleaned floors and random holes in the yard, to small rocks and various debris in the washing machine. Not because they have any malicious intent, but because that's just how kids roll.

I'd noticed in the US that some adults had taken the Leave No Trace principles to an extreme and sometimes lectured children for infractions as small as collecting rocks or picking common flowers, telling them that "the flowers are food for the bees" and asking the classic question, "What would happen if everybody picked a rock?" Some researchers believe this strict interpretation of Leave No Trace can limit children's opportunities to make meaningful connections with the natural world and may even exacerbate the perceived separation of humans and nature. Thomas Beery, an assistant professor in environmental science at Kristianstad University, Sweden, is particularly interested in children's fascination with collecting things. He says that collecting natural objects can foster play and creativity as well as knowledge about the outdoors. In one study, he showed that over 80 percent of college students had collected items like rocks, shells, or insects, or foraged for food in nature when they were younger, and that the collectors in the group perceived themselves as more connected to nature than the noncollectors.

Collecting is technically a violation of Leave No Trace, which says that you should "leave what you find" in nature, but Beery believes that it can be done responsibly and lead to a dialogue about environmental stewardship. "For example, when we collect tadpoles from the pond, what's our responsibility to keep them alive and get them back where they belong after we learn a bit about them?"

Similarly, at Nora's preschool, the children sometimes bring things back from their outings, and the teachers usually see their curiosity as an opportunity for learning. "If the children collect things, we encourage it, but of course you can't bring home the whole forest," says Barbro. "We had one little boy who was really interested in rocks and he would fill his pockets with them. Once we got back to the preschool we would count how many he had and maybe sort them by size. I think that's something very positive."

Beery, who has taught Leave No Trace in the US, thinks having an outdoor code of ethics is a good thing, but he also believes that it needs to allow children more freedom in their interactions with nature. "Of course if we're talking about an endangered species that has a very fragile habitat, that's a place where we don't play. There are places where we don't build our forts. That's a given. But I think we've started overusing the idea of Leave No Trace in the context of children's play spaces in nearby nature."

As Beery and other researchers have pointed out, children explore nature in a more sensory way than adults, and when doing so they will inevitably cause some damage to the environment. In school forests like Nora's, some of the plants have been trampled where the kids have run over them, the soil is compacted in the heavy-traffic areas, and some of the weaker lower branches on popular climbing trees have broken off when children scaled them.

But just how much harm do children really do to popular nature play areas? Matthew Browning, an environmental scientist and assistant professor in recreation, sport, and tourism at the University of Illinois, Champaign-Urbana, set out to find out. In 2009, Browning, a former state park ranger whose conservation ecologist mother raised him to love and respect nature, went to Sweden to study forests around schools, where a lot of children gather to play with little to no adult intervention. After collecting and crunching the data and comparing it with similar nature play areas in the US, he found that although there is some initial damage from the children's activities—mostly loss of soil and ground cover, and some harm to trees—it plateaus after the first couple of years. As he had suspected, the areas very much remain functioning ecosystems. He also noticed that in Sweden adults didn't seem to be all that concerned about children's rampages through the woods. "There is not this 'leave no trace' mentality here," he says, and adds that the US code of ethics is misunderstood. "Leave No Trace is really about promoting land ethics. It's not saying that you should never, ever have an impact when you're going out and recreating. It's more about reducing that impact and knowing what it does."

Back at Nora's school forest, Barbro is finishing up one of the homemade muffins she brought for her coffee break while the other teachers keep an eye on the kids. Nora has finally come down from the tree, and a boy has taken her place. Another boy is playing with a charred piece of wood from the fire pit and contentedly shows off his blackened hands. In Barbro's opinion, it is all good. "I think it's very important for children to feel joy in nature," she says. "We want them to have positive memories from this, and hopefully later they will become interested in protecting it."

Among Swedish early childhood educators, Barbro is far from alone in feeling that children should regularly be given an opportunity to learn in and connect with nature. In fact, in Scandinavia this idea is so pervasive that it has birthed a revolutionary preschool model that places the classroom directly into the heart of nature: the forest school.

The Forest School: Trolls and Tree Climbers

At eight o'clock in the morning on an overcast and chilly late-winter day, about a dozen children are getting ready to start the day at their preschool in a residential neighborhood on Lidingö, an island just east of Stockholm. Except instead of having their morning gathering on an alphabet rug on the floor of a classroom, they are sitting on cushy pads in a teepee, seeking warmth from a fire that is burning in the middle. For a while, they talk about the weather and sing songs about snow. Then, when the gathering is over, they disperse in the yard, a large, craggy space that besides the teepee sports a rustic shelter, a woodshop, some log steps, a chicken coop, a few pine trees, and some homemade toys, like a train made of pallets. A line of prams, where the youngest children take their naps, sit under a small roof that is attached to the wall of the main building, a low-slung house with red wood siding. In the center of the yard, the few remaining patches of ice have become a popular sledding course. Five girls, who look like they are between the ages of three and four, grab a couple of sleds and start tying them together, then race down the hill. On the other side of the yard, a boy is surreptitiously circling the shelter while holding a piece of bark up to his ear, like a cell phone.

Preschool teacher Anna Mållberg takes the children at one of Sweden's many forest schools for a walk in the woods.
Linda McGurk

"Calling all ninjas!" he shouts into the phone. "There are snakes on the loose in town; can you come over?"

Another boy, who has climbed up in a gangly pine tree, jumps into the game:

"Danger in town! Tons of pythons on the ground! Be careful!"

Scenes like these play out daily at Mulleborg, the first forest school in Sweden. Most days, the children and teachers spend their entire day in the nearby forest, where the children themselves have come up with names for some of the most popular spots: Blueberry Mountain, Sunny Hill, and Silja Line. Naming their favorite spots is not the only way they take ownership of these places.

"Whenever we go to a new place in the woods, the first thing the kids do is to collect sticks and build a fort," Maria Mårtensson, one of the pedagogues at Mulleborg, tells me while she watches the children playing from a distance. "It's almost like they're marking their territory."

Four boys at a Swedish forest school play and look for frogs in a creek that meanders through the wooded property.
Linda McGurk

There are about forty-five thousand residents, eight forest schools, and countless forts on the island of Lidingö, making it a hub for this type of early childhood education in Sweden. It all started in the 1980s, when two outdoorsy preschool teachers dreamed of immersing children in nature and educating them about the environment on a daily basis.

"When you spend time in nature you learn to understand and take care of nature," says Susanne Drougge, a self-proclaimed entrepreneur and cofounder of Mulleborg. "It's almost impossible not to. You automatically create an interest in nature and the environment, without preaching to the children."

The first modern forest school was founded in Denmark in the 1950s, but when Drougge and her colleague Siw Linde proposed the idea in Sweden in 1983, it was a radical break with the prevailing traditional municipal preschool model of the time. The premise behind the forest school philosophy was simple: Stimulate children's physical, cognitive, and social development by spending as much time as possible in nature, every day, all year-round. At forest school, nature becomes a classroom with no walls, where children learn through self-directed play by using their whole bodies and all of their senses, in an environment that nurtures their curiosity and strengthens their self-esteem. In the process, the thinking goes, they will become responsible stewards of the land. Drougge and Linde—who met at a car repair class and immediately hit it off—quickly got local parents and the Swedish Outdoor Association to support the idea. Convincing the local Lidingö government was tougher, but after the pair jumped through all the regulatory hoops, Mulleborg opened its doors in 1985.

"When I feel that something is right for the children, for society and nature, I'm hard to stop," Drougge says.

Through the forest school, she found a perfect outlet for her love of nature and the outdoors. The practical aspects of keeping kids outside most of the day, often in the woods away from the preschool building and any type of indoor or outdoor plumbing, didn't scare her. On the contrary, she felt like being outside was often easier, as there were fewer things that interfered with the children's play, and they had more space to move around.

"You become really good at changing diapers outside and cooking food using a camp kitchen," she says. "Everything becomes so simple when you're outside, and there's always something for the kids to do. Ultimately I think it comes down to whether you're willing to get out of your comfort zone and learn new things in life."

The opening of Mulleborg, which translates to "Fort of Mulle," had a ripple effect, and today there are more than two hundred forest schools in Sweden and thousands more internationally, sometimes under names like nature kindergarten, nature-based preschool, outdoor school, forest kindergarten, *Waldkindergarten*, and bush school. Outside of Scandinavia, forest schools are particularly popular in the UK and Germany, but interest is also growing considerably in Japan, Australia, Canada, and the US.

A vast majority of the forest schools in Sweden have a waiting list, and the parents who seek them out generally fall into one of two categories: They're either very outdoorsy themselves, or they want their kids to enjoy the healthy benefits of an outdoor lifestyle but don't feel like they have enough interest or time for it at home. Many parents also enroll their children in forest schools because they want them to learn how to take care of nature.

Just how popular the Swedish forest school model is became clear in 2014 when it came time for Sweden's heir to the throne, Princess Victoria, and her husband, Prince Daniel, to choose a preschool for their two-and-a-half-year-old daughter, Estelle. It was a sign of the times that they chose not an academic prep school but a local forest school. "For us it is extremely important that nature becomes a natural part of our children's everyday life," Princess Victoria told reporters at the time of the enrollment. "[Forest schools] use a pedagogy that I think is very sound, especially when it comes to their attitude toward nature." Because only in Scandinavia is playing with sticks, eating your lunch under a piece of tarp, and pooping in a hole in the woods considered a life fit for a princess.

To teach students—princesses included—how to take care of the environment, Swedish forest schools have a special tool at their disposal. His name is Mulle (pronounced *moo-le*), and with his shaggy moss-green hair topped by a cone-shaped hat made of birch bark, he looks like a subtler, more domesticated version of a good luck troll. Mulle, or Skogsmulle (Forest Mulle), is a symbol of outdoor ethics and is generally recognized as the father of outdoor education for children across the country. (The closest American equivalent might be Smokey Bear, who educates the public about forest fires.) Conceived in the 1950s by Gösta Frohm, who at the time was the director of the Swedish Outdoor Association, Mulle uses stories, songs, and games to teach children about nature and how to take care of it.

"Mulle is a pedagogical tool that we use," says Kajsa Källström, the manager of Mulleborg. "The children read books about him and they know that it's somebody that dresses up as him. Mulle almost has a Santa Claus effect; he triggers their imagination."

Gösta Frohm, the original "Mulle," the friendly
forest troll who educates children about nature.
Svenne Nordlöf

By the Swedish Outdoor Association's accounting, as many
as two million children have at some point been educated by
this raggedy forest troll either by going to a forest school or joining one of the association's many nature groups for children,
so-called Skogsmulle schools. It's hard to overestimate the influence of Mulle on outdoor education in Sweden, and the phenomenon has spread internationally, to Norway, Finland, Latvia,
Russia, the UK, and Germany. In Japan, he's led the upswing of
outdoor education and almost garnered a cult following as more

than five hundred Japanese educators have flocked to Sweden to receive training in Mulle's simple philosophy, which goes something like this: "If you can help children love nature, they will take care of nature, because you cherish things you love."

Drougge, Mulleborg's cofounder, goes as far as calling this doctrine the "pedagogy of Mulle." "Mulle teaches children to care about nature and how to see the difference between different plants and animals," she says. "We need this today more than ever. We need adults who still have one foot in nature, who understand how nature works. We can't go on using up all our resources without giving anything back to the planet. With Mulle, this comes automatically, without preaching. You just create an interest in nature and the environment."

Where Did Your Breakfast Come From?

If Mulle helps establish an environmental ethos for the youngest children, their education soon gets more sophisticated than that. Today environmental education is a mandated part of the national curriculum not only for preschool but also for grade school in Sweden. And the message in the curriculum is clear: Understanding how your own lifestyle affects your health, the environment, and society at large is considered just as important as, say, mastering math problems and knowing the difference between past and present tense. This message is reinforced by the media as children's programming on TV regularly brings up different environmental issues. In the months that we spend in Sweden, the young reporters in one of the most popular kids' shows, *REA*, will investigate the consequences of food waste, show how computers are recycled, question why children don't have more influence over land use (for example, when a forest is threatened by development), and sample worm burgers, as protein from insects is sometimes touted as part of the solution to world hunger.

By the time they hit third or fourth grade, many Swedish kids already sound like budding environmental activists. When Mattias Sandberg, an associate senior lecturer of cultural geography at the University of Gothenburg, interviewed ten-year-olds in Gothenburg and Stockholm for his doctoral thesis, he found that those who played regularly in nature near their homes felt strongly about protecting their own neighborhood and the environment as a whole. Several were concerned about littering, land exploitation, and pollution. Most of them also felt ambivalent about cars, which on the one hand are useful for getting around, but on the other hand contribute to pollution.

One boy named Benjamin said, "I didn't like it when we were in preschool and they cut down a forest there. And then they built weird houses."

When Sandberg asked the children why they don't like it when the forest is cut down, he noted that the children weren't just concerned about losing a place to play. They also made connections to larger global environmental issues like pollution and climate change. "China and many other countries don't have a lot of forests, they have more cities, and that causes the air to become polluted. In the forest the air is cleaner," said a girl named Lina, who wanted to write an ad to encourage people to ride bikes.

Another girl, Natalie, chimed in, "If we cut down all the forests and build roads, we take the freedom from the animals, and then there will be a lot of pollution and cars."

"That's not good; haven't you heard about the earth's surface and the warming effects?" Lina responded.

Growing up in Sweden, I, too, had been acutely aware of environmental issues from an early age. Six days after my eighth birthday, on April 26, 1986, an explosion in reactor number four at the Chernobyl nuclear power plant in Ukraine caused radioactive fallout to quickly spread over Europe. Five percent of it fell over Sweden, lacing our milk, fish, venison, reindeer meat, and wild mushrooms and berries with the radioactive compound cesium 137, limiting our ability to forage for food in the wild. The cesium levels in these foods eventually came down, safety restrictions were lifted, and life went on, but as a child I couldn't help but notice that something sacred had been tainted in the worst possible way.

And it didn't stop there. Acid rain, species extinction, the thinning ozone layer over Antarctica, and the clear-cutting of the rain forest were other threats du jour that became harder and harder to ignore. In the span of a decade, the environment went from being a marginal issue for most Swedish voters to being a top concern. At school, a surefire sign of this green awakening was the rain forest purchase certificate that every self-respecting classroom in the country at one point had on proud display.

Global climate change is undoubtedly a more complex and difficult concept for this generation of children to grasp than the threatened rain forests that we fought for in the '80s. After all, you can't buy an iceberg, and even if you did, how would you stop it from melting?

Maya is still blissfully unaware of the potentially life-altering effects of climate change, but at her Swedish school she is already being prepped to fight it and other threats to the environment, one small personal act at a time. Some of these acts are happening in an unexpected place—the school cafeteria. My own children rarely rave about the food I cook at home, unless it's pancakes, so when Maya writes to her classmates in the US that she likes the school food in Sweden, I decide to come try it myself.

The cafeteria at Maya's school is definitely homey; only forty-some children eat at a time, and in the center of each white-cloth-covered table sits a glass vase with a fake pink daisy. The food is served on ceramic plates and eaten with real silverware. Since the school is a small one, the kitchen staff knows the students' names as well as their likes and dislikes. Most days, the students can choose between a meat or fish dish and a vegetarian dish, but on the day I visit both options are vegetarian: a potato-and-leek soup served with bread and cheese, and a bulgur-and-vegetable casserole. I choose the soup and find that it's hearty and full of flavor, and has a homemade texture to it. Maya, who's notoriously picky, chooses the soup, too, and eats every spoonful of her serving. When I ask the kids, they all say that they like the food, but can't explain why. Sure, the menu contains some given kid-pleasers, like meatballs and macaroni, but many of the dishes are heavy on vegetables and some are downright exotic, like the Asian casserole with coconut flakes and bamboo shoots, and lasagna New Delhi.

Perhaps what's most noticeable about school lunch in Sweden—and maybe why the kids like it so much—is that none of the food is prepackaged, not even the milk, and there is little to no processed food or refined sugar. "We don't roll our own meatballs and we don't bread the fish, but everything else is pretty much made from scratch—soups, sauces, casseroles," says Eva, one of three food workers at the school. This reminds me of conversations I had with Maya's teachers back in the US. "If it doesn't look like it came out of the microwave, the kids won't eat it," one teacher had complained to me. Another staff member once jokingly said that the cafeteria workers might as well throw the vegetables straight in the garbage, without even serving them to the kids, because that's where they'd end up anyway.

As Maya and I go to put our dishes away after we finish eating, I make another discovery: The stainless steel bowl in which the children scrape their leftovers before putting their bowls in the dish rack by the kitchen is nearly empty. Eva the kitchen worker tells me that the children are always encouraged to try everything and are welcome to come for seconds, but are told not to take more than they think they can eat. But that's not the whole story.

School lunches are free in Sweden, so food waste directly affects the city's wallet. Plus, it's taxing for the environment. Producing and transporting food from the farm to the end consumer takes a lot of resources—agricultural land, energy, water, chemicals, and fuel—and the later in the food cycle that it gets wasted, the greater the impact on the environment. Globally, food waste causes over three billion tons of carbon emissions every year, according to the UN's Food and Agriculture Organization. To put that in perspective, if food waste were a country, it would be the third-largest emitter of greenhouse gases in the world, after China and the US.

When food is discarded in the school cafeteria, not only has it been produced in vain, but it also takes resources to dispose of it. To save money and lessen its environmental footprint, the city launched a competition in 2012 challenging all schools in the district to reduce their food waste. The top school stood to win a little over a thousand dollars, and the city vowed to use the rest of the money saved to buy a greater share of organic foods. The children took the challenge to heart. In the three years that the competition has run, Maya's school has placed in the top three out of nearly forty schools for reducing waste, and in 2014 they also had the least amount of waste per plate: 0.04 ounces per student, which is basically the weight of four large peas.

The kids in Maya's class were noticeably proud of this achievement. "We don't waste any food at our school," one of the boys had casually informed me while we were waiting in line to get served, while another girl had chimed in, "We don't take more than we can eat." Winning a citywide contest had proven to be an incredibly effective way to inspire change and make the students own it. "We've seen a lasting effect of the competition," says Chatrine, who handles much of the school's environmental education, when I catch her after school one day. "They influence each other and remind each other not to take more than they can eat."

The cafeteria is central to the school's environmental work in other ways. The menu is now "climate adjusted," which means that each meal is carefully composed based not only on its nutritional value but also on its impact on the environment. Because of this, beef has more or less been eliminated from the menu, as it has been blamed for causing a substantial amount of greenhouse gas emissions and takes much more land and water to produce than other types of meat. Hamburgers are pretty much out, and fish burgers made from certified sustainable fish are in. Rice, a crop that is a source of major methane emissions and has to be shipped long distances, is only served about once a month. Potatoes and pasta have mostly picked up the slack.

Swedish schools also try to buy as many organic products as possible. The city of Borås, which handles all purchases for the preschools and schools in the district, has over the past few years gradually increased the share of organic foods, which was set to reach 40 percent in 2016. Maya's school and several others have already surpassed that goal. "The pasta, bread, milk, fruit, vegetables, cheese—it's all organic. It's almost harder to think of things that we buy that are nonorganic than organic," says Eva, the cafeteria worker. "We buy organic both because it's better for the environment and because there are fewer toxins in it. It's the same reason why I buy organic for my family at home."

Beyond the cafeteria, Maya's school emphasizes the connections between personal decisions and the environment in other ways. This year the students are working with the theme "Climate and Energy," and the school has found some creative ways to introduce the concept. In the fall, students were asked to think about what they had for breakfast and find out where their food came from. They also looked for certifications, like *organic* and *fair trade*, then entered all the information into a PowerPoint presentation on an iPad. A gray map with a little white airplane illustrated how far the food had traveled. In one group, all the food amazingly enough came from Sweden, while in others it came from several exotic locations from far away, such as oranges from Argentina or cheese from Germany. This sparked a discussion about energy: what it is, how it is spent, and how it affects the climate. Often, these discussions continue when the children get home.

"The kids turn into little environmental police—they go home and nag their parents about conserving energy," Chatrine says. "They tell them to hang out the laundry instead of drying it in the tumble dryer, turn off the lights when they leave a room, and not let the water run when they brush their teeth. The older ones talk about climate change too."

While I'm ecstatic over the thought of Maya eating homemade and mostly organic food every day and learning all about the environment in the classroom, environmental education in Swedish schools is so ordinary to the other parents that nobody even thinks to mention it to me. It reminds me of a friend of mine in Indiana who used to work as a high school science teacher and faced a huge battle with some parents over an eighth-grade curriculum that focused on human-induced climate change. Even though her unit followed the state standards, one of the parents went so far as to accuse her of spreading propaganda and complained about it to the principal and school board. "It was incredibly stressful," she says. "I've talked to multiple teachers who have struggled with the same thing, especially in small, rural towns." In Sweden, however, teaching kids about climate change and the environmental costs of development and economic growth is not something parents seem to consider political or controversial. Instead, they embrace it as a matter of self-preservation of the human species.

What really amazes me, though, is that the school's climate-adjusted menu has slipped through without vocal protests.

When I do some digging around, I find a couple of mildly critical voices whose main complaint is that the school should prioritize local food—for example, beef produced in Sweden—over organic. But overall, eating a vegetarian diet, or at least cutting down on red meat, apparently has become mainstream—so mainstream that when an old friend and I decide to catch up over lunch, the first place she suggests is the new vegan raw-food café in town. "They have such good food there," my friend, whom I remember as a devoted carnivore, tells me.

I can only assume that when it comes to saving the environment, there are no sacred cows in Sweden. Not even in the form of a steak.

A Special Friend Named Towa

The changing of the seasons is an important part of life's steady rhythm in Scandinavia, and each is celebrated for its own merits. Tourists, however, typically don't come to Scandinavia to "meet the spring" the way they would go to, say, Paris or New York. Which is understandable, since this season sometimes feels like a long, slightly warmer extension of winter, just with less snow. The objective, meteorological spring in Sweden occurs after February 15, whenever there are seven days of rising daily temperatures averaging between thirty-two and fifty degrees Fahrenheit. This objective start of spring may or may not coincide with the subjective signs of spring. Chain saws revving in the forest. Alfresco dining with wool blankets. The distinct smell of dirt, evaporating rain, and freshly cut pine trees. The return of life and growth. And, if the snow doesn't melt fast enough, the collective race to put out the patio furniture, as if this act alone will force out warmer weather.

"Reducing spring to a matter of weather is like reducing love to a series of chemical signals in our brains," says a speaker during valborg, a celebration of the arrival of spring that I attend with the girls. A pagan tradition with roots in the Middle Ages, valborg occurs on April 30 every year and, in its modern form, usually involves choral singing, racy student parades, and enormous bonfires. "I've been told that spring will come tomorrow," the speaker says, trying to boost morale as we huddle around a paltry fire by the clubhouse in the pouring rain, "but meanwhile, let's enjoy the beauty of nature and let the warmth come from within."

We have no choice but to do exactly that. The cheap plastic chairs on the small patio outside the Shack are set up and ready for use, but the warmer temperatures evade us. At least it's getting visibly lighter every day, and by the end of April, it stays light well past nine in the evening. The light more than anything creates a visual bridge between winter and summer and gives us all a much-needed serotonin boost. All of a sudden it seems like people have lost their gloomy winter veil—the normally reserved Swedes all seem happier, friendlier, more hopeful. The light also sets my children on the fast track to insomnia. "How can it be eight o'clock already? It only feels like six!" Maya complains every night as I attempt to start the bedtime routine. Nora, who usually predictably conks out around seven and sleeps for twelve hours, bounces out of the bedroom two, three, even four times to tell me that she can't sleep. The blackout curtains do absolutely nothing to fool her brain into thinking that it's time to go night-night. Two massages and three bedtime stories later, she's still awake. Lying in bed with her for forty-five minutes and reassuring her that the Sleep Fairy is going to come and sprinkle her magic slumber dust any minute now doesn't do the trick either. Finally, I decide to throw in the towel and wait until nine o'clock before I even attempt to put them to bed.

Springtime also marks the start of the gardening season, an event on par with Christmas for my mom, who grows vegetables in a greenhouse about the size of a small apartment. One day the girls and I drive out to her house, a nineteenth-century homestead about twenty minutes from the Shack, where she lives quasi–off the grid with her husband. As we pull up in front of the carport, where firewood is stacked in neat rows all the way to the roof, she comes out and greets us dressed in her soiled gardening pants and a mustard-colored button-down shirt, her frizzy, henna-dyed hair temporarily tamed in a knot. Her hands are dirty too; she's spent this sunny morning planting potatoes in the raised beds in her backyard, and she's oozing a gardening high. Some people connect with nature through epic hikes through the mountains or cross-country skiing through the wilderness. Meanwhile, my mom finds inner peace by filling her sunroom with tomato seedlings and lemon trees.

"Come on in, I've got something to show you!"

The last time she said that, she and her husband had installed a modern underground root cellar for food storage in the backyard. I really don't know what to expect this time. We follow her to the first-floor bathroom and she opens the door. "We call her Towa," Mom says affectionately and points to something on the floor. And it is not the new furry kitten Maya and Nora were hoping for. Whatever it is looks like a large green watering can with a heart-shaped opening at the top and a long plastic handle hanging down on one side.

"We use Towa to collect pee to fertilize the garden," Mom explains proudly as she shows off her latest internet purchase. "Did you know that urine is known as the liquid gold of gardening? It's completely insane to flush such a great resource down the toilet!"

Then she starts instructing us on how to create the magic potion for the garden.

"From now on you only need to use the toilet if you're doing a number two. For number one, just use Towa, and throw the toilet paper in the trash can. After she's been used a few times I dilute the urine with water and sprinkle it over the plants."

Nora and Maya are way more excited about the custom-made pee bucket than I ever could have imagined and race each other to it. Little sister comes out on top this time. She quickly pulls down her pants and smiles with delight as a light yellow stream hits the green plastic with a splash. I'm slightly less enthusiastic.

"I think I'll just use the toilet if that's okay."

Mom looks disappointed and dumbfounded.

"Why would you? This is the most sustainable and ecologically sound way to handle urine. And my vegetables are going to grow like weeds. It's a win-win."

She's right, of course. Fertilizing produce with human urine is ingenious, as it is both sterile and chock-full of nutrients, not to mention free, and the supply never ending. Several pilot projects are already up and running in Scandinavia to see if urine can be used as an agricultural fertilizer on a larger scale. Securing the supply will probably be the greatest challenge, since few Swedes would be willing to go as far as my mom to set up their own chemical-free fertilizer production. My mom, who has a sharp eye for cutting-edge gardening practices, is as usual ahead of the curve.

Even though she came of age in the '60s, my mom was never

a hippie. Unlike me, she never walked in demonstrations and shouted homemade slogans against atomic bomb testing or protested the Norwegian seal hunt. But at this point I realize that my mom may be the most radical environmental activist I know. One small action at a time, she's doing her share to save the planet by voluntarily forfeiting conveniences that even I balk at giving up. Here she was, growing and burying her food in the backyard like a pioneer woman, while I was still going to the grocery store every week like an unenlightened conformist. And as I'm standing there, watching my daughters running around barefoot in my mom's yard, enthusiastically giving their grandmother's plants golden showers with a green watering can named Towa, I think to myself that maybe this is the best environmental education they could ever wish for.

Scandinavian Parenting Tip #4
The best way to raise an eco-conscious child is to be an eco-conscious parent. Live by the principle of the three R's—reduce, reuse, recycle—and involve your child in the process. Talk about how your personal choices can impact the environment and look for opportunities to make a difference—for example, by volunteering for cleanup days at a nearby park, using public transit or riding your bike instead of taking the car, and shopping for organic, locally grown food.

Suggested reading: *Beyond Ecophobia: Reclaiming the Heart in Nature Education*, by David Sobel. Orion Society, 1999.

5

A LITTLE DIRT WON'T HURT (NOR WILL A LITTLE RAIN)

Why go inside when it rains? That's when the mud makes the best globs.
—SWEDISH OUTDOOR ASSOCIATION

By springtime, keeping track of Maya's social calendar has turned into a part-time job. She has had more playdates in three months than she had in her entire life before we came here, and she uses my cell phone to set them up herself. To my surprise, the Shack soon becomes a popular meeting spot for the kids in Maya's class. I didn't think we had much to offer, just a tiny old house with no more entertainment than what the girls had brought with them from the US—a few coloring books, a box of crayons, a pile of books, and as many stuffed animals as they could squeeze into their carry-on luggage. Still, the kids keep coming. Unless it's pouring down rain, they're out the door within a few minutes of getting home on most days, even though they've already been outside for several hours at school and *fritids*. If they're not playing with the neighbor's dogs or petting the horses that are grazing behind the Shack, they're climbing trees or playing in the woods nearby.

At one point, I have as many as six of them running around outside. There, it seems like both gender and age barriers are shattered. Often, boys and girls play together, and Nora, who is four years younger than most of them, is keeping up with them all. Sometimes they gravitate more toward games with rules, like

141

chasing games and soccer, other times rough-and-tumble play. Other times they collect things, like slugs, flies, or other bugs, and build habitats for them. (At one point a few of the girls even create an insect club at school and spend every recess period "rescuing" injured bugs, which they name after the big soccer players, like Messi, Ronaldo, and Neymar, then negotiate custody over them and bring them home.) Often they delve into imaginative play, pretending that they're singers putting on a concert one minute, riders taking their horses into the woods the next. Theoretically, at their age, they're well past their peak for imaginative play, but of this I don't see any evidence.

"We're pretending that Milton is a thief who stole our horses, and now he's going to poison them," Maya explains one day when I ask her what happened to the classmate that she had brought home from school, since I hadn't seen him for a while. (As it turns out, Milton has been jailed indefinitely under the climbing tree, charged with said attempted horse theft and poisoning.) Or, as I casually try to strike up a conversation in the unusually quiet car on the way home from school one day: "Ssshhh, Mom! We can't talk right now: we're horses riding in a trailer, we're on our way to a race."

Back in Indiana I had always been the one orchestrating outdoor play as soon as the girls got home in the afternoon, trying to entice them with sidewalk chalk, creek investigations, and picnics at the park. Some days it didn't matter how hard I tried; they still weren't up for it. It may also have been a result of the inevitable Law of Parenting: The more I wanted them to go outside, the more they dug their heels in. I don't know how many times Maya and Nora had dissed my suggestion that they build a fort in the woods behind our house. Here in Sweden they come and ask for my help to make one, and often spend time playing in it in the evenings. For the first time, they will spontaneously stay out and play for hours, and I'm the one saying no when they want to go back outside after dinner.

Something has happened and I think I know what it is. I was a good enough playmate for them for years, but what they needed was other children to inspire them. In Sweden, we find a rich culture of outdoor play, and it is upheld through an unspoken agreement among the parents.

"I let them play Minecraft for half an hour or so," Nellie's mom, Therese, reports almost apologetically when I pick Maya up from her house one day. She quickly adds, "But they were outside for an hour jumping on the trampoline as well."

Nora too has made plenty of new friends at preschool, but it takes a little longer for her to get set up with playdates, partly because I don't know any of the parents at her school. Finally, I pick up the phone and call the mom of Kerstin, a girl whom Nora has bonded with. Her name is Mari and she says sure, the girls can play. Even though we live in a small community where people generally trust each other, contacting strangers out of the blue and then leaving your kid there to play for a few hours feels a little bit like going on a blind date. What kind of parenting choices have they made? What are their likes and dislikes? What will they think of my child? You just don't know who's going to show up when you ring the doorbell.

In this case, it's a friendly former professional shot-put athlete turned IT manager named David, also known as Kerstin's dad. David is tattooed up to his neck, speaks six languages, and, as I'm just about to discover, is a storyteller extraordinaire. While Kerstin and Nora run off to play, David invites me to join him and Mari for *fika*. While holding and comforting his and Mari's two-year-old daughter, Rakel, he makes coffee and tells me about his upbringing in northern Sweden and Saudi Arabia, where his father worked for a multinational company; his subsequent stint as a broke exchange student in Louisiana; his massive weight gain after giving up his sports career; and getting told by five doctors that he would have to take statins for the rest of his life. Then he explains how he went on a raw vegan diet and started exercising madly, dropped eighty pounds, and proved them wrong.

"I'm a problem solver. I just don't like it when shit comes to me too easily," he says.

David and Mari's home, a one-of-a-kind former church community building with an open floor plan and eighteen-foot ceilings, was once featured in an interior-décor magazine and is nothing short of stunning. As I sit at their dining room table made out of massive slabs of reclaimed wood and drinking tea out of a cup with no handles, I'm thinking that we're a mismatch. These people are clearly way too stylish and 100 percent more hipster than me.

Then a different narrative emerges—our mutual passion for the outdoors. David tells me that he and Mari moved here a couple of years ago from Gothenburg, the second-biggest city in Sweden, following some green-wave dream to leave the city and go "back to the land" or, in this case, back to the forest. When David's not busy managing over a hundred programmers, some of his favorite pastimes are exploring nature with his daughters, looking for frogs, fishing, foraging for berries and mushrooms, and geocaching, a form of modern-day outdoor treasure hunt using GPS-enabled smartphones. Once he signed up for a survival course in the wilderness to prepare himself for solo camping with his dog and ended up spooning random strangers through the freezing night.

"When Rakel was younger I would put her in a sling on my back, push Kerstin in the stroller with one hand, and hold the dog with the other," David says. "There's always a way to get outside."

When I come back to get Nora a few hours later, David is cooking dinner (vegan Mexican/Middle Eastern fusion rolls with mint sauce) while his wife, Mari, is enjoying the sun with Rakel on the expansive back porch. Nora and Kerstin are digging holes in the sandbox, where they have spent the better part of the afternoon, and they're so absorbed by this activity that Nora doesn't even notice my presence. Her jeans are caked in filth and she has sunk her hands deep down in the mud, carefully massaging it. Periodically she pulls her hands out of the hole for inspection. "Look, Mommy, I've got brown hands!" she says elatedly once she finally sees that I'm there.

Mari, who works as a school counselor, watches calmly as Kerstin and Nora proceed to smear mud on their arms and faces, war-paint style. "Dirty kids are happy kids," she says. "All play is based on creativity, and I think this is creative if anything. This is all a part of the exploratory process that is such an important part of being a child."

This creative process unfortunately needs to come to an end before Nora gets into the Saab, so Mari sets out a tub of soapy water and some wet wipes on the deck for the girls to wash off with. They strip down and start to clean themselves up, still playing and giggling madly.

David, Mari, and I are chatting in the kitchen that is adjacent to the deck when Kerstin, butt naked, comes up to the open patio door and informs us that she needs to go potty.

"Just go in the grass, honey," David says.

As Mari brings out towels for the girls to dry off with and helps them get dressed, I notice that she doesn't scold them for getting just about every square inch of their clothes and bodies dirty, including the lining of their nostrils. I'm not surprised. Messy, wild play is seen as a perfectly natural, even cherished part of childhood in Scandinavia, and the way I was raised, muddy hands, piles of filthy clothes, and wet boots were almost considered badges of honor, a testament to a day filled with adventure, new experiences, and lots of trial and error. The adult me has a slightly more complex relationship with messes. I wouldn't exactly call myself a neat freak, but I like my house orderly and clean, and my kitchen counter free of clutter, craft glitter, and traces of homemade salt dough. Outside, however, it's a different story. I have no problem whatsoever with my children wading knee-deep in a creek, carousing with filthy farm animals, or walking barefoot through a muddy field. They can wrestle in mud puddles all day long, as far as I'm concerned. It's almost as if nature itself manages to pacify my type A tics. Or maybe I'm just calmed by the knowledge that the kids will leave their muddy clothes in the garage on their way back inside the house, thereby keeping the mess contained and manageable. Either way, I truly feel like sending kids outside to play and then barring them from getting dirty is like giving them an eight-week-old kitten and telling them they're not allowed to pet it. It's just not right.

Mari was apparently a kindred spirit, and in Sweden we were far from unique.

"Of course children should be able to get dirty when they play outside; it goes without saying," says Johanna, a mother of two preschool-age girls, whom I meet at an outing with a nature play group. Her husband, Marcus, agrees: "There is this fantastic invention called a washing machine. We have one and it runs a lot."

"I think jumping in puddles is part of childhood," another mom tells me. "It's also a form of risk assessment. 'How much can I splash around before I get wet?'"

This acceptance of children being a bit wild and getting dirty likely originates in the Romantic era, when nature was glorified by thinkers and philosophers like Jean-Jacques Rousseau, who was a vocal critic of civilization. He argued, somewhat radically, that the purest people were found in primitive societies rather than civilized ones. The farther removed humans were from what he called the original "state of nature," the more morally corrupted and decadent they would inevitably become. Children were viewed as close to nature because they hadn't yet become broken down and destroyed by civilization, and according to Rousseau's logic it was desirable that they stay in that natural state as long as possible.

The idea that children are natural was popularized again in the twentieth century, and eventually nature became a symbol of the good childhood in Scandinavia. Children's books, like the ones written by beloved Swedish author Astrid Lindgren (in the US most famous for her stories about Pippi Longstocking), helped reinforce the idea that wild, free, messy play outdoors is the ultimate childhood experience. In Lindgren's story collection *The Children of Noisy Village*, based on her own childhood in southern Sweden in the early twentieth century, seven boisterous kids race bark boats down a creek, spontaneously try to ride a docile bull, have tea with their dolls in a cow pasture, dance around a bonfire, jump in the biggest mud puddles they can find, and wade in ditches until their boots are filled with water.

The ideals from Lindgren's books very much prevail in Sweden today, partly thanks to the Swedish Outdoor Association, which holds that all children enrolled in its forest schools have a right to "become dirty, stay active and be inspired by nature," Although the forest schools blazed a trail for messy play, these ideas are now embraced by more traditional day cares and schools as well. Swedish veteran preschool teacher and author Ann Granberg sums it up well when she writes that "too much order and cleanliness hampers play. Children must be allowed to get muddy, get in the water with their clothes on, make a mess and be rowdy; they should be spontaneous, improvise and do things that are not thought-through."

Interestingly, the difference in attitude toward dirt in Scandinavia can also be traced semantically. The Swedish equivalent of *shit*—widely considered one of the rudest swear words in the US—is *skit*. Except in Sweden, since this is synonymous with *dirt* or *poop*, it's not really considered a swear word at all. Both kids and adults use it as an interjection no worse than, say, the word *oops* in English. The only problem is that, since most Swedes are excellent English speakers and more fascinated by American pop culture than most Americans, children and adults both gravitate toward using the English version of *skit*.

"It just means dirt! It's not a cussword!" my mom will protest every time I scold her for loudly dropping the s-bomb in the checkout line at the grocery store while visiting us in Indiana, regardless of how many times I've explained to her that it *is* in fact considered a cussword and I would very much appreciate it if she would start treating it as such. During our time in Sweden, Maya and Nora are in for a reverse culture clash.

"One of the boys said the s-word three times today!" Maya reports in dismay after one of her first days of school. "I told the teacher and she told him off, but I heard him say it again later."

The next day, it's somebody else. And the next day. I tell Maya that her classmates may just not understand that the s-word is a really bad word in English and suggest that she explain it to them. She does, but fails to convince them. After complaining to the teacher again, the issue of the s-word usage makes it all the way to the school's Great Council, a monthly gathering where all the students and teachers meet to discuss policies and current events. There, the teachers again reinforce that cussing is not appropriate at school, even if it happens to be in English. For a few days after the meeting, it seems like the situation has cooled off, but it doesn't take long before things revert to the old order. Maya soon realizes that she's fighting a fruitless battle. Once again, some things just don't translate well.

Dirt Is Good

When North Dakota native Ania Krasniewska enrolled her daughter in a Danish forest school, she didn't quite know what to expect. Ania, who lived in Copenhagen for several years while her American diplomat husband was stationed there, initially leaned toward one of the international schools that are typically favored by expat families. But then she decided to look at some options that were closer to their house in the exclusive suburb of Charlottenlund. The forest school, she was told, was a "very traditional Danish school," one where children spend most of their day outside in the forest and, inevitably, come home dirty.

The first time she saw the school her eyes welled up with tears, which she did her best to hide.

"When I saw the crates that were full of dirty toys, that looked like they were some castoffs, it reminded me of the orphanages around the world that I used to volunteer at," she says. "I've always been a hands-off type of parent, but when I saw all the dirt at the school, it took me a while to separate the two different types of dirt—the dirt that comes from playing outside and the dirt that is due to neglect."

Ania's experience is not unique. To the outsider, Scandinavians' affinity for messy play can be perplexing. Ebba Lisberg Jensen, a human ecology researcher at Malmö University whose research focuses on the relationship between humans and nature, experienced this firsthand when she brought a Vietnamese friend to a dinner at the home of a middle-class family in southern Sweden. As is typical for a Swedish dinner party, the children were running around outside in somewhat raggedy summer dresses, barefoot, dirty, and with messy hair. The parents thought everything was dandy, as it fit right in with their romantic ideas of a perfect childhood experience. But the Vietnamese dinner guest was confused.

"She discreetly whispered to me, 'Why do the children look like that? Why are they dirty and barefoot? Why are these people not taking care of their children?'" says Lisberg Jensen. "And that's when I realized that dirty, barefoot children with ripped clothes is maybe something you can allow yourself to have when that's not tied to your prestige."

To me, the story sounds familiar. When we're invited to a dinner party at my friend Malin's house together with a couple of other families, the patio doors by the kitchen and dining area are wide open so that the kids—about ten of them in all—can run in and out. It's drizzling, but the kids couldn't care less. One girl, who's just about to turn four, is maneuvering a ride-on backhoe digger in the sandbox, barefoot and wearing a pink flowery dress that looks more suitable for a tea party than a mud session with the neighborhood kids. Her mom, Emilia, shrugs.

"It's no big deal. I can always wash out the stains. You've got to let them be kids. You know, let them play, even if they're in their nice clothes."

On the big wooden deck, Einar, three years old, is throwing a small tantrum because he doesn't want to wear the rain boots and waterproof pants that his mom has brought for him to wear in case of inclement weather. Eventually, she decides to let it go. After all, it's just rain. Einar elatedly joins another of the boys, who's already barefoot and riding around on the deck on a toy tractor. After a while, Malin's oldest daughter, Elin, comes running with a bloody knee and torn stockings.

"My bad for not making her wear her shell pants," Malin sighs, and unceremoniously puts a Band-Aid on the wound.

My own kids are down by the swing set, singing and spinning around in the light drizzle. Nobody is telling the kids to come inside, clean up, calm down, or stop playing in the mud. Instead, after dinner, they are sent back outside, and they are more than happy to comply. If it hadn't been for the rain and the fact that Malin's patio lacks cover, dinner would've been served outside as well, since most Swedes tend to have an unstated goal of eating as many meals as possible in the open air during the warmer months. This time, however, we have to settle for eating in the dining room.

"Maybe it'll clear up before it's time for dessert," Malin says, and optimistically looks for signs of blue in the sky.

It's a typical Swedish dinner party in the country.

Our reaction to dirt very much depends on our upbringing, social class, cultural context, and personal experiences. Attitudes toward hygiene have also shifted back and forth during different time periods. Before the eighteenth century, neither parents nor doctors in the Western world cared much about personal hygiene; in fact, many people believed dirt protected children against disease. In France, for example, washing a child's head was even believed to hurt his intelligence, and leaving a layer of dirt was believed to protect against injury. In Sweden a couple of hundred years ago, it was standard practice to bathe your whole body only once a year, usually around Christmas. The turning point came in the middle of the nineteenth century, when poor sanitation was linked to the disastrous spread of cholera. Up until this point, cleanliness had been considered a privilege reserved for the upper classes. Now it became a public health concern. But it would take almost another hundred years, until after World War II, before indoor plumbing became standard in Swedish homes. In the '50s and '60s, the importance of cleanliness grew. For the working class, keeping your kids neat and tidy, even if they didn't shower every day, became strongly tied to a woman's honor and even viewed as a way to stave off poverty.

Improved sanitation, combined with the invention of penicillin in the 1940s, successfully helped to drastically reduce the spread of infectious disease, in Sweden and elsewhere. Soon thereafter, however, incidences of allergy and asthma started climbing in the entire industrialized world, reaching epidemic levels in the past thirty years. The highest rates of allergy and asthma are found in the English-speaking developed countries: Australia, Ireland, New Zealand, the UK, and the US. Today, about one in ten children in the US has asthma, a disease that kills three thousand people in the country every year, and as many as 40 percent are affected by allergies. Combined, allergic disease, including asthma, is the third-most-common chronic condition among children under eighteen years old in the US. Meanwhile, asthma and allergy remain very rare conditions in many developing countries.

The changes have happened too fast to have been caused by a genetic shift in the population; instead, the culprit is likely a variety of environmental factors. Many researchers believe that smaller family sizes, increased antibiotics use, less contact with animals, more time spent indoors, and an obsession with cleanliness have all contributed to our immune systems slacking off in the past fifty years.

Our lives may be cleaner than ever—*too* clean, if you ask most immunologists—but our germophobia keeps reaching new heights. Corporations have found creative ways to profit from this fear, successfully marketing products like bleach-based toy sanitizers, shopping cart covers, and UV sanitizers for cell phones as necessities for parents in modern-day society. (And they're more than happy to point out that the cell phone your toddler just licked has eighteen times more bacteria than a public restroom.) There are now enclosed "no-mess" indoor sandboxes that children access through holes with attached rubber gloves: "all the fun of playing in a normal outdoor sandbox, but without the mess and sandy clothes!" and are marketed as completely worry-free for the parents, since "bugs, dirt, and water are no longer an issue." Some bloggers have even stopped using empty toilet paper rolls—one of the most popular recycled crafting materials of all time—simply because their readers are grossed out by the thought of the roll at one point being located within reach of a toilet.

As if parents weren't already freaking out enough, headlines like "Playing with Danger: Germy Playgrounds" and "Children's Playgrounds Are Dirtier Than Toilets, Study Shows" help fan the fears. Whether the viruses and bacteria found on the play equipment in public parks are actually dangerous (most of them are not) or whether it's possible to protect the children who play there from getting sick (it is, with regular hand washing), the damage of knowing that a baby swing or a seesaw can have as much as fifty-two thousand times more germs than a typical home toilet seat is already done. As the old adage goes, perception is reality. And that perception holds that all germs are bad and should be eliminated at any cost, preferably by a bucketful of bleach or, at the very least, by a liberal dose of hand sanitizer.

In reality, our modern, sanitized lifestyle has wiped out a lot of beneficial microbes in our gut that help us stay healthy. Being exposed to certain microbes in the womb and early childhood can actually strengthen our immune systems and protect us from illnesses later on. When the immune system is not challenged enough, it might start looking for stuff to do, like overreacting to things that are not really dangerous, like pollen and peanuts.

This is believed to cause allergies, asthma, eczema, childhood diabetes, and inflammation later in life.

In academic lingo, this is called the hygiene hypothesis, and it's been around since 1989. Many studies have supported this hypothesis, most famously a comparison of children in West and East Germany before and after the fall of the Berlin Wall. The researchers were surprised to find that the children in the poorer, dirtier, and less developed East were less likely to suffer from asthma and allergies than the children in the more affluent and sanitary West. More recently, studies have found that Amish children have remarkably low rates of asthma and allergies. The reason? Likely what European scientists call the "farm effect." Breathing in the microbes found in manure from cattle and other farm animals every day is beneficial to the immune system and could explain why only 7.2 percent of the Amish children in one study had an increased risk for allergies, compared to 50 percent of the general population. The Amish kids also had more siblings among whom to pass around the germs, which means they build more immunity. And the earlier we are exposed, the better the protection.

One group of microbes in particular has gotten researchers' attention. Some research suggests that low- or nonpathogenic strains of mycobacteria can help regulate the immune system and protect against allergic hypersensitivity. One of them, *Mycobacterium vaccae*, seems to have the ability to trigger our serotonin production, effectively making us happier and more relaxed. *M. vaccae* occurs naturally in soil and water, and is inhaled or ingested when we come in contact with dirt. Our exposure to mycobacteria has decreased considerably due to sanitation and water treatment in Western urban areas, but by regularly playing outside or helping out with a backyard garden, children can still get in contact with it.

A recent study on mice also revealed that *M. vaccae* can improve cognitive functions, like learning. When researchers Dorothy Matthews and Susan Jenks at the Sage Colleges in Troy, New York, fed the bacterium to one group of mice, they were able to navigate through a difficult maze twice as quickly as the control group while being half as stressed. After the mice were taken off the *M. vaccae* diet, the effect of the bacterium gradually tapered off for about three weeks, at which point it disappeared. The researchers speculated that the *M. vaccae* not only helped the mice feel less anxious but also made them concentrate better.

"Gardeners inhale these bacteria while digging in the soil, but they also encounter *M. vaccae* in their vegetables or when soil enters a cut in their skin," Matthews told Therapeutic Landscapes Network after the results from the study were published. "From our study we can say that it is definitely good to be outdoors—it's good to have contact with these organisms. It is interesting to speculate that creating learning environments in schools that include time in the outdoors where *M. vaccae* is present may decrease anxiety and improve the ability to learn new tasks."

Integrative pediatric neurologist Maya Shetreat-Klein also makes a good case for letting our children acquaint themselves with microbes early in life in her book *The Dirt Cure: Growing Healthy Kids with Food Straight from Soil*. "It turns out that all the things that are messy and dirty in the world, the very things we thought we needed to control or even eliminate to stay alive, are actually the very elements necessary for robust health," she writes. "Bacteria, viruses, parasites and fungi play a critical role in developing and maintaining a healthy gut and immune system. Playing outside, digging for worms, planting vegetables, and essentially coming into contact with plenty of dirt and livestock are actually good things. Not just good—essential."

While American preschools and schools use chlorine disinfecting wipes like they're going out of fashion, and many moms consider keeping a travel-size bottle of hand sanitizer in their purse nothing short of a survival strategy for the early years, Swedish parents have a slightly more relaxed relationship with germs. Hand sanitizer is mostly found at hospitals, and bleach is rarely used in the household or at schools for cleaning purposes. In fact, it's rarely used at all, since it's considered so toxic to the environment that several of the big chain stores have stopped selling it.

"I used bleach to unclog the bathtub drain once," my friend from high school, Linda, who has a nine-year-old son, confesses. "That tells you something about how strong it is. I felt really guilty about it afterward." Another friend says she's never even had it in her home, although her husband reportedly used it once to bleach jeans sometime in the early '90s. "Why would you want to use bleach for anything?" she asks me. "It's harmful. If the kids' toys are dirty I just use soap or run them in the washer. But, honestly, I rarely wash their toys."

Nor is it the norm for babies and children in Sweden to take a nightly bath. The official recommendation from the nurse-midwives who advise Swedish parents on an ongoing basis until their child starts school is to give young babies full baths just once a week. "For the parents the bath is often a special time with the baby, so some people want to do it every night. But babies who take baths several times a week risk getting dry skin," says Lotta Bohlin, the nurse-midwife in Borås. "Some parents want to use a lot of shampoo and soap, too, but that's not necessary, because babies don't get dirty the same way we do. Instead we recommend using just a little bit of oil in the water. In general, I think we're too clean."

Older children get baths or showers on an as-needed basis, ranging from every night in the summer if they've gotten dirty while playing outside to two or three times a week if they're not visibly filthy. In the US, on the other hand, the virtue of cleanliness is so ingrained that newborn babies are sometimes bathed by nurses at the hospital within hours of being born, before they've even had a chance to latch onto their mother's breast, even though research has shown that the waxy coating that covers the baby's body in fact acts like a moisturizer and natural cleanser that helps ward off infection.

Of course, nobody's suggesting that we should go back to the days of bathing once a year, drinking filthy water, and dying from simple, treatable illnesses. Vaccinations, antibiotics, and the improvements in sanitation and personal hygiene in the industrialized world have been key to curbing outbreaks of infectious diseases and have saved a lot of lives. Unfortunately, beneficial microbes were the unintended casualty of this progress. How to bring them back in an age when most people don't have a barn with farm animals conveniently located in their backyard is a question that vexes scientists. Our relationship with parasites, bacteria, and viruses is complicated to say the least, and researchers don't necessarily know what type of dirt can help protect us against asthma and allergies. But if being too far removed from nature is the main reason for the epidemic, as so many scientists seem to believe, one easy way to support children's health and strengthen their immune system could simply be to let them play outside as much as possible and not panic if they sample a clump of dirt or lick an earthworm. The ick factor may be high, and for small children rocks and other small loose parts can be a choking hazard, but the risk of them getting sick from such things is extremely low.

"I watch out for cigarette butts and choking hazards," one mom tells me. "But chewing on sticks and pinecones never killed anybody; kids have done that since the beginning of time. That's how they get to know the world around them. They usually discover pretty soon that sticks don't taste that great."

Exposure to microbes is not the only way children can benefit from messy play in nature—it's also the ultimate sensory experience. Walking barefoot across a log, sinking your hands into a pile of mud, listening to the birds singing, and feeling raindrops land on your forehead are all stimulating to children's senses. This is important because good sensory integration—i.e., our ability to process and organize the information that we get through our senses—means that our body and brain are functioning at their optimal level.

According to pediatric occupational therapist Angela Hanscom, the recent rise in sensory issues in children can at least partly be explained by the fact that many of them don't have the opportunity to get in direct contact with nature. To many of the children that she has seen over the years, walking barefoot or making mud pies is not something that comes naturally. "There's a lot of anxiety and fear among children [regarding] getting dirty because they haven't had that practice and exposure," she says. "Mud gives you tactile input. The extra bonus is that when you're digging and carrying heavy buckets, you're getting proprioceptive input in your joints and muscles and that overrides the feeling of light touch, which feels yucky to some children. With practice and repetition, they're going to be able to tolerate getting muddy."

In a clinical setting, therapists often use sensory bins and sensory bottles to stimulate children's sensory input, but according to Hanscom some sensory experiences can't be replicated indoors. She says any outdoor play is beneficial, as it helps kids stay active, but natural areas have one big advantage. "Being in wild places is going to be more therapeutic. For one, there is no noise pollution. In nature, you can hear the birds sing and figure out where your body is in space. Also, it's going to be more calming, even though you're in an alert state. Calm but alert is actually the perfect state for sensory integration to happen."

Sometimes it's adults' own fears that keep children from having sensory experiences in nature. Hanscom says preschool teachers who bring classes to her TimberNook nature camps often order the children to keep their boots on out of fear that they will step on something and get hurt. And parents who do let their children kick their shoes off in public run the risk of getting shamed. Going barefoot, like so many other things that used to be a common part of childhood in the US, has now become controversial.

"We're a barefoot family and we get a lot of negative comments," says Lee, a reader of my blog who lives in New Hampshire. "People have always made comments about it, especially when I didn't put shoes on my son when he was a toddler. That apparently made me a bad mother." Now fifteen, her son still gets comments about walking barefoot. "Last summer he was told by a random stranger that he was going to get parasites from going barefoot, that worms were going to burrow through his feet," Lee says.

Sue, a friend in Indiana whose three-year-old son was stung by a bee while playing barefoot in the grass at his babysitter's house, was lectured by a nurse practitioner after she sought treatment for the swelling. "Keep his shoes on at all times outside and don't let him walk through clover" were the nurse's terse instructions. In other words: Have fun playing in the driveway the rest of the summer.

Many Americans have had these strict hygiene standards drilled into them from an early age, and breaking out of the mold can be difficult. When Ania, the American mom in Copenhagen, enrolled her daughter in a Danish forest school, she didn't just have to battle the prejudices of some of her US friends and acquaintances. She also had some of her own.

"If you had asked me two years ago what I was looking for in a school, cleanliness would have ranked pretty high on the list.

To me, cleanliness was a pretty good sign of how much a school and its teachers look out for its students and how much they teach children to be mindful of their person and the environment around them," she says.

But, much to her own surprise, her daughter's experience changed her perspective entirely. Even though her car is now regularly caked with dirt and sand, her hallway littered with little twigs and crumpled leaves, and her washing machine running constantly, Ania embraces it and has become a fierce advocate for forest schooling and messy outdoor play.

"I learned that the kind of dirty that you get in forest school isn't the kind of dirty that really bothers me," she says. "This is the kind of dirty that you earn when you're out exploring and learning and challenging yourself. That's different from the kind of dirty caused by neglect or apathy or not knowing better. And it's a kind of dirty I'm willing to encourage. As an adult, you must have the judgment to know which one of the two kinds of dirty you're seeing on your child, and ultimately the children will learn to tell the difference too."

THE DISH ON DIRT

In a society where nothing is considered really clean unless it's been doused with chlorine, and hand sanitizer is hailed as the greatest thing since sliced bread, researchers now believe that keeping our kids' environment sterile may not be so good after all. These ideas can help bring back some beneficial microbes into your child's life:

* Let your kids play outside and get dirty as much as possible. Most germs in our environment are completely

harmless, and some are even beneficial to our health and well-being.

* Don't pressure your doctor for antibiotics at the first sign of a cold. Chances are the infection is viral and won't be helped by antibiotics anyway. Overuse of antibiotics leads to drug-resistant bacteria, which is a major public health threat, as it makes it harder to prevent and treat a wide range of infections.

* Let your child spend time with dogs and farm animals early on in life. As gross as it may sound, being around the microbes found in animal poop is believed to help protect against allergies later in life.

* Wash hands to avoid infections, but ditch the antibacterial hand soap and nonalcoholic hand sanitizer. They don't do anything that regular soap and water can't take care of, and most of them contain triclosan, a harmful hormone disruptor that is believed to create bacteria that are resistant to antibiotics.

* Stop that bleach-infused house-cleaning routine. There's no need to use the nuclear option of cleaning supplies when old-fashioned soap and water does the same job without harming the environment and killing beneficial bacteria. Plus, contrary to popular belief, a study involving children in Spain, Finland, and the Netherlands showed that exposure to household bleach may actually increase the risk of infections like influenza and tonsillitis.

* Support your child's gut health by feeding her natural probiotics like kefir, yogurt, and fermented vegetables. The more diverse our gut flora is, the better able it is to support important bodily functions, like the immune system and digestion.

Dress for the Weather

Along with a more relaxed attitude toward dirt, Scandinavians are known for their insistence that children "dress for the weather." It was the logical extension of "There is no such thing as bad weather, only bad clothes," and if I heard it once, I heard it a million times growing up. In fact, the clothes are the means that make it possible to play outside every day, all year-round, in the Scandinavian climate. Proper outdoor gear is mandatory both at preschool and at school, and the kids usually bring them to their playdates, indicating that there's an expectation of outdoor play, even when the weather is cold or wet. When I ask the mother of one of Nora's friends to bring her rain gear to a playdate on a particularly dreary day, she responds, "Of course!" without hesitation. When I return her wet and muddy child after an hour-long session at the playground in the rain, she is equally enthusiastic. "It's so nice for them to get out for a little bit, even if it's raining!"

According to parents here, no weather conditions are so bad and no mud puddle so big that they can't be conquered with some good coveralls, waterproof mittens, and a pair of fleece-lined muck boots. The idea that it is good for children to play outside in all types of weather—assuming that they have proper gear—is pretty unique to the Nordic countries, and it applies to adults too. Ask a Scandinavian, "Why would you want your child to go outside when it rains?" and she'll likely respond, "Why not?"

"What's so special about Sweden is that we have a long-standing agreement that it's good for children to be outside, regardless of the weather, so that's not something teachers need to discuss with the parents," says Eva Kätting, director of studies for the master's program in outdoor environmental education and outdoor life at Linköping University. This is often not the case in other countries and cultures. "When I've worked with Turkish teachers, for example, they tell me that the parents become furious if they take the children outside in the rain. They'd rather keep them home than allow it."

To some extent, the Scandinavian attitude is probably a reflection of the belief that being able to cope with different types of weather will make children more resilient.

"I like that the soccer practice is rain or shine," one mom told me after her son got back from playing soccer on a muddy gravel field on a typical spring day featuring pouring rain and forty-degree temperatures (4.4°C). "That makes them tougher. And the kids don't care. I think the rain bothers us adults more than it bothers them."

Lisberg Jensen, the human ecology researcher, points out that the moral argument—that it's healthy and strengthening for children to play outside—hasn't always been the leading one. In the 1950s and 1960s it was customary for homemakers to send their kids outside to play regardless of the weather, simply because the mothers wanted them out of the house.

"Mothers back then didn't watch the kids after they turned four or five; they were supposed to go outside and play, and bad weather was no excuse for staying inside. I think it was a matter of convenience for the parents more than anything."

Today, parents and early childhood educators often raise other arguments for dressing kids for the weather and letting them play outside all year-round. Nature looks and acts differently depending on the season and the weather, and in order to understand these changes, you need to experience them firsthand. Plus, different types of weather inspire different types of play. Rain means that you can build canals and run your tricycle through deep puddles. Best of all, you can make mud.

Hanna, a mom who says that she's not really gung-ho about getting outside in inclement weather, still thinks it is important that her children experience it.

"Often, we'll make an activity out of it. I'll say, 'Let's go outside and jump in the puddles.' The kids love that," she says. "Even if I think it sucks that it's raining, I don't want to convey that feeling to my children, because it's more harmful to sit inside than to be outside in the rain. I don't have a problem with them getting dirty either, either at home or at preschool. When the preschool says that they go outside every day, rain or shine, I think it's great."

Another mom says that although she thinks it is easier to get outside in the summer, when it's warm out, she insists on taking the kids outside every day, regardless of the weather. "In the summertime it feels like a victory when you stay outside all day long. In the wintertime the kids don't always feel like going outside, and nor do I, especially if it's dark and slushy. But then I remind them how nice it is to come inside after being outside."

Sweden's forest schools are where you find some of the most enthusiastic advocates for outdoor play in all weather. I meet one of them, Anna Mållberg, while visiting the forest school outside of Borås that my friend Malin's three children attended. The legend of Mållberg holds that she is the kind of person who won't let anything stop her from getting outside. One day, Malin tells me, the kids wanted to eat their lunch in the forest. Not only did Mållberg single-handedly carry out all the pans and dishes to a suitable spot in the woods, she then came back for a five-year-old girl who had broken her leg and was on crutches. Since the girl was having trouble walking in the woods, Mållberg simply threw her up on her back and carried her to the lunch spot in the woods, cast, crutches, and all.

When I visit the school, the weather couldn't be much more

idyllic. As the sun breaks through the clouds and dapples the birch trees with bright morning light, four stereotypically blond boys wearing heavy-duty rain boots are slopping around in the small, muddy creek that meanders through the property. They're looking for critters and one of them just got lucky. "I've got a frog!" yells four-year-old Benny triumphantly. "Does anybody want to hold it? Come on, it's not dangerous!"

Benny's older brother, Victor, who is eight, takes him up on the offer. Before too long, they have not only fashioned a ramp for the frog out of a piece of wood but also made a complete habitat for it in a bucket filled with water, rocks, and grass.

"What do you like best here at school?" I ask Benny. "Catching frogs. Holding frogs," he replies, stating the obvious. "Sometimes we find salamanders too," his brother chimes in.

"The kids here are happy, fit, strong, and full of energy," Mållberg says heartily as we watch the frog study unfold. "We've never had to explain to a parent why the kids are outside. Everybody understands that it's good for them—the fresh air, the big space. There are fewer conflicts and infections, because the kids are not on top of each other all the time. We may have a couple of cases of stomach flu, but we don't get the epidemics that other places have. There's also less noise. We see a lot of advantages to being outside."

That's of course easy to say when it's sunny and a balmy sixty degrees Fahrenheit, but I'm curious to find out how they handle the cold, wet season.

"Everybody wonders how we do it in the wintertime but I think that's the best time of the year to be outside with the kids," Mållberg says. "The youngest children sometimes struggle with the heavy clothing, but we adjust our schedule accordingly. The temperature and the amount of precipitation are the factors that guide us. If the kids are soaked, we have to go inside, but if everybody is dry and happy, we eat outside. In the winter we change clothes a few times a day, and periodically our two drying cabinets run around the clock. But, regardless of the weather, we *always* go outside. If a child is not healthy enough to go outside, he or she needs to stay home. The parents know how it works. We don't stay inside because somebody has a runny nose."

Mållberg has that calm, pedagogic demeanor about her that often seems to be present in those who choose a career working with children, a characteristic that I, by the way, both admire and envy. At this forest school, it seems like she has found her perfect fit. Enthusiasm for nature and being outside is not something that can be faked, especially when you are roughly on the same latitude as the Gulf of Alaska and your job description includes putting snowsuits on twenty-some toddlers and preschoolers, then following them around, looking at squirrel tracks and blueberry bushes for at least five hours a day, regardless of season or temperature.

Suddenly, one of the other teachers rings a cowbell, which signals to the children that it's time to gather for a morning snack, or fruit time. The children line up by a faucet on the outside of the building to wash their hands, then gather around one of the picnic tables, where Mållberg is cutting bananas in halves and apples in quarters and then doling them out to eager hands.

"Hmmm. I wonder if Victor really washed his hands after playing with that frog," Mållberg muses out loud to one of the other teachers after most of the kids have already finished their fruit and returned to the creek. "Oh well, a little dirt won't hurt."

I try to channel the spirit of Mållberg when cooler, wetter weather rolls in once again that spring, but I'm struggling to find the enthusiasm to get outside. Then one day, as I look out the window, I see that my elderly neighbor is heading out of his house. The rain is pouring down from leaden skies, and to make matters worse, he's on crutches. At first I assume that he's just limping out to get the mail. Then I realize that he's heading out for his daily—and sometimes twice daily—walk.

That's it. I'm going out. I throw on my rain gear and yell a cheery hello as I pass him a little farther down the road. He slows down and turns his head in my direction, visibly startled. Then he gives me a gracious nod before reverting to inspecting the pavement. Of all the times I've run into him during my walks, this is the first time that he's even acknowledged my presence. It feels like a victory.

I walk in the rain to the nature preserve down the road, where a path lined by beech and maple trees, still in their barren winter garb, takes me up a steep hill. At the top, I come upon a waterlogged clearing where the mushy ground is covered by blunt rocks and green grass. A lone knotty oak with long, twisted branches and a trunk so massive that two adults holding hands barely could reach all the way around it towers over the meadow. With its roots firmly planted in the ground, it's been standing guard here for centuries before I was born, and it will likely still be here long after I'm gone. There's something about the way the dim afternoon light hits the old oak tree and the grayish lichens drooping from its veiny branches that makes this place feel magical. I loosen the hood of my rain jacket and pull it back, letting the rain flow freely over my face and make trickling streams on my forehead, cheeks, nose, and chin.

My hiking boots sink down in the wet, muddy ground as I walk past the old tree and back into the forest. It feels different in the rain. Gloomier, but also more serene. Before I turn around and go home, I stop and listen to a small stream from a freshwater spring trickle through the trees. My feet are damp, but my mind is still. Silently embraced by the forest, I am alert, contented, calm. *This*, I think to myself, *is what it feels like to be truly alive.*

Scandinavian Parenting Tip #5

Try to embrace the weather for what it is, and let your child run wild and get dirty while playing outdoors. If possible, reserve a spot in the backyard where your child is allowed to dig in the dirt or create a simple "mud kitchen" with some old pots, pans, cups, and other kitchen utensils. If the dirt on your child's hands and clothes bothers you, remember that in general the problem isn't that kids today are too dirty but that they are too clean.

Suggested reading: *Let Them Eat Dirt: Saving Your Child from an Oversanitized World*, by B. Brett Finlay and Marie-Claire Arrieta. Algonquin Books, 2016.

6

FREEDOM WITH RESPONSIBILITY

You don't remember the times your dad held
your handle bars. You remember the day he let go.
—LENORE SKENAZY

One Saturday, when the skies can't seem to decide whether to stay in drizzle mode or open up the faucets to a full downpour, I take Nora and Kerstin, Nora's friend from preschool, to a small local park in town. It's the kind of day when you don't really expect kids to flock around the monkey bars, but as I pull up in my Saab I notice two boys and a girl running down the grassy hill toward the swings. They're all geared up in polyester rain clothes, boots, and hats, and both of the boys carry toy bows and arrows.

"That's Maya's mom," I can hear one of them say as we exit the car. I recognize him as Teddy, one of Maya's classmates. Teddy is eight, the other boy is seven, and the girl, Teddy's little sister, is five. And they're here on their own. The American in me does a second take and starts to look around for the parents. The Swede in me, however, is not surprised.

I tell them hello and make small talk while Nora and her friend get busy relocating an earthworm from the sandpit to the grass.

"Do you come here often by yourselves?" I ask.

"Sometimes," Teddy responds.

"Where do you live?"

"Over there," he says, pointing vaguely in a direction past the apartment complex on the north side of the playground. "In the house up the road."

"Where else do you go by yourselves in town?"

"It just depends. Sometimes over here, sometimes over there," he says, at this point clearly losing interest in my questions and turning his attention to his friends on the big spiderweb swing.

After a while, they take off, on to new adventures. It was an ordinary scene, one that I had seen played out many times before. After all, I used to be that five-year-old girl exploring the neighborhood and the woods behind our house with my friends. Yet on this rainy day in Sweden it struck me as oddly extraordinary.

The year before, on April 12, 2015, two American children, ten-year-old Rafi Meitiv and his six-year-old sister, Dvora, had also been playing without their parents at a park about a mile from the family's home in suburban Maryland. Except they didn't make it home. Instead, on their way back from the park, they got picked up by the police and were handed over to Child Protective Services. After holding the children in custody for several hours, CPS eventually notified the parents, Danielle and Alexander Meitiv, and proceeded to charge them with child neglect, referring to a Maryland law that makes it illegal to leave a child under the age of eight unattended in a building or vehicle. The Meitivs had been investigated by CPS once before, in December 2014, after somebody had spotted the children walking home from a different local park and called the police.

The Maryland case sparked outrage and a national debate about child safety, government overreach, and so-called free-range parenting. The Meitivs' case is perhaps the most publicized incident in which parents have come under suspicion from CPS for letting their children play unsupervised, but it's far from the only one. "Seeing kids playing outside unsupervised has become so rare in a lot of parts of America that people immediately call the authorities because they think the kids are in danger," says Lenore Skenazy, founder of the Free-Range Kids movement, who has defended the Meitivs and other parents on her popular blog. "Also, because the kids don't have their parents with them, people automatically think that the parents are bad, because only bad parents put their kids in danger. What I've been trying to do by highlighting these cases is point out that this was the norm a generation ago, and just because the kids are outside unsupervised doesn't mean that they're in danger. It just means that their parents trust them and their community."

The Meitivs were eventually cleared of both charges, and state officials clarified that playing or walking alone is not reason for CPS to get involved "unless children have been harmed or face a substantial risk of harm." But the debate about their parenting choices kept raging in the media, with news outlets inviting readers to weigh in on whether the case constituted neglect or not. Although a majority seemed to think CPS had overstepped its bounds, there were also quite a few people who thought the parents had been irresponsible for letting the children walk alone. Amid the debate, the media attempted to explain the "controversial" parenting technique known as "free range parenting."

Or, as it is also known in Scandinavia, "parenting."

If you hear people mention the term *free-range* in Scandinavia, they are most likely talking about egg-laying hens. What in the US has become a parenting subculture devoted to consciously letting your children play or walk unsupervised outside is viewed in Sweden as a normal part of children's growth and development. That doesn't mean Scandinavian parents just open the front door one day and let their toddlers loose on the street. Just as Vygotsky's "scaffolding" gradually enables a child to get to the next stage of learning, many parents live by the notion that children need a certain amount of freedom—both freedom of move-ment and freedom to take reasonable risks while playing—in order to become independent, confident human beings. To gain more freedom, you have to demonstrate that you are responsible enough to get to the next level. In Sweden, parents logically call this "freedom with responsibility."

In order to understand this common parenting tenet, it helps to know that independence, resilience, and self-esteem are highly coveted qualities in children in Scandinavia. Unlike academic facts, these qualities can't be taught; they must be learned through firsthand experience over time. It's also a com-monly held belief among parents and educators that young chil-dren practice these skills best by playing freely in nature.

"I think playing in nature is great for children's develop-ment. They become so independent and trusting in their own abilities," says Linda, whose three children have all attended a nature-based after-school program. "Nobody will help you up on that big rock—you have to get up by yourself. And when your body is ready for it, you will."

This attitude is common across Scandinavia, as both parents and early childhood educators have traditionally had a higher tolerance for children's risk-taking than in the US. "In Denmark, parents try to intervene only when it is absolutely necessary," write Jessica Joelle Alexander and Iben Sandahl in *The Danish Way of Parenting: What the Happiest People in the World Know About Raising Confident, Capable Kids*. "They trust their chil-dren to be able to do and try new things and give them space to build their own trust of themselves."

In preschool, learning to stay within eyesight of the teachers in the forest, a place where there are no man-made boundaries, fosters both independence and self-control. Instead of being confined by a fence, the children learn to adhere to natural borders, like a fallen log, a creek, a steep hill, and so on. Of all children, none seem more apt at mastering their environment than the children who go to nature-based preschools. The first time I watched a two-year-old boy at a forest school amble around on top of a rather high rock wall, it was nerve-wracking. It wasn't exactly like he was teetering on the edge of the Grand Canyon, but the drop-off was high enough that he could have gotten injured had he fallen off. The preschool teacher in charge of him, however, remained completely calm.

"He knows where he can go and where he can't," she said when I voiced my concern. "They learn surprisingly quickly how much they can handle."

Several other forest school teachers have told me similar things.

"The more time they spend in nature, the better they become at self-control," says Maria Mårtensson, a forest school teacher in Stockholm. "You can tell that they have a good grasp on their own ability, because they don't get themselves into situations that they can't handle."

At home, Swedish children may hone these skills first by playing in the backyard without adult supervision and then, as they get older, around the neighborhood in the company of older children. Once they reach school age, many start walking or riding their bikes to school and each other's houses. The kids that we saw at the playground that rainy Saturday were no anomaly: Every time I drove through town—and the countryside, too, for that matter—I saw children either playing outside without adults or moving about by themselves on foot or by bike.

A study of a midsize city in southern Sweden showed that 74 percent of fourth graders there either walked or rode their bikes to school, while 21 percent were chauffeured, either by bus or car. Although more children today get a ride to school than was the norm thirty years ago, the study notes that school-age children in Sweden have among the highest physical activity in the world. PE and organized sports contribute to some of this activity, but the most active children were the ones that played the most with their friends outside. Other everyday activities such as traveling independently to school, running errands, and doing chores like walking the dog also contributed to overall activity. Or, as the study notes, "good levels of physical activity reflect a varied everyday life at large in which they play and move about on their own accord."

"I'm a fierce believer in children's ability to pull on their boots and go outside on their own," says Fredrika Mårtensson, the environmental psychologist who conducted the study. "There's an enormous difference between walking and getting a ride somewhere. I believe you have to let transportation take its time in order to gain appreciation for the way the world works. It doesn't necessarily have to be a scenic walk. Nature is everywhere when you're outside, even just the wind blowing in your face."

Free-Range Days

I grew up in Dalsjöfors, a small town with around three thousand residents, about a ten-minute drive from the Shack. Our burgundy brick house was located in a middle-class '70s subdivision just a two-minute walk from a spring-fed lake, where I spent most of my summers. I learned how to swim in that freezing water, and how to catch crayfish after dark by blinding them with a flashlight and plucking them from the water with my bare hands. Behind our house was a big hill with a few more houses scattered around it, including my cousins' home, then endless forest consisting of mostly pine trees, but also some birches, oaks, and maples, with a few meadows and clear-cut areas scattered in between. We didn't know who owned this forest, but since Swedes have the right to roam over private land, it didn't matter anyway.

Like most other kids our age, my two cousins and I roamed freely in these woods from a young age. Here, we made up our own games, played horse, skinned a few knees, and spent countless hours racing our pet rabbits—a popular pastime among Swedish kids at the time. Most of the time we were savvy. We knew that we were supposed to stay away from cow moose with calves, red mushrooms with white spots, and uprooted trees. But inevitably we sometimes pushed our boundaries. One summer afternoon, the three of us deliberately decided to explore one of the marked trails that meandered through our woods. I'm guessing I was around eight at the time, which means my cousins would have been six and ten.

There were three trails: red, yellow, and green, each color representing a different distance. We started following the green trail, thinking that it was the shortest one, at only about one and a half miles. We walked deeper into the woods, trudging along old logging roads, over hills, and across rocky creeks. After a couple of hours or so we were far out of our comfort zone, realizing that we had no idea where we were and wondering why the trail hadn't taken us back home. Then it dawned on us that we had gotten the trail markings mixed up and in fact had embarked on a six-mile hike into strange territory. Tired, we kept walking, careful to stay on the trail, thinking that we eventually would come upon a residential area. Finally, a yellow brick house appeared along a rural dirt road and we knocked on the door. An elderly lady opened it and was nice enough to explain where we were and let us borrow her phone to call home. Shortly thereafter, my dad showed up in our green Volvo and put an end to our misadventure.

We didn't lose any privileges over this episode, probably because our parents figured that we had already learned our lesson. They were right—we never did it again. Besides, stretching your boundaries and making mistakes was considered par for the course. Interestingly, my parents hardly remember the event when I bring it up with them thirty years later. If they were worried sick at the time, what happened was clearly not traumatizing enough to leave a lasting impression. Since they were used to us playing outside for hours on end, I'm not even sure they realized that we had gone missing until they received our phone call. "It does ring a bell now that you mention it," my dad says when I tell him the story. "But it doesn't really stick out as a big deal."

Just about any of my friends can tell similar stories. During a trip to Stockholm I stay for a couple of nights with my friends Björn and Jeanette and their eighteen-month-old daughter, Clara. Cecilia, another mutual friend of ours, joins us for dinner one night. As the subject of risky play and the freedom to roam comes up, we take turns telling stories that reek of equal parts childhood nostalgia and awe of our parents' nerves of steel.

Cecilia, whose family owns a summerhouse on an island in the archipelago outside Stockholm, knew how to drive her parents' motorboat by herself by the time she was six. In the summertime, she and her brother, who is three years her senior, would take the boat out to a smaller island together, where they would grill hot dogs and hang out on their own.

"Mom thought it was better for us to go to the small island rather than somewhere on the main island, in case we accidentally started a fire," she says, and laughs.

Her own daughters, who are eight and six, have not learned to drive the boat on their own yet, but it's a matter of time.

"We're working on it. They're going to learn how to whittle and use an axe too. I think it's important to know those things when you're in the country," she says.

Björn recalls how, from when he was six years old, he and his classmates would spend their lunch breaks cross-country skiing for several miles in the woods behind their elementary school, unaccompanied by adults. At home, they raced their sleds over a steep cliff and sometimes landed in the middle of the road. As a five-year-old, while riding his bike on the gravel roads around town with his older cousins, he once raced down a steep hill, lost control of his bike, crashed, and flew over the handlebars. Afterward, the doctor had to use tweezers to get all the rocks out of his face. He remained unfazed.

"I think it's healthy for kids to try things, have some responsibility. Sometimes you scrape an elbow or bruise a knee, but you learn from your mistakes," Björn says.

However, his wife, Jeanette, begs to differ.

"You still get hurt all the time, so you obviously didn't learn a damn thing," she retorts curtly. "I never want you to tell Clara these stories."

Later, after Jeanette goes to bed, Björn wants to clarify his position. In hindsight, he realizes that he was probably lucky not to have gotten seriously injured performing some of his more spectacular stunts. But he also believes that the freedom he had to experience different things on his own early in life was ultimately what had given him the confidence to broaden his horizons and eventually leave his small hometown to study in Australia for several years, setting the stage for a career in the media world that would eventually take him to London and then back to Stockholm, where he currently works as the head of digital advertising sales at a big publishing house.

"Will you give Clara the same freedom that you had?" I ask him.

He rests his dimpled, bearded chin in his hand and is silent for a moment.

"I don't know yet. I guess that depends on Clara."

With Clara only being eighteen months old, he still had some time to ponder all of this. I, on the other hand, was already in the middle of it with my girls.

The Tree House

Somewhere in the woods behind our house, as a child, I had formed a lifelong bond with the natural world. The subtle scented vapors from those pine trees and the crystal-clear freezing water in the lake forever made an imprint on me. They became part of my fabric, or what Richard Louv likes to call those "special places in nature that we pick up as children and carry around in our hearts for the rest of our lives." Louv believes those are the places that shape us, that make us take ownership of the natural world and, ultimately, give us a desire to protect it.

After I moved to the US, I had returned to this place every time I visited my dad in the summer. When I myself became a mom I started visiting more often—in my mind's eye and through my memories—because as I was trying to figure out what kind of childhood I wanted my daughters to have, I kept returning to my own. I must have talked to the girls about these woods more than I realized, because one day, when Maya was six and Nora three, the inevitable happened.

"I want to do what you did when you were little, Mommy."

Maya was standing in the hallway at my dad's house, fully decked out in rain gear and ready to enjoy the Swedish summer.

"What do you mean?"

"I want to go to the woods. By myself, like you did."

"Uhmmkay."

"Can I? Please!"

"Me too," Nora chimed in, and started to put her rain gear on.

I normally wasn't a worrier and I purposely tried to be a hands-off type of parent. I let Maya and Nora push their limits on the playground equipment. I gladly let them climb trees and boulders and take reasonable physical risks whenever we were outside. I had even let Maya play unsupervised from a fairly early age in our unfenced wooded backyard in the US. I had preached about my own free-range childhood to anybody who cared to listen. I knew Maya was reliable and they were both savvy for their ages. Yet I hesitated when faced with letting Nora out of my sight in this forest for the first time. On the one hand I felt that she was ready for more responsibility and freedom, but on the other hand I didn't know if my nerves could handle letting go. My parents had done it, sure. In the '80s. As my friends and I had also established, it was widely known that parents back then either must have been popping Xanax to cope with our antics, or simply hadn't known better. They gave us a lot of freedom to explore and play on our own, which made us independent, confident, and resilient. They also put us to sleep on our stomachs, didn't care much about bike helmets, and let us roll around in the back of the family station wagon like a bunch of human-size bowling balls while chain-smoking Marlboros (which, by the way, we were able to purchase from the store, no questions asked, by age nine approximately).

I looked at my dad for guidance. He just shrugged.

"Why not? What could go wrong?"

I didn't really know. But I didn't know if I could trust the guy who used to smoke his pipe in our Volvo either. This neighborhood was about as safe as it gets and there was very little in the woods that could realistically hurt them. They knew not to eat mushrooms or pick up snakes. (Maya had learned this the hard way when she was four and tried to pet a harmless water snake.) I doubted they would be able to climb very high in any of the trees and if, against all odds, one of them got hurt, it would be easy enough for the other one to come and get me. My biggest fear was probably that my kids would do exactly what I had done with my cousins that one time—simply decide to walk off—the difference being that they were not at all as familiar with these woods as I had been at their age. Then I remembered that Nora hated walking and demanded to be carried whenever I tried to take her on a hike that lasted for more than a quarter of a mile. Her walking anywhere that wasn't in the direction of home seemed highly improbable.

"Okay. It's okay," I said, more to myself than to the girls. "Just don't go any farther than to the tree house."

The girls had found the tree house the year before, when we were out in the woods together. It was a rather elaborate structure that had been put together by two of the neighbor boys and their dad. A short ladder led up to the main floor; then another ladder provided access to a rooftop, which was enclosed with pieces from an old picket fence. The tree house even had a real window and its own mailbox. Although it wasn't visible from my dad's house, it was within shouting distance, less than three hundred feet away. It seemed like a sensible enough place for them to start practicing a little freedom with responsibility in the forest.

"Promise!" Maya said.

Then they were gone.

My dad was right, of course. Nothing was going to go wrong. But just to be perfectly sure, I went out on the front step every fifteen minutes or so, to make sure I could still hear them chattering among the trees. When they came back, about an hour later, they were wet, happy, and emboldened by the experience. Pretend play had taken them to a land far, far away, where there were giant snakes and monster dinosaurs. Luckily, they had fought them all off, and now they were in need of ice cream, they told me.

A while later, I noticed a little boy standing in the street outside my dad's house, straddling his bike. He didn't look like he intended to come knock on the door, but he didn't look like he was planning to go away either. If stares could open doors, he would have barged through ours long ago. Finally, I opened the door to make sure everything was all right.

"Can the girls come out and play?" he said before I had the chance to say anything.

"I'll go ask," I told him.

His name was Colin, and, as it turned out, he and his older brother lived down the street and were the proper owners of the tree house. He must have spotted the girls when they were outside earlier. Maya and Nora got dressed to go outside again and approached him, shy at first, but clearly excited. I looked around for adults or other children, but there was nobody else in sight.

"Are you by yourself?" I asked him.

"Yes."

"How old are you?"

"Four."

For a second I felt like I had stepped out of a parallel universe. Here was a four-year-old searching for playdates while biking on his own down the street, and yet nobody was as much as batting an eye. The boy's confidence and matter-of-fact behavior told me this was far from the first time he'd been out on his bike alone, but I decided to let his parents know where he was, just in case. Maybe he had sneaked out without telling them, and maybe they were worried and looking for him. While the girls and Colin disappeared to the tree house, I walked down to his house and found his dad, Magnus, ambling around in the yard with some tools. He seemed unconcerned. If he was looking for anything, it was his power drill, not his son. Magnus, a friendly thirty-something with a shaved head, explained that the neighborhood had gone through a rejuvenation phase lately, bringing in a lot of families with young children who all played together.

"We've got a bunch of kids in this neighborhood, two in the house across the road, the neighbors over there have two girls, and then it keeps going that way," Magnus said, pointing toward the road.

"How much freedom do the kids have?" I asked.

"Well, they have this zone, where they're allowed to move around on their own," he said.

The perimeter of the zone consisted of the road that looped around the neighborhood. In all, the loop was probably a little over a quarter mile long, and since it ended with the cul-de-sac by my dad's house, it had little traffic. As the kids got older, like Colin's brother, Charlie, who was eight, they graduated from the zone and were allowed to expand their range, eventually exploring the town independently. "In the summertime we sometimes don't see them all day. But often the neighbor kids all come over here, since we have a pool. It turns into a bit of a day care," Magnus said, and laughed.

I hadn't expected it, but at least in this middle-class suburb, children seemed to have the same freedoms that we had enjoyed in the '80s. They had two things going for them: little traffic and a high level of what researchers call "social trust," which is generally defined as "a belief in the honesty, integrity and reliability of others," according to Pew Research Center. In communities with a high level of social trust, children are generally given greater independence and mobility. "Having social trust means that if problems arise, we trust that we solve them together, as a community. In places where the attitude is that everyone minds their own business, children have less mobility," says Mårtensson, the environmental psychologist.

In some ways, it seemed like time had stood still in the neighborhood where I had grown up, the main difference being that all the kids now wore bike helmets and some of the older ones had cell phones. Soon, Maya and Nora were the ones running down the street to ask if Colin could come out and play. Both girls were clearly proud to have made a new friend on their own, without any assistance or intervention by adults. I, too, made a friend, as Colin's mom turned out to be an old classmate from seventh grade. By the end of our visit that year, we had all grown. I was no longer (or at least was less) nervous about letting the girls play on their own in the woods or down the street. Maya became a lot more confident about meeting new people and started asking if they could "go and find new friends" whenever we went someplace new. And even if it was only for a few short weeks that summer, the girls had gotten a taste of what it was like to live in a neighborhood where kids still stay out and play until it is time to come in for dinner.

Risk and Resilience

As parents, we're wired to worry. But today, in many places, allowing children to play outside on their own has become a controversial parenting choice or, worse, criminalized. A 2014 survey of a thousand American parents showed that 68 percent want to ban children age nine and under from playing unsupervised at parks, and 43 percent want a law prohibiting children who are twelve years and under from doing the same thing. This represents a radical shift from attitudes just a couple of decades ago, illustrated by another widely cited study that notes that although 70 percent of American mothers played freely outside daily when they were young, only 29 percent of their children do. Instead, many children have become part of a "backseat generation" that spends a significant amount of time getting transported to various organized activities and has little time for unstructured outdoor play. But according to the Centers for Disease Control and Prevention the most dangerous place for a child to be is neither the playground nor the woods. It's in a car, as motor vehicle accidents are the most common cause of death among the more than twelve thousand American children who die due to unintentional injury every year (followed by drowning, the majority of the time in the family pool).

Research also shows that three-quarters of all American parents worry that their children will get abducted, despite the fact that violent crime against children has been decreasing steadily since the 1990s and the risk of being kidnapped and killed by a stranger is so minimal—around 0.00007 percent, or one in 1.4 million annually—that experts call it effectively zero. And in a vast majority of sex abuse cases against children, the perpetrator is somebody close to the victim—a family member, relative, or acquaintance—and not a stranger off the street. Still, these numbers have done little to alleviate parents' fears that their children will get snatched and hurt by a stranger.

According to David Eberhard, chief psychiatrist at the emergency psychiatric ward in Stockholm, our brains have a tendency to overestimate two types of events that may occur to our children: those that have disastrous consequences and those that are out of our control. Both types encompass kidnapping. No matter how extremely rare it is, our brains are simply not that good at judging this type of risk. And fear is a powerful thing. When stories about child abductions lead the evening news, it is easy to believe that the same thing is going to happen to your child. "The reason why these things make such big news is that they virtually never happen," Eberhard says. "But the human psyche finds that type of information very hard to handle."

If the risk of letting children play unsupervised outside hasn't changed in the past generation, it appears that moral attitudes have. As the researchers behind a 2016 study at the University of California conclude, "Americans have adopted a parenting norm in which every child is expected to be under constant direct adult supervision. Parents who violate this norm by allowing their children to be alone, even for short periods of time, often face harsh criticism and even legal action." The researchers brought this shift to light through a series of experiments in which participants were asked to judge the level of risk associated with leaving a child unsupervised in five different hypothetical scenarios. The ages of the children and the circumstances during which they were left were the same in all the studies, but the parent's reason for leaving the child varied. In some cases, the hypothetical parent had left the child unintentionally or to go to work, in other cases to relax or to rendezvous with a secret lover. As it turned out, participants consistently rated the situation as more dangerous to the child when the reason for the parent's absence was deemed morally unacceptable—for example, seeing a lover. "People don't only think that leaving children alone is dangerous and therefore immoral. They also think it is immoral and therefore dangerous," the authors write. Playing outside unsupervised is far from the only childhood activity that used to be considered perfectly normal that has been demonized lately. Climbing trees, walking barefoot, playing tag, waging snowball war—the list of abolished pastimes goes on. A study by Play England showed that half of all British children have been stopped from climbing trees and one out of five has been banned from playing tag or chase, even though in 2007, children were nearly three times as likely to be admitted to the hospital after falling out of bed than after falling from a tree.

Ironically, in a time when our children are statistically safer and more secure than ever, removing all perceivable risk from their lives has become a mainstream parenting strategy. Human ecology researcher Ebba Lisberg Jensen at Malmö University believes the anxiety over so-called risky play is a result of the fact that society has become so safe and secure. "The safety becomes a little bit of a trap. We want more and more safety, and it's just never safe enough. This is what we call 'care anxiety,'" she says. "Once you've secured your children's safety, you somehow feel like you've succeeded, and that in turns creates positive reinforcement."

Erin Kenny, who cofounded the first forest kindergarten in the US, Cedarsong Nature School, on Vashon Island, Washington, says that the prevailing culture mistrusts children's ability to assess risk to the degree that they're missing out on learning opportunities and physical skills. "If every surface around a climbing structure is soft and spongy, it gives children a false message that they can fall and they may climb higher than they actually should. They don't learn how to assess risk," she says about the ever-stricter safety regulations for playgrounds. "As a culture, we don't trust our children at all—we basically live their lives for them. Up until age seven or eight they're so bubble-wrapped and helicoptered that they don't get to practice any of their physical skills, and now there's huge fallout. Public kindergarten teachers are reporting that kids don't even have the hand strength to hold a pencil. Eighteen-year-olds are in physical therapy because they don't have any upper-body strength. It's shocking."

Kenny's words reminded me of a time when I stood at the local playground back in the US and noticed a mother barking at her daughter, who was maybe six or seven years old, to immediately get down from the monkey bars. "You're going to break a leg and we don't have time to go to the emergency room today!"

The girl, visibly disappointed, obliged and promptly got down from the equipment. And who wouldn't, considering the threat of impending orthopedic surgery?

I don't doubt that this mom had good intentions. After all, no parent wants to see their child get seriously hurt. It can be extremely tempting to hover over children and implore them to "be careful," "slow down," and "get down from there." But there are many good reasons why children seek out risky play, and why adults should allow it.

Ellen Sandseter, an associate professor of physical education at Queen Maud University College of Early Childhood Education in Trondheim, Norway, describes risky play as "thrilling and exciting play that can include the possibility of physical injury." She goes on to identify six different types of risky play: those involving, respectively, great heights, high speed, dangerous tools, dangerous elements, rough-and-tumble play, and disappearing/getting lost. When Sandseter reviewed several studies on risky play, she found that children who played unsupervised or had independent mobility are more physically active and have better social skills than their peers. They're also better at judging risk, which can help them later in life, when they're no longer monitored by adults. Sandseter argues that the overall positive health effects of risky outdoor play are greater than those associated with avoiding it. She also notes that risky play makes children better able to master peril. When adults restrict children's risky play, it hampers their ability to seek out the challenges and stimulation that they need for normal physical and mental development.

A study led by Mariana Brussoni of the University of British Columbia in Vancouver also showed that children who were allowed to engage in risky activities like climbing and jumping, rough-and-tumble play, and exploring alone had greater physical and social health. Brussoni points out that risk-taking during play "helps children test their physical limits, develop their perceptual-motor capacity, and learn to avoid and adjust to dangerous environments and activities." Simply put: Allowing some risky play actually makes children safer and less prone to injury.

I think of Brussoni's words as I watch Maya and Nora play one day at a new playground in Ulricehamn, one of the bigger nearby cities. The girls are off playing on a modern piece of equipment that looks a bit like the swing carousels that you would normally find at amusement parks, except this one is human powered and has a motley collection of swings, some for standing up in, others for sitting in or hanging from. Nora is hanging upside down on some sort of rope contraption and Maya is standing up on one of the swings. It doesn't look like any other piece of playground equipment I've seen before. Four or five other kids have their own ways of hanging on to the remaining swings. One unfortunate dad has gotten stuck acting as the engine and ends up pulling the carousel around and around, until it gains enough speed and momentum to go around a few laps on its own. "Again! Again!" the ecstatic children shout until he grabs the carousel and makes it go again.

Meanwhile, I'm watching them from a distance with the carousel dad's wife, Anette. She shakes her head and smiles as her daughter goes around, lap after lap, showing no signs of wanting to slow down. "As long as they don't do anything life-threatening, they're okay as far as I'm concerned," she says. "We've never told our kids, 'No, you can't do that,' and they've never broken anything either. I think they get better coordination from trying things and staying active. Even if they did break something, a broken bone heals quickly. The most dangerous thing of all is to sit still."

I had heard many other parents in Scandinavia say the same thing. "Of course you don't want your child to get seriously injured," says Magnus, a father of two, "but it's normal for kids to get bruised legs and scraped knees. That's what we call 'summer legs.'"

According to researchers, at least part of the reason for this common attitude is that Scandinavians regard nature as a much-needed, unrestricted "free zone" for children, a necessary counter-weight to adult-led, organized activities and predictable routines. In nature, children face physical and mental challenges from powers much greater than themselves, and Scandinavian parents believe that doing so fosters prized traits like self-restraint, resilience, and problem-solving skills. One of the most renowned advocates of risky play, Peter Gray, research professor of psychology at Boston College, says that not only is risky play beneficial to children's health and development but that depriving them of it can cause harm. According to Gray, risky play is nature's way for children to teach themselves emotional resilience and learn how to manage and overcome their fears. Gray draws a straight line from the decline in children's freedom to play and embrace risk to the dramatic rise in childhood mental disorders like anxiety and depression that has occurred since the 1950s.

"The story is both ironic and tragic. We deprive children of free, risky play, ostensibly to protect them from danger, but in the process we set them up for mental breakdowns," he writes in *Psychology Today*. "In the long run, we endanger them far more by preventing such play than by allowing it. And, we deprive them of fun."

Resilience is often defined as the ability to recover from setbacks, adapt well to change, and keep going in the face of adversity. Educators and CEOs alike often tout this grit, determination, and ability to learn from failure as essential for coping with challenges at school and at work. Resilience, it turns out, is key to academic and professional success, not least for children, who face a considerable amount of adversity.

In order to foster these traits and encourage physical activity, researchers suggest a shift from the prevailing attitude to keep children "as safe as possible" to the more nuanced approach of keeping them "as safe as necessary." Scandinavian forest schools are an excellent example of a place where children are allowed to take manageable risks on a daily basis, whether by climbing trees (great heights), poking sticks in a fire (dangerous elements), or using hammers and saws (dangerous tools).

"Our children are independent because we let them do things—not hazardous things, but real things," says Siw Linde, cofounder of Sweden's first forest school, Mulleborg, as she shows me a woodshop in the yard where the preschoolers are in the process of making their own stick horses. "I think children need to use real tools in order to create something real. Yes, they may hit their thumb with the hammer, but there's something to be learned from that too. I think we need to let them try things; we can't protect them against everything that's dangerous."

Free play in nature can potentially involve all six of Sandseter's risky play categories. However, Scandinavians have been curiously unaffected by the fear of nature that seems to have spread to many parents elsewhere. "The one thing that I worry most about is traffic. But in nature? No, I feel like nothing could happen to my kids in the woods," one mom tells me.

This is a shared view, and it can partly be explained by the fact that Scandinavians have lucked out with flora and fauna that are pretty harmless. Mosquitoes, the deadliest animal on the planet, don't harbor any dangerous diseases here, and the woods are even spared from the nuisance of poison ivy. But here, too, nature is a wild place that offers its fair share of risk. In Sweden, moose are common, as are ticks, wasps, and the country's only poisonous snake species, the European viper. Wild boars have become prevalent in some areas, and once in a blue moon predators like wolves and lynx are spotted near urban centers. Uprooted trees, noxious weeds, tall cliffs, slick rocks, fast-moving water, sinkholes, and poisonous berries and mushrooms are more common potential hazards to a young child.

The difference is that in Scandinavia fears regarding such dangers are fought with familiarity, both at preschool and at home. When you grow up going to the woods on a regular basis, climb those trees, roll down those hills, cross those creeks, scramble up those boulders, those activities don't feel any more dangerous than sitting on your couch. (Which, it could be argued, is actually far riskier, considering the very real and serious effects of a sedentary lifestyle on children's health.)

"In the forest there are poisonous berries and mushrooms, but instead of telling the children that they can't pick any of them, we teach them which ones are poisonous," Linde says. "Otherwise they won't know once they get out in the woods on their own."

Coffe, a father of two young girls, is thinking along the same lines regarding risks in nature. "We want our daughters to learn how to climb trees, because if you know how to climb, you don't fall. We want them to feel safe with it, because it's when you're scared that you fall."

The potential pitfalls of nature also pale when viewed in light of other risks. For example, approximately thirty children die in traffic every year in Sweden, whereas poisonous snakes kill on average one very allergic person every eight years. The last fatal wolf attack in the wild occurred in 1821. A few people do get attacked by moose every year, and in 2008 a sixty-three-year-old woman in southern Sweden was fatally injured by an unusually aggressive animal. (The woman's husband was jailed for a year, suspected of her murder, before DNA evidence from moose saliva found on the woman's clothes solved the mystery.) But logically, the risk of getting hurt or killed by a moose is by far the greatest when you are in a car, since there are roughly five thousand traffic accidents involving moose in Sweden every year. (As a side note, more people in the world died while taking selfies than from being attacked by sharks in 2015.)

The idea that nature is an ideal and safe place for children to play is so prevalent that it is even embraced by self-proclaimed worriers like Emilia, a friend of mine from high school. When I catch up with her and her husband, Christos, who live in a trilevel brick home in a small town outside of Borås, both their children are playing in the woods adjacent to the house. Estrid, who is six, is weaving pine branches through the small, cone-shaped den that she and her four-year-old brother, Oscar, have built with the help of their dad, while Oscar is filling a bucket with water from the small creek that runs through the wooded area. The kids don't have any set boundaries in the forest, but "they rarely go very far," Emilia says.

A few blocks from Emilia and Christos's house is a small playground with a couple of slides, a climbing structure, a sandbox, and a swing set. The playground is a popular gathering spot for the neighborhood children, and, like many of the other kids in the area, Estrid is allowed to walk there as well as to her friends' houses by herself, sometimes with her little brother in tow.

"It was scary the first time," Emilia acknowledges. "But she's very good about following instructions. We really feel like we can trust her. We could tell that she was really proud afterward."

Traffic is not much of a problem on these quiet streets. But what about strangers with malicious intent? Those who are every parent's worst nightmare and one of the main reasons why so many children are no longer allowed to play outside on their own in the US? It's one thing to recognize how far-fetched it is, statistically speaking, for a child to get snatched off the street, and another to be able to let go of these deep-seated fears.

"I've never heard anybody worry about kidnappings. That just doesn't happen," Christos says.

His statement surprises me a little bit. Christos grew up in a rough part of Borås and had not enjoyed the sheltered middle-class upbringing in a small town that I had had. Plus he works as a policeman.

"What do go in waves are reports about perverts. All of a sudden we'll get a tip about a white van that's parked outside a school and then it's all over the grapevine. Because of social media, it takes five minutes for the news to reach the whole town, and then everybody is seeing white vans everywhere. Of course, about ninety percent of all contractors drive white vans, so it's not very strange that people see them everywhere. Or it could just be somebody's grandpa who's sitting outside the school, waiting."

Naturally, in Sweden, as in the US, there are people who could pose a threat to children, but according to Christos they are fairly few. "Of course there are mentally ill people out there, but most of them aren't dangerous. They mostly stick to themselves. Children run a much greater risk of getting bullied or beat up by a classmate than running into a pervert on the street."

At first glance these stories may only prove that Swedes are lax on safety, yet they are anything but. This is the country that invented the modern version of the three-point seat belt, where you can't as much as smell a beer and legally get behind the wheel, and finding a place to smoke indoors besides your own home is about as easy as finding a smiling person on the Stockholm subway at seven o'clock on a Monday morning. Children are recommended to ride in a rear-facing car seat at least until their fourth birthday, and bike helmets are mandatory by law until you turn fifteen. Most adults use them too. In fact, when I show up to a bike-riding meet-up with a group of friends one day, I'm the only one who's not wearing one and I'm immediately scolded. "You know me, always living on the edge," I joke defensively. They are not amused. Instead, one of them proceeds to tell me a heartbreaking story of a workmate who had fallen off his bike and ended up paralyzed from the neck down. The next time I see them, they've pooled money to buy me a helmet.

In Sweden, if anything is perceived to be at all dangerous, it's usually soon regulated by decrees and laws that are supposed to make the citizens' lives simple, secure, and safe. This shows in the statistics, as Swedish children have the fewest number of deaths by injury among all developed nations, just over five per hundred thousand children, according to UNICEF. The US comes in fourth from the bottom, with an injury death rate that is almost three times that of Sweden. Even so, the study notes that "the likelihood of a child dying from intentional or unintentional injury is small and becoming smaller" across the developed world, despite parents worrying more than ever.

Just as Scandinavians generally feel safe in nature, many parents think that playing in the local neighborhood is safe for children, especially in smaller towns where the social trust is high and traffic is less of a problem. It's also a practical issue. Children need several hours of physical activity every day to stay healthy, and for many families it's neither feasible nor desirable for a parent to constantly tag along.

When I ask Hanna, who lives in an apartment in Halmstad, a city of sixty thousand residents, why she and her partner have made a point of letting their seven-year-old daughter, Siri, play unsupervised with other kids at the neighborhood playground, she says that they see it as a way to build her confidence and make her more independent. "I want Siri to be able to play out here and feel like this is her street and that she's safe out here. If she feels safe, I feel safe," Hanna says. "She knows she's not allowed to leave the area, not even with a friend, without telling us. We haven't talked to her about perverts yet, because we don't want her to start distrusting everybody, but she knows that she has to stay near our house. And we trust her—she doesn't go anywhere."

In bigger cities, where there is generally less social trust and more traffic, parents tend to be more protective and more likely to give their children a ride to school than was the case a generation ago. But there are also forces at work trying to reverse this trend. In Gothenburg, a city of half a million people, the streets and traffic department recently mailed out a brochure encouraging parents to let their children walk to school by themselves. "In our effort to be good parents, we sometimes forget that children actually can handle a lot by themselves. Like walking to school," the first spread of the colorful booklet states. "Children actually learn a lot when they are allowed to explore the neighborhood on their own, take responsibility for being on time, and plan things with their friends." In addition to appearing in the brochure, the message aired as a commercial at local movie theaters. It may seem odd that the local government would try to influence parents' decision on whether to give their kids a ride to school. But it has good reason to. More parents driving their kids to school means more traffic around the school, leading to a greater risk that a child on foot or on a bike will get hurt. Ironically, what many parents perceive as the safest option for their kids is making the area around the school less safe for other children.

Mathias, a father of three who lives in central Gothenburg, really liked the brochure and commercial from the city and says they sparked conversation for him and his friends. "I think it will make more parents reevaluate how they look at traffic sense, cars, and safety in general. And I like the idea of children learning things by gradually figuring out how to get around on their own." Mathias, who usually bikes with his kids to school, says his ten-year-old son, Nelson, has free range within a mile-wide radius from the home, and his eight-year-old son, Dante, is allowed the same mobility when he's with his older brother, whereas Otis, who is seven, is allowed to play by himself on the street but is not to go any farther than that. "I think we're some-where in the middle of the pack when it comes to the amount of freedom we give our kids," Mathias says.

Eberhard, the psychiatrist, who himself is a father of eight, let his children start walking to school by themselves at age seven, in Stockholm, a city of over one million people. This is not nec-essarily the norm anymore, but by the time they're in second or third grade, it's not unusual for children even in the biggest cit-ies in Scandinavia to ride public transportation by themselves, and many still walk or ride their bike to their after-school activi-ties. In contrast, when Lenore Skenazy let her nine-year-old son ride the subway home on his own in New York City, she was chastised for her decision and dubbed "America's worst mom," eventually spurring her to found the Free-Range Kids movement in the US.

Young children naturally need protection in order to survive, but Eberhard believes the level of risk in children's lives should be increased steadily in order to successfully prepare them for adulthood. "Children are not going to be children for the rest of their lives," he says. "If you overprotect them and don't let them take risks and have a certain amount of responsibility, they'll have a shock when they head out into the world later. This is not something you learn overnight; this is something you have to learn gradually. There's a high risk that children won't learn how to behave in traffic and in nature if they don't learn this early."

Small children should be served small portions of risk, but they, too, need to explore the world, Eberhard says. Having said that, he is careful to point out that he does not advocate letting toddlers out willy-nilly without supervision. It's all about taking baby steps, using good judgment, and practicing often. "We need to understand that children, too, are different individuals. What goes for one child doesn't necessarily go for another," he says, and adds that his own children don't all enjoy the same privileges or go by the same rules at the same age. "I think a good approach is to constantly challenge yourself, because this comes down to what you can handle as a parent, not what your child can handle."

Skenazy believes that challenging yourself to allow your children to have unsupervised time can be just as beneficial to the parents as it is to the kids. "Parents need to experience what it's like to let go of their kids and not have them supervised for a little bit of time, for them to realize that it's not the end of the world," she says. "The ones who are afraid to do it are afraid because in their mind they ask themselves, 'What if?' I call this 'worst first' thinking. You come up with the worst-case scenario first and proceed as if it's likely to happen."

The Freest Kids in the World?

Just a two-minute walk from the Shack is another small red 1800s homestead that's owned by the local church. I had noticed that the traffic on our normally quiet road increased exponentially every Wednesday a little before six o'clock at night, and then again at seven thirty, and sometimes I would hear children's voices through the trees. When I take a closer look at the woods one day, I discover signs of human activity throughout. Large tripods made from long, straight tree branches that have been lashed together with meticulous knots. Rustic, low-slung shelters with names carved on the inside walls. Multiple fire pits with blackened leftover pieces of wood strewn about.

Something was going on up there. But what?

One Wednesday night, while Maya is at choir practice, Nora and I walk up the road toward the homestead, where a tall man with a long ponytail stands in a circle with about forty children ranging from about nine to sixteen years old. He waits patiently until all the children are quiet and standing completely still with their right hands raised.

"Hello, Scouts!" he yells.

His name is Magnus, and like many others he joined the Scouts when he was nine years old, back when scouting and soccer were more or less the only after-school activities available to the kids here. A few years ago, he chose to come back as a leader. He says that even though today's parents are more likely to give their kids a ride to activities in the big city, the scouting tradition remains remarkably strong.

"The parents think it's a good thing. They have nice memories of it themselves, and they like that we're outside a lot," Magnus, who is in his early forties, says. "We're actually outside more now than when I was in the Scouts as a kid."

They don't really have a choice, since there is not enough space for the whole group in the old homestead. Meetings are outside, rain or shine, and each troop has its home base by one of the shelters. Getting kids outside to enjoy *friluftsliv* is one of the main goals of the Swedish Scout movement, not just for the sake of their personal health, but also to foster an understanding for nature and environmentally sustainable practices. But their idea of getting to know nature is more about survival skills than about bird-watching.

"We get to know nature in order to utilize it. We build towers, we burn things," Magnus says. "When we set up camp, our first priority is to make sure that the group can survive. Then we'll worry about the recyclables and make sure that we do as little damage as possible."

One element stands out as particularly important: fire. "If we don't burn something at a meeting, everybody becomes disappointed, including the leaders," Magnus jokes.

Whoever said that kids should never play with fire obviously never saw Swedish Scouts in action. Today, they're supposed to practice for a competition appropriately named "Hundred-Meter Fire." In this game, the troops first make a fire, then move it a certain distance—for example, a hundred meters. Along the way, they have to make several stops and complete assignments, like burning off a piece of string, bringing a pot full of water to a boil, popping popcorn, and, finally, lighting a torch. The youngest kids are allowed to use matches, precut wood, and a metal grill for moving the fire. The oldest are only allowed to use a fire striker and have to collect wood from the forest and figure out their own way of moving the burning logs.

As soon as they get the go-ahead from their leader, several of the children pull out their knives and start making kindling by cutting small wood shavings from logs. Others take to the woods to look for tinder. A girl who looks to be no older than ten years old starts chopping wood using an axe like nobody's business. How to handle knives, axes, and fire are some of the first skills they learn when joining at age nine, and many Scandinavian parents believe that these practical basics—how to survive in the outdoors—are an important part of a well-rounded education.

"The whole point of these exercises is to show them the usefulness of these skills," says Torbjörn, a leader whose daughter joined the Scouts five years ago. "If they can't get the fire started, they end up eating their hot dogs cold. That's happened before."

Soon, several fires are burning around us, and the first

troop to burn through the string begins to move their fire. Two girls lift it up using two long, straight branches that they have placed underneath the metal grille that holds the burning logs. For a few seconds, the fire rests precariously on the grille while the girls cautiously move forward with their load over the rocky ground. Then they lose their balance and the fire starts falling apart. *Thump, thump. Thump.* Burning logs hit the ground (which is moist and not at risk for catching fire) and sparks fly in all directions.

This doesn't seem to throw anybody off.

"That's okay, you can put it down right there," says Jacob, one of the younger leaders, calmly and without a trace of sarcasm.

Meanwhile, Nora is poking a stick into another fire, then pulling it out and pretending it is a torch. Instinctively, I feel like telling her to put it down and stop playing with the fire. Then I realize that if there ever was a place where this is considered acceptable, this is it, so I let it go. But she is not content with this. She wants to use a knife. I ask Magnus if he thinks it would be okay for her to borrow one. He cracks a big smile. This is a request he's more than happy to heed.

"Of course you want a knife," he says, and pulls one up from his pocket. "Here you go."

It takes a couple of tries and a little bit of frustration, but eventually Nora is able to whittle away a few chips from a small pine branch. She works on it fastidiously until darkness falls and only reluctantly returns the knife when it is time for us to leave. As we walk home, a thick smell of wet pine and burning wood fills the air. The sound of children laughing and yelling eventually dissipates, but Nora keeps talking about her experience until she falls asleep that night, tired and happy, her hair reeking distinctly of campfire.

I knew that Nora's encounter with the Swedish Scouts had

left a lasting impression, and during a trip to Copenhagen a few weeks later I become even more convinced that the Scandinavian approach to risky play and freedom with responsibility is essential for children.

The first thing that stands out to me when I arrive at the central train station in Copenhagen is the sight of dozens of preschool children in high-visibility vests walking through the main hall with their teachers. They're walking in pairs, holding hands, nonchalantly chatting and seemingly oblivious to the fact that they are navigating one of the biggest transportation hubs in Scandinavia. Then again, they have been groomed for this since the day they started walking.

The second thing that strikes me, once I walk outside, are the bikes. Hundreds, maybe thousands, of bikes stacked in two stories in designated bike-parking areas similar to the outdoor parking lots for cars that I had seen in New York. The streets, too, are packed with bikes. I'm thankful that I'm not driving but instead riding shotgun with Danish native and filmmaker Daniel Stilling through the city. Daniel and his American wife, Aimie, are the creators of the award-winning documentary *NaturePlay*, which takes on the high-stakes testing that has come to define early childhood education in the US, and instead advocates for the Scandinavian tradition of letting preschoolers spend their days playing in nature.

At a little less than twice the size of Massachusetts, Denmark has ten thousand cycle routes, and many of the bike riders are children. Some of them are on their way home from school; others are heading to their *skolefritidsordning*, or SFO, an after-school program for children of working parents (the Danish equivalent of Maya's *fritids*). We're heading to Regnbuen, "Rainbow," an SFO where kids come to play with fire, hammers, and nails. And rabbits. Although usually not all at once.

While Daniel, who is darkish-blond and has a neatly trimmed goatee, effortlessly navigates through the narrow, busy streetscape, Aimie tells me that the two of them met on a movie set where Daniel was filming and Aimie, a former backcountry rescue ranger with expertise in wilderness medicine, was in charge of safety. The first time Aimie visited Daniel's native country, she got a crash course in the Scandinavian way of raising children. Daniel recalls how, when they went to a museum in the city of Roskilde, they saw a toddler climbing all over some low boulders in front of the museum.

"The parents were not concerned at all, but Aimie was horrified," Daniel says.

"I was like, 'Where's the rubber surfacing?'" Aimie chimes in and laughs.

After the couple had a daughter of their own, Bella, Aimie became a self-proclaimed helicopter parent who watched her daughter's every step. That all changed after the couple decided to leave their home in Florida for an extended stay in Denmark, where they enrolled Bella in a forest kindergarten for a few months. Now Aimie says her helicopter tendencies are almost gone—she jokes that she's "recovering, with bouts of regression." The experience also led to the filming of *NaturePlay*, some of it right here at Rainbow.

Established in 1984, Rainbow today has 150 children ages nine to sixteen years, who come here after, and sometimes before, school on a regular basis, on foot or by bike. Although an SFO is only open to the children who are enrolled there, Rainbow is modeled on the concept of public adventure playgrounds— or "junk playgrounds," as they were initially called—which originated in Denmark. The first adventure playground was built in Emdrup in 1943, in the midst of the German occupation of Denmark during World War II. The prominent landscape architect Carl Theodor Sørensen is usually credited with having come up with the idea after noticing that children liked playing with leftover building materials at construction sites. From Denmark, the idea spread to several countries, and today there are more than one thousand such playgrounds in Europe.

Bella Stilling walks through the construction zone at Rainbow, an after-school program in Copenhagen, Denmark, that is modeled on so-called junk playgrounds.
Linda McGurk

Never mind the fact that we're in the middle of Copenhagen and flanked by a school on one side and a row of high-rises on the other—as we get out of the car we're immediately greeted by a couple of geese and a free-range potbellied pig who are patrolling the place like they own it. A brown-and-white Danish country goat that is tied to a tree stump and sweeping the ground for edibles looks up at us when we walk by with Klaus Nedergaard, the SFO's manager of thirty years. He introduces us to all the animals one by one, including two horses and two smaller ponies in a small enclosure. At first he strikes me as reserved, but then I realize that he is just the kind of person who doesn't engage in trivial small talk. When he speaks, he is direct and to the point, each word carefully weighed and measured.

"The brown pony bites," Klaus tersely informs us.

"Don't touch it, honey!" Aimie quickly implores Bella; then she immediately corrects herself. "Helicopter parent, step back!" she says to herself, and laughs. "Some habits die hard."

"She'll learn," Klaus responds calmly.

Then we enter the construction zone. Here, muddy paths lead past tall stacks of pallets, chicken coops, piles of lumber, heaps of random junk, and smoldering fires. And everywhere are colorful asymmetrical tree-house-like structures that the children have designed themselves and built with a little help from Klaus. Some have one story; others have two. The only firm rule is that the structure must be safe. Many of them never get finished, but each becomes a unique fixture in this ever-growing ramshackle village of childhood dreams.

"The houses actually get used very little after they are finished. For the kids it's more about the process than the product," Klaus says.

Even if the children have a lot of freedom and the place may look chaotic and random, there is structure, and there are rules to follow. There's a checkout system for the tools, and those who leave tools lying around are suspended from using them for a week. The children can come and go as they please, but those who have chickens or rabbits are responsible for their care.

"We have animals here, so we need to come every day, otherwise they won't get food or water," a nine-year-old girl named Mia explains. "I love this place, especially the animals."

Not all SFOs are like Rainbow, but the place pretty well reflects the general attitude toward risk, freedom, and responsibility that prevails in Denmark. Having small accidents here and there, getting bruises and skinned knees, stepping on a nail, or cutting your hand are seen as normal parts of childhood. Even though the children here use real tools, climb trees, and start fires, all under little supervision, this is all seen as something that helps them manage risk, and serious injuries are rare at Rainbow.

"In thirty years we've had maybe two broken legs. We explain to the parents from the start that our kids play with fire and use tools. If they can't deal with that, they need to go to a different SFO," Klaus says. "And I refuse to hear complaints about dirty or ruined clothes. If the kids smell bad and come home dirty, then you know they had fun."

After we leave, Aimie tells me about her mom, who let her play outside by herself from an early age, which set her on a path to a career in the National Park Service. For Aimie, a pivotal moment came when she compared the lives of children in Denmark with what was going on in her and Daniel's own community in Orlando. Even though their neighborhood is gated and extremely safe, she rarely saw children playing outside.

"I realized that I had to be proactive. Our mothers' generation could be relaxed about it and just let us outside. But today in America you always have that fear that somebody will call the cops if you give your child too much freedom, so now we have to construct that reality for our children—for example, by creating nature play groups where we can set them free within the construct of what we've set up."

A Test for Maya

One of the after-school activities for children in our town was a gymnastics class in the school's gym on Thursday evenings. There were two classes: one for preschoolers at four thirty, and one for the school-age children at a quarter past five. Both Maya and Nora wanted to go, and I figured they would just have to wait around for each other. Then I ran into Jenny, the mom of one of Maya's classmates, Hannes, and his little brother, Love, who lived within walking distance from the school. She had other plans.

"I was thinking that Hannes would stay home by himself while I go up to the little kids' gymnastics with Love, and then he can walk himself to the gym. Maya is more than welcome to come and stay at our house after school and then they can walk together," she said. "Hannes would love that!"

She said it so matter-of-factly, as if it was a given that they could handle it. As if it was a given that this wouldn't make her a bad parent. As if this was actually completely culturally acceptable. I had let the girls play unsupervised in the woods before, but since our home in the US was in the countryside, for them to walk places other than to the mailbox down the road had not really been an option. And I had never left them alone in the house, aside from when I had taken short walks with the dog.

"Have you ever left him alone before?" I quizzed her.

"Oh yeah, for about an hour or so at a time, while I'm out walking with Love or doing something nearby in town."

"Does he know how to lock up the house and all that kind of stuff?"

I wasn't sure what other "stuff" might be involved, just this seemed like a big responsibility for an eight-year-old.

"No. But he'll figure it out."

Her confidence was contagious, so I told her that I would ask Maya, although I already knew what her answer would be.

"I'm going to stay with Hannes by myself?"

Her eyes widened and her face lit up with an incredulous smile.

"Yes. Would you like to do that?"

"Yes!"

"Do you think you can handle getting to gym class on time?"

"Mmm . . . yeah," she says, not at all convincingly.

Either way, I decide to give it a try. When the first Thursday arrives, I go over to Jenny's house so that we can prep them together. Before we leave, Jenny gives Hannes one last rundown in the hallway.

"You need to lock the door when you leave. The key is over here, your gym clothes are over here," she says, pointing first to the key rack on the wall, then to the gym bag on the floor by the door. "You need to leave at five after five to make it on time. Got it?"

Hannes nods, although his gaze is wandering and it's unclear whether he's actually paying attention. Then both of them run back outside to play on the zip line that he's just gotten for his birthday. And that's where we leave them.

It would be dark by the time they left, but Hannes lived less than a five-minute walk from the school, and the route they would take had no traffic. I was not particularly worried about them staying home by themselves or walking to the school. The worst thing that would likely happen was that they would lose track of time, making them tardy for the class. As I glance at the clock on the wall in the gym at ten after five, and Maya is nowhere to be found in the changing room, I'm starting to think that this is exactly what has happened. At close to fifteen minutes past five, I go outside to look for them. I can hear them before I see them, giggling and racing each other up the small hill by the soccer field behind the school.

"We forgot to lock the house," Maya shouts when she sees me, "so we had to go back!"

They barely made it on time, but they did make it. By the time gym class season came to an end, a couple of months later, I didn't think twice about giving Maya the responsibility to get there by herself. Before long, she and Nora were walking by themselves to their cousin's house, a little over half a mile down the street from the Shack.

It had all started with baby steps.

Scandinavian Parenting Tip #6
Refuse to give in to the culture of fear that has quashed outdoor play as we used to know it. Dare to trust your child and, as he matures, gradually give him more unsupervised time around the house, in the backyard, and in the neighborhood. Network with neighbors and other families to increase social trust in your community.

Suggested reading: *Free-Range Kids: How to Raise Safe, Self-Reliant Children (Without Going Nuts with Worry)*, by Lenore Skenazy. Jossey-Bass, 2010.

7

OUTSIDE, THERE IS A
BETTER CONNECTION

The mountains are calling and I must go.
—JOHN MUIR

Spring has been building steadily for a while when summer comes in with a bang in May. The forest explodes in a sea of green as budding leaves burst open with unfettered zeal almost overnight. A week ago I was wearing mittens; now children are running around barefoot and the roads are clogged with camper vans en route to the ocean. At the local cemetery, blooming daffodils, pinkster lilies, and pansies have replaced the simple pine branches that usually adorn the gravesites in the winter. Shaded by towering Scotch pines and with two purple pansies in my hands, I walk down the paved path toward the spot where Farmor and Farfar, my paternal grandparents, lie buried. The girls are zigzagging through the gravesites eagerly searching for their headstone, but run right past the inconspicuous granite slab without noticing. The stone, a natural smooth rock with a pink tint, lies flat on the ground and is barely two feet wide. In front of it, ten yellow daffodils stretch toward the sun, next to a small sign that reads, MAINTAINED BY THE PARISH.

I sit down in the damp, moss-riddled grass by the grave. Then it all comes back to me. I'm three years old and tumbling around in an adult-size navy-blue sweatshirt in a parklike green space, my family basking in the late-summer sun on the benches behind me. We're in Swedish Lapland, 165 miles north of the Arctic

209

Circle, and the sweatshirt belongs to my grandmother. During this trip, I would cross some of the most epic wilderness in Sweden in a carrier on my father's back, and see the midnight sun hover over one of the most photographed mountain scenes in Sweden: Lapporten, a valley shaped like an enormous half-pipe carved out by a glacier during the last ice age. These images, and most everything else that happened during this trip, remain hazy and have only been partly reconstructed thanks to the mandatory vacation photo slide shows in my grandparents' basement. I guess my three-year-old self only had so much appreciation for beautiful scenery. Instead, what I remember most clearly is my grandmother chasing me around and both of us laughing hysterically as I clumsily tried to make a getaway in her much-too-large shirt.

At six foot two and 220 pounds, my grandfather was of imposing stature and had a perpetually tanned face full of wrinkles that ran deeper than ancient canyons. His steely hair was slickly combed backward in a style that remained the same from when he was a teenager until the day he died. He liked change about as much as a vegetarian enjoys a bloody steak and was punctual to a T, probably as a consequence of his lifelong career as a bus driver. He ran his bus like certain authoritarian leaders run countries, and had little interest in making jovial small talk with passengers. This, combined with his well-known annoyance with tipsy teenagers (he was a longtime teetotaler himself), eventually earned him the nickname Stone Face.

As his only and much-adored grandchild, I rarely saw that side of him, aside from when he ranted about communism or the magpies that had hijacked his meticulously maintained bird feeders on the back porch.

"Here, I have a surprise for you!" he would say, secretively stretching out his clenched right hand toward me. Then he'd slowly open it, revealing a handful of wild strawberries that he had picked fresh from the garden. "I saved them all for you."

If my grandfather could be a little crotchety, my grandmother, a seamstress working from home, was anything but. Submissive and good-natured, she never raised her voice to me. In fact, she rarely ever told me no. She spoiled me rotten and I knew it. But the toys and the cupboards that were always fully stocked with candy weren't the main reason why I loved going to her and Grandpa's house when I was little. It was because my grandmother gave me something way more precious—her undivided time and attention— and played with me like a peer. She never told me it was too cold to go outside; instead, she helped me dig tunnels through the snow. In the summer we played hopscotch in the driveway and badminton in the backyard. We went for walks around the neighborhood and ate fresh strawberries and ice cream on the porch. I was my grandmother's world and she was mine.

My grandparents were not exactly what you would call expert outdoor adventurers or hard-core environmentalists. They didn't own any expensive gear. They were never particularly athletic. And they definitely didn't dream of conquering any fourteen-thousand-foot peaks. Still, the outdoors was a constant presence in their lives, and their relationship with nature was steady and loyal, not unlike the one that my grandfather had with Volvo cars and the evening weather forecast on TV.

My grandfather died when I was in high school, but my grandmother lived until I was thirty-five years old. After she passed away in 2013 at age eighty-five, I went through the entire stockpile of old slides that she had kept on a shelf in her closet for years. The pictures roughly date from the time my dad was born, in the '50s, through the late '80s, and are pretty typical snapshots of the highlights of my grandparents' life: traditional celebrations like birthdays and Christmases mixed in with vacations and visits from relatives. But after going through hundreds of speckled frames, I notice a different trend. A disproportionate number of the pictures seem to be what I can only describe as some sort of nature-centric portraits: my grandmother sitting on a rock surrounded by a sea of wood anemones, a common wildflower, to mark the coming of spring, or my grandfather standing next to a giant snowdrift in order to document a particularly heavy storm. Some show both of them posing in the mountains of Lapland, wearing jeans and clunky rubber boots—standard hiking gear of the time. Sometimes my grandmother would even photograph the plants in her garden, just to memorialize a particularly heavy bloom. In the small things in nature, she found a lifelong source of fascination and wonder.

Many of the slides also show my grandparents eating outside, sometimes on a blanket in the grass, sometimes sitting in chairs at a small folding table that my grandfather used to haul around in the trunk of his yellow Volvo 240, along with a maroon leather shoulder bag packed with a thermos of piping-hot coffee, *saft*, cheese sandwiches, and cinnamon rolls. In some of the pictures, my grandparents have set up their table and chairs in a no-frills rest area near the road; in others, they have scored a million-dollar view over rolling pastures and farmland separated by ancient stone walls and dotted by tiny red houses with orange clay tile roofs. Sometimes they just pulled all the patio furniture from their small back porch and put it in the grass in the backyard. It was a simple setup, but judging by the looks on their faces, they might as well have been sitting in a five-star restaurant, sipping vintage Cristal and feasting on exquisite Russian caviar. To them, eating under the open sky was the finest dining experience imaginable.

Later, I begin to appear in the images as well: petting a goat at the zoo, balancing on my first cross-country skis in my grandparents' backyard, standing on a big rock in an old-growth forest. When I was little I didn't reflect much on this, but as I got older I realized that they had taken me to just about every nature preserve, cultural heritage site, and national park within a two-hour drive, and then some. When they took me to Lapland, they made their infatuation with the flora and fauna of the rugged mountain landscape mine to keep forever.

Back at the cemetery, I dig a hole for one of the purple pansies I'm holding while Maya hovers over my bent back, hoping to spot an earthworm. She immediately finds one and puts it in the palm of her hand. "Look, Nora! A worm!" she exclaims with such excitement that you'd think she'd found a tiny rainbow-colored unicorn. Luckily, I soon find another one for Nora, who holds it up against the sun and carefully inspects it. After I've planted both of the pansies, Maya and Nora gently put the worms down by the flowers and watch, transfixed, as they make their escape into the damp, dark soil. Then the girls take off to collect pinecones and lichens to decorate the grave. When they're done, Maya examines it contentedly.

"It looks nice. Too bad Farmor can't see it," she says.

"Well, who knows? Maybe she can," I offer.

"Yeah, true. Maybe she can see us from up in the air."

Before we leave, Maya and Nora kick their shoes off, grab each other's hands, and start walking around in an ever-faster spinning circle on top of the headstone, making an impromptu game out of my grandparents' final resting place. My gut reaction is to become dismayed, and worry that somebody may see it and frown upon it. But then I think of Farmor and Farfar, and I know they would never find it disrespectful. In my mind I can almost hear my grandma saying, "Keep playing, my little trolls. Just keep playing."

The Digital Generation

There is a popular meme circulating on the internet, stating that "kids don't remember their best day of television." The meme has been re-created in many forms but usually features romantic images of an ideal childhood: kids with vintage backpacks walking down a wooded path; a boy and his dad sitting on a horse, watching a herd of cows; silhouettes of children running across a field toward the sunset. The author is unknown but the meme has been shared thousands of times, so the message obviously resonates with many. Although I clearly remember the day that I binge-watched *The Thorn Birds* while home sick from school in fifth grade as well as I remember frolicking in Lapland, there's some truth to this meme. Studies show that we're more prone to remember events that engage our whole body and all our senses. Nature, it turns out, is just the right place for that. That's why, when researchers ask people to share memories from childhood, they often think of things that took place outdoors. Playing with friends in special hideouts, going on family camping trips, experiencing the elements.

The meme also says a lot about our desire to give our children quality experiences in real life, away from screens like TVs, gaming consoles, DVDs, tablets, computers, smartphones, and the distractions of social media. Because if there was one thing my grandparents had going for them, it was the fact that they didn't have to compete with an iPad.

Maya was two years old when I bought my first iPhone, and it took her about that many minutes to figure out how to work it. Later, I installed a few games, thinking that they might come in handy while killing time at the dentist's office. That was before I realized that touch screens were an electronic form of kiddie crack, more addictive to her than chocolate was to me. When she was three or four, we bought our first tablet, a Kindle that I figured could help us get through the roughly twenty-hour-long trips to Sweden now that I had both a preschooler and a baby in tow. Bad move. By the time she was five, Maya would wake me up at six o'clock on Saturday mornings, desperately pleading for her tablet so that she could get to the next level of Candy Crush Saga. The sound track alone made me long for the days when "I Love You" by Barney the purple dinosaur was the most commonly played tune in our home—no small feat, considering that this was allegedly the CIA's preferred song for torturing prisoners at Guantánamo Bay and other detention centers in Iraq and Afghanistan.

At that point, I sorely regretted ever having brought the tablet into our house and secretly wished that I could send it back to where it came from, but not before I had obliterated it with a few choice tools. When Maya was six I got what I had hoped for, but not in the way I had expected. I was in the middle of navigating a rental car through a busy roundabout in Italy, complete with honking drivers, frantic lane changes, a nonfunctioning GPS, and two different exits with signs pointing to Rome when it happened. First, the tablet made Maya carsick. Then it died. Fortunately, the girls' cousin Oliver, who was also in the car with us, still had a functioning iPad, which he somewhat reluctantly shared during the remaining two hours in the car. But there was enough grief over the dead Kindle and bickering over the iPad that I vowed never to let my kids become dependent on electronic entertainment in the car again.

For a full year, the Kindle was tucked away in a drawer and left for dead, mostly because I had no idea how to dispose of it in an environmentally sensible way. The girls got used to life without it, going on six-hour-long road trips with nothing but a few toys and some crayons in the backseat without complaints. Then, unexpected resurrection. "Mom! The Kindle is working!" Maya shouted excitedly one morning. Somehow the tablet had come back to life.

I tried to embrace it, telling myself that even though I had been born in the Jurassic era, screens were going to be a part of my children's future, and I knew that digital media would serve them well later in life. Plus, I figured that banning the Kindle outright would only make it more appealing. Instead I deleted Candy Crush, limited video games to the weekend, and tried to steer the girls toward some educational apps (most of which they quickly lost interest in). Eventually, as I grew tired of the girls squabbling over the only tablet in the house, I decided to buy Nora a Kindle of her own.

Even with our new rules in place, it took a conscious effort on my part just to match their screen time with "green time," and when Maya was seven and Nora four, shortly before we left for Sweden, I started to wonder if I wasn't fighting a losing battle after all. When Nora's preschool class got to make wish lists for Santa, her classmates listed things like a GI Joe, Legos, and a pet turtle. Meanwhile, Nora's list was topped by an iPhone, followed by a laptop. Shortly after that, Maya told me, "I like playing outside, but I like playing Minecraft more."

I knew I was dealing with a first-world problem. But still, I felt like a failure.

According to a 2010 study by the Kaiser Family Foundation, the average American eight- to eighteen-year-old racks up over seven and a half hours of recreational media use per day, not including texting. That's nearly fifty-three hours per week—more time than they spend going to school. Younger kids are not that far behind. A 2009 survey by Nielsen showed that American children age two to five years spend over four and a half hours per day in front of a TV screen, not counting time spent playing video games. And this was at a time when smartphones were still a novelty and the iPad had yet to be released. In comparison, preschoolers in Scandinavian countries spent just one to one and a half hours watching TV every day in 2014. Excessive use of digital entertainment has likely contributed to the epidemic of children who "don't know" how to play outside, as I often hear Americans who are my age and older complain. Plus, it doesn't take a rocket scientist to figure out that a child who spends over four and a half hours in front of a TV every day—on top of playing video games, going to preschool or school, attending after-school activities, doing homework, eating, and sleeping—simply doesn't have much time left for building forts in the backyard.

My children were nowhere close to those numbers, but there were still several reasons why I decided to enforce strict limits on screen time at home. Aside from all the physical and mental benefits of playing outdoors, I didn't want my daughters to lose their fascination with the "slow" entertainment mostly available in nature, or their ability to play imaginatively and creatively with very simple means (in Italian rental cars and elsewhere). I also spent enough hours working in front of screens every day to know that I didn't want them to gobble up my kids' childhoods.

By the time we left for Sweden I was sick and tired of constantly negotiating and policing screen time, and I was wondering how our move would change the dynamics of this balancing act. Scandinavians are known to have a voracious appetite for new technology and Swedes have managed to digitize nearly every aspect of their lives, from the battery-driven robotic lawn mowers that roam in every other homeowner's yard in eerie silence, to the stores and restaurants that have completely abolished cash in favor of electronic payments with cards or smartphones. Ninety percent of Swedes have broadband in their homes, and 97 percent have a cell phone. Many of the most popular computer games and apps, including Minecraft, Candy Crush Saga, and the Battlefield series, were developed by Swedes, as were the free call service Skype and the music-streaming app Spotify. In 2005, the average Swedish child started using the internet at age nine, according to the Swedish Media Council, a government agency that gathers data on children's media use and is tasked with protecting minors from harmful media uses. But since then, the popularity of tablets has increased dramatically and made games and the internet more accessible to younger children. Today, a majority of three-year-olds have used the internet and 15 percent of the two-year-olds are online daily. In 2014, as many as 80 percent of Swedish two- to four-year-olds used a tablet at home, and 12 percent had their own, a number that has quadrupled since the last survey in 2012–2013.

Swedish children watched a lot less TV than their American peers, but when it came to new technology, they seemed to be at least as plugged-in, if not more so.

Considering how ardent Swedes are about fresh air and outdoor play, I'm surprised when I initially can't find any consistent national guidelines on media use for young children. Turning to experts for advice on the topic is a little bit like listening to a PETA activist and a hog farmer discussing the merits of pig slaughter. On the one hand, there's Hugo Lagercrantz, a renowned pediatrician and senior professor at Karolinska Institutet in Stockholm, who claims that children two years and under should have no screen time at all, since they need direct contact with a caregiver more than anything. Too much screen time for young children "fragments their lives and can lead to concentration difficulties, impaired language development and reading skills, and obesity," he writes. On the other hand, some experts accuse Lagercrantz of fearmongering without good scientific basis for his advice, and argue that what you do in front of the screen is more important than how long you do it. Some even believe that the term *screen time* is outdated and obsolete, since so many of us pretty much walk around with powerful computers in our pockets and can access the internet at any time.

Lagercrantz based his restrictive screen time recommendation on the guidelines from the American Academy of Pediatrics, the gold standard that I myself had tried to live by. But at the end of 2015, the AAP announced that the organization was planning to moderate its recommendations, acknowledging that "in a world where 'screen time' is becoming simply 'time,' our policies must evolve or become obsolete." The new guidelines, which came out in 2016, lower the age at which electronic media may be introduced to eighteen months and lift the restrictions on video chatting for children of all ages. For children aged two to five, the new AAP guidelines keep the previous limit of one hour per day of high-quality programming. Some tech buffs and media outlets made the updates sound like a major game changer for attitudes toward children's media use, but AAP's core message for parents and other caregivers essentially remains the same: "In summary, for children younger than two years, evidence for benefits of media is still limited, adult interaction with the child during media use is crucial, and there continues to be evidence of harm from excessive digital media use." Meanwhile, the Swedish Media Council has declared that it is not planning to referee the debate about screen time, leaving parents to figure things out on their own.

When we arrive in Sweden, I'm not surprised to see that a lot of Swedish ten-year-olds have newer smartphones than I do, and it doesn't take long before Maya notices too. "Can I have a cell phone? Pleeeeeaaaase? *Everybody* else has one!" The last part is not quite true, but I do notice that smartphones and tablets are ubiquitous. Most preschools, including Nora's, even have an iPad or two these days.

"We don't let them sit by themselves with it and we don't use it to comfort them if they're upset, but we do sometimes let them play an educational game together," Barbro reassures me when I quiz her about it one day. "And we only let them use it for short periods of time. It's a pedagogical tool, not something to kill time with."

Many of Maya's classmates are allowed to use their tablets every day, even if it's only for half an hour or an hour while their parents are cooking dinner, and initially I feel like I'm the only parent in Sweden trying to limit my children's screen time, akin to the cultural reactionaries who claimed that jazz music was the work of the devil or that train travel would cause women's uteruses to fall out. Luckily, my sister Susanne is there to make me feel like a cutting-edge technology maven. Since she's concerned about electromagnetic radiation, all laptops and tablets at her house are plugged into the wall and the Wi-Fi is turned off most of the time. This doesn't fully eliminate her kids' screen time, but it does make it a lot more inconvenient to get online. Especially since, in order to turn on the Wi-Fi, you have to make a treacherous climb up the cluttered, dark stairs that lead to the attic, where the router is placed on the dusty floor like a rejected Christmas present from Aunt Edna.

My sister is far from a typical Swedish parent in her approach to screen time, but the more I talk to others, the more I realize that many of them are also concerned about the impact of electronics on their children's lives. A few, like my sister, worry about radiation, but far more have noticed that digital entertainment is addictive and cutting into their children's outdoor play and physical activity.

Sara, the special education teacher whose daughter is in the same class as Maya, says that her five-year-old and nine-year-old have tablets, but that she has fairly strict limits on how often and how long they can use them. "I work with kids who come to school bouncing off the walls on Monday because they spent all weekend inside playing video games. I keep thinking that that's going to happen to my kids, too, if I don't set limits," she says. "My five-year-old son would sit all day if I let him. After a while I get so stressed-out that I just say, 'Now we need to put away the tablets and go outside.' I think it was easier for our parents, because we didn't have that kind of entertainment inside. We would go out on our own and stay outside for hours."

Petra, whose son Oscar is in Maya's class, says that she appreciates her son's iPad because it helps him learn English and practice reading. She likes that he knows how to use FaceTime when they're apart and that he often plays video games together with friends, rather than isolating himself. But she also recognizes that the tablet comes with a downside. "We noticed that some games became addictive," she says. "Oscar would panic and start to cry when it was time to put away the iPad. That's when we decided that something had to change. We didn't want him to become enslaved by it, so now we have a ban on the iPad during the workweek, at least when it comes to playing games."

Petra and her husband didn't stop there. As they both work long hours—she as a middle manager and he as the head of his own advertising agency—they decided to put away their own phones and iPads from the time they get home until the kids go to bed. "When we're home, we want full focus on being together as a family, and we want the kids to be outside and play, because I think it's good for them."

As Petra and her husband had already discovered, it's not only children's overuse of digital media that can cause problems. A British State of Education report found that four-fifths of teachers are worried about children not being prepared for starting primary school (which in the UK happens at age five) due to poor social skills and delayed speech, which many of the teachers attribute to *parents'* excessive use of smartphones and tablets. "There is limited parent/child interaction," one teacher writes, according to the *Guardian*. "Four-year-olds know how to swipe a phone but haven't a clue about conversations." According to the survey, as many as a third of the students who are enrolled in primary school are not ready for the classroom.

Pretty much every new technology that has revolutionized our everyday lives has been followed by some sort of moral panic, especially when it comes to how it will affect children and women (remember those flying uteruses?). But even though the claim that total abstinence from electronics is best for the youngest children has been called into question, experts seem to agree that what infants and toddlers need most for healthy development are interactions with caring adults in the real world. Occasionally playing with a tablet or watching a show on TV will not cause brain damage in young children, as some of the more sensational headlines have claimed. It can even boost cognition if done with the guidance of an adult. Moderation, however, is key. The side effects of too much screen time—increased risk of sleep deprivation, attention problems, anxiety, depression, and obesity, according to the National Institutes of Health—are real.

Considering this, I find that the best advice regarding screen time comes from the national handbook for the nurse-midwives who counsel all Swedish parents during regular checkups from their child's birth until he or she starts school. Acknowledging that it's inherently hard to give advice about screen time, since it can encompass everything from playing educational games on an iPad to passively watching a movie, the handbook notes that both can benefit the child in multiple ways "as long as the family also spends time communicating more actively, stays physically active and spends time outdoors."

When, how much, and what type of screen time is appropriate comes down to the individual child, his or her age and personality, and how much he or she engages in other activities. The handbook suggests having set rules around screen time in families where the screens tend to cause conflicts—for example, by having a maximum amount of time per day or avoiding screens during certain days or times every week. It also helps to have screen-free zones in the home, like the children's bedrooms or at the dinner table during meals.

Lotta Bohlin, the nurse-midwife, says that the topic of screen time can be touchy for some parents, since it's often a way for them to get some much-needed time to themselves. "For children under three years we suggest keeping screen time to a maximum of half an hour per day, and preferably in the company of an adult. Some programming for children is very intense and action-filled, so we recommend choosing quieter shows. Then you can gradually increase the time that they watch."

When I first started planning our trip to Sweden, I toyed with the idea of leaving the tablets at home and unplugging completely for six months. Then I decided that the girls would have enough changes to adjust to, including living in a tiny homestead with just a few of their regular toys. So the tablets came with us, along with the same limits on screen time that we had had in the States. But after a couple of months in Sweden, I find myself relaxing the rules a little bit. Nora spends most of her day at preschool, where there is no TV and the iPad is used sparingly, so her screen time is cut significantly and her outdoor playtime is increased dramatically. At Maya's school, tablets are rarely used in the lower grades, and she's already getting a lot of physical activity outdoors at recess, at *fritids*, and at home after school. We still save computer games for the weekend, but during the week both girls sometimes use the tablet to work on math problems, dance to music videos, curate their individual Spotify playlists, and occasionally look up information. Back in the States, the challenge for me had always been to get the girls outside enough after my workday was over, when I also had to prepare dinner, do laundry, help with homework, run errands, and do all the other little things that make a home go round. We made it outside every day, but not always for as long as I'd have liked. Now I had all kinds of help making it happen throughout the day, every day. To say that it was nice would be the understatement of the year. And for the first time I feel like we're successfully able to strike a healthy balance between green time and screen time.

One Friday, Maya's friend Liv comes over after school for a sleepover. They play outside as usual, and after a while I notice them coming back from the woods with a motley collection of nature items: a small bouquet of yellow coltsfoot and white wood anemone, three pinecones (one intact and two that had been decimated by a squirrel), some pine branches, a twig from a blueberry bush, and various leaves. They line up all the items on the front porch, then come in and get white paper, colored pencils, and Maya's Kindle. Maya is in high spirits.

"We're going to make a nature journal!" she announces. "We're going to look up facts on Google and write our own book. We're going to be authors!"

For an hour and a half, Maya and Liv secretively labor with their project on the porch. Then they present the result, a twelve-page nonfiction book called *Facts About Nature*. On each page, they have meticulously drawn one of the items that they have collected and written a few sentences about it. "This is a fun book. It is about nature," the summary on the back of the book declares.

"We're going to read it to the class tomorrow and make extra copies of it. We might even ask if we can put a copy in the library," Maya says, visibly proud of her achievement.

Sure enough, the next day I'm stunned to learn that my normally shy child and her friend have read their work aloud to their entire class at school.

I was as proud of the book as Maya was, but the pride I felt was of a different sort than the kind I had felt back home when she made the honor roll in first grade. Building on academic, digital, and real-life skills, and using her creativity and imagination, she had conceptualized this project herself. She then collaborated with a friend to execute and present it, without any prompting or help from me. They owned this project from beginning to end and, moreover, they'd had fun doing it. To me this represented real, self-directed learning at its best.

So far, I'd been able to stave off Maya's pleas for a cell phone, but some of her friends back home were starting to get them, and I knew that soon enough the day would come when she would too. Before then, I wanted to make sure I had done everything in my power to preserve her sense of wonder—that amazing feeling of curiosity and boundless possibility that we're all born with—and keep her feet firmly rooted in the humus-clad forest floor in our backyard. Limited screen time aside, I knew that the best way to foster a love for nature and counteract a sedentary lifestyle was to give my children quality experiences outdoors as often as possible. They were off to a good start, but once Maya was introduced to the world of Snapchat, Instagram, and incessant texting, all bets would be out the window. At that point, my influence over her digital media use would be limited, and I could only hope that I had set her on a path of healthy habits. Some of that brave new world I would never understand. Some of it she would probably grow out of. Some of it would forever shape her identity in ways it had never shaped mine, simply because it was not the way of my generation. Somewhere deep inside I felt a gnawing urge that now was the time to cement her love for nature, nurture her sense of outdoor adventure, and help her to form memories that would last a lifetime.

Now was the time to take her to Lapland.

A Personal Pilgrimage

Humans have evolved in natural environments for 99.99 percent of history, so it's not surprising that nature still affects us in profound ways. In the 1980s, the American researcher Roger

Ulrich discovered that simply having a room with a view of a natural environment rather than a brick wall helped patients at a Philadelphia hospital recover more quickly from gallbladder surgery. They also reported being less depressed and having less pain. Other studies have shown that being immersed in nature can lower blood pressure, reduce stress, and lessen ADHD symptoms.

In Sweden, gardening is becoming an established form of therapy for treating mental burnout, with one project at the Swedish University of Agricultural Sciences in Alnarp successfully rehabilitating three out of four participants who had been on long-term sick leave, in some cases for as long as ten years. In Japan, *shinrin-yoku*, which literally means "forest bathing," has been a part of the public health system since the 1980s and is growing in popularity. Breathing in phytoncides, volatile antimicrobial substances derived from trees, during these recreational trips to the forest can increase the activity of natural killer cells, which in turn fight tumor cells and release anticancer proteins. In the US, some physicians have started to prescribe nature time for a variety of conditions, including post-cancer fatigue, obesity, high blood pressure, and diabetes.

For children and adults with mental disorders and developmental disabilities, nature often has a soothing effect. When the girls and I meet up with Linda, a mother of three who works with people with disabilities, she tells me about an autistic man whom she took care of for several years. As part of their daily routine, they would walk to a forest near the man's home.

"I could tell that he felt good in the woods," she says. "At first I thought it was because of the silence, but then we found this bubbling creek and he was completely transfixed by it. He could stand there and just watch the water run through the creek for half an hour. Sometimes when I could tell that he had a lot of anxiety, I'd take him there first thing in the morning, and his anxiety would dissipate right away." Nature is no cure-all, but there's something about sinking your hands deep into the dirt, watching a leaf slowly make its way down a stream, or breathing in the aroma of wet soil after a light spring rain that makes us relaxed, calm, and less prone to feel anxious, angry, or depressed. Many scientists believe that these feelings are caused by what they call "soft fascination" with natural elements, which—unlike the directed attention needed to navigate through busy traffic or solve a complicated math problem—can help keep our minds at rest. A related theory holds that our sense of well-being in natural environments can be traced to a phenomenon called *biophilia*, our biologically innate tendency to feel affectionate toward and seek a connection with other life-forms and living systems.

I had intuitively turned often to nature as a form of therapy long before I had kids or even heard about soft fascination and biophilia. As my daughters got older, I wanted them, too, to feel that nature was a constant fixture that they could always rely on for a break from the pressures of modern life. Children may not appreciate nature for its meditative or spiritual qualities, but the habit of seeking emotional support, recreation, and inspiration from nature is established in childhood.

I'd entertained the idea of returning to Lapland for years, but when Farmor died it went from being a vague bucket-list item to a personal pilgrimage, a journey I had to undertake to find closure and honor the legacy of a life that had ended. It would also in a tangible way connect my grandparents' lives and my own childhood with the life of my oldest daughter. For a while (actually, about a second) I considered bringing Nora as well, as her appetite for outdoor play seemed to have grown, thanks to the routines at her new preschool. Her commitment to hiking was still fly-by-night, however, and highly dependent on her mood for the day. Some days I could take her on a four-mile hike and she'd be all smiles and sunshine; other days she would dramatically drop to the ground and scream that she had broken her leg when asked to walk five hundred feet. She'd have to sit this one out, and she wasn't particularly sorry.

When I tell my mom about my plans and ask her for advice, she gets excited.

"Of course you want to go to the mountains!" she says with a sly smile. "That's where you were conceived, in a tent in Norway. I remember exactly where and—"

I cut her off before she is able to finish.

"I was thinking more along the lines of whether you have any recommendations on lodging or hikes, stuff like that."

But of these my mom has no recollection. At least she'd had a good time in the mountains.

My sister's memories of Lapland are slightly less romantic.

"I remember the mosquitoes. Big. Frigging. Mosquitoes. Make sure to stock up on mosquito spray."

Dad, who had gone to Lapland with his parents many times growing up, is a little more helpful. He tells me about the lodge in the small resort of Björkliden, which back then was held by the government-owned railroad company and used to provide rest and recreation for state employees, like my grandfather. We talk about the perils of big ice melts from the mountains that sometimes create powerful and hard-to-cross whitewater downstream. Then he advises me not to get overly ambitious and camp on the mountain with Maya.

"It's going to be cold up there at that time of year, especially at night. Torneträsk will probably still be covered with ice," he says of the 550-foot-deep body of water that is a remnant of an ancient glacier and one of the longest lakes in Sweden.

At least we won't need to worry about mosquitoes. At the start of June, when we'll be going, it still won't be warm enough in Lapland for them to flourish.

The trip will effectively cap our time in Sweden; the day after Maya and I return from Lapland we'll fly back to the US. But we still have a few weeks and some loose ends to tie up before we leave for our trip. First up are parent-teacher conferences for both girls. Or, rather, parent-teacher-student conferences, because in Sweden the child is an active part of these conversations.

As we walk into her classroom, Maya is hyper and bubbly, so different from the shy, apprehensive, and quiet girl who started at the school just five months ago, although it feels like a lifetime. Her teacher, Suzanne, starts out by asking her questions about school, what she likes, what she thinks she is good at, how she perceives the adults at the school, who she plays with, and how she feels about coming to school. She even asks her what she thinks of the school lunches.

"Our students' well-being is so important," Suzanne explains. "We want them to feel good about coming here and being here, because if they don't, nothing else is going to work either. It's so important to play and have friends and enjoy school."

Swedish students don't get any letter grades until sixth grade, but the teachers do record their progress and whether they are below, at, or above the requirements for their grade level, as specified in the national curriculum. Eventually, Suzanne hands over a piece of paper with Maya's report card; she's at grade level in all subjects, and above level in English and—of all things—Swedish. But the most important progress has probably come in areas that are not easily objectively measured.

"In the beginning I could tell that you were very quiet," she says, and turns to Maya, "but I think you've come a really long way when it comes to standing up and talking in front of the class. I can tell that you feel safe here, and when that's the case, it's natural to become more assertive."

Later that same week, it's Nora's turn. She, too, gets to participate in part of her parent-teacher conference, and is asked to share what she likes at the preschool and whether there's anything that she misses about the US. First, though, Ellen, the preschool teacher, dives into a set of questions that the teachers use to evaluate the children. How does Nora show interest in collaborating with others? How does she show consideration for others? How does she express her thoughts and opinions? She tells me that Nora seems happy at preschool and always finds something to do, often with friends like Kerstin, but also by herself. She likes to do crafts, draw, weave, play in the sandbox, and sculpt with play-dough. Ellen commends her motor skills and her command of the Swedish language and says that she's creative and imaginative. Ellen is not interested in whether Nora can count to ten, twenty, or a hundred, but we talk at length about how she's showing interest in math.

Ellen tells me that a few weeks ago Barbro, the other preschool teacher, had worked with some of the children on that topic. She had brought out a tray with some random items: a butterfly, a roll of tape, a brush, a troll doll, and some things from the toy kitchen. The children were then tasked with pairing two of the items and explaining why they thought they belonged together. Nora was first up, and she picked the butterfly and the troll.

"At first Barbro was surprised and didn't understand why Nora made that association," Ellen said. "But then Nora explained that they both belong in nature. We thought that was a really clever answer."

If previously I had thought of preschool math as being "one plus one is two," Nora's teachers showed me that it can be a lot more.

A few weeks before we are to leave for Lapland, I pull up in front of the preschool and park the car. The children are all outside as usual, some of them racing each other on trikes back and forth on the paved path that goes through the yard, others building castles in the sand play area. As I've been doing lately, I stay in the car for a moment and observe the scene from a distance. It takes me a while to spot Nora, but then I see her, on a red trike. She's wearing jeans that are worn thin over the knees, a red T-shirt, and her pink *Frozen* baseball hat, and she's spinning fast in ever-smaller circles, obviously enjoying the thrill of speed and the small risk of tipping over. Her face is caked in sandbox dust and her jeans are covered with grass stains. She's only five years old, but she's gotten visibly taller over the past few months. Her baby belly is disappearing quickly and she's already asking to get her ears pierced. In three short months, she'll be starting kindergarten. All I can think of at this moment are all the lasts—the last days that she'll spend hours on end outside making mud pies, riding her trike, painting sticks, lounging in a tree. Of course I want her to grow up, but I can't help but wonder if, once we get back to the US, her childhood is going to slip away too fast.

As I walk up to the green metal gate and see her face light up in a big grin when she sees me, I fight back tears.

Goodbye, Shack

For nearly six months we had lived in a five-hundred-square-foot house with one shared bedroom and a tiny bathroom with four minutes' worth of hot water. My wardrobe made minimalism master Marie Kondo look like a hoarder, and the girls had survived with fewer toys than I ever could have imagined. Even more remarkably, they hadn't once told me they were bored. There had certainly been times when I missed our "old" life (sleeping in my own bedroom, with all lights turned off, now seemed like a luxury), but I'd also discovered a new kind of simplicity, and it was liberating.

During our last week, we pack up our lives in three suitcases and six carry-on backpacks and wheeler bags. Whatever is left goes in paper bags: three for recycling, two for items to donate, and two with leftover food for my mom. She would get the pepper plant that Nora planted at preschool in a cut-off juice carton as well.

Before we move out we go for one final walk through the nature preserve down the road. As usual when both girls are with me, we don't move fast. There are simply too many things that constantly require their full attention. A beetle dragging another beetle around. A fallen tree that's begging to get climbed. An ant trail crossing our path.

"Look, Nora! The ants are collaborating to get the food to the anthill!" Maya shouts as she takes a closer look. Nora, however, ignores her, as she's busy devouring a stand of wood sorrel, a kid favorite among wild edible plants. I'm taking it all in from a moss-clad stump, letting each passing moment warm me, along with the afternoon sun.

On our way back, near the Scout cabin, a small frog jumps across the trail. Like an expert hunter-gatherer, Maya effortlessly sweeps it up with one hand. The girls love on it for a few minutes; then I suggest that it's time to move on.

"We have to let it go, Nora," Maya tells her little sister in a serious tone. "It belongs here in the woods."

"But I really want to keep it as a pet," Nora says, disappointed and on the verge of tears.

"That's okay, Nora. Don't be sad. We can order another one from Facebook."

Nora is not completely clear on what Facebook is, nor does she know that, in fact, the social media site is typically not where one would go to purchase pet frogs, but none of that matters. She's comforted by her big sister's words and we're able to finish our walk, embraced by the evening sun and the knowledge that summer is upon us.

A few days later, it's time for Maya's school's commencement ceremony at the local church. The pews are decorated with purple lupines, and the program is full of hymns that lionize nature and summer, evoking images of flowering meadows, wild strawberries threaded on grass straws, and cows that have just been released for their summer grazing. Several of the songs are the same ones that I used to sing during my own commencement ceremonies, eons ago. One of them, "The Barefoot Song," is exactly what the title implies: a celebration of running around without socks and shoes. When it's time for the school's principal to give her traditional speech, this is also one of her main themes.

"You've been cooped up way too long, and your feet have been trapped in shoes," she says as she addresses the school's eighty-some students. "Now is the time to throw them off and walk around barefoot. Promise me that you will do that!"

Chances are she won't need to ask them twice.

After the ceremony we go to my mom's house to prepare for my and Maya's flight to Kiruna, Lapland, later that night. In my former life, before I had kids, I used to be organized. I used to plan ahead and make checklists. I'd been that rare (and, admittedly, somewhat annoying) breed that would even arrive early to parties. Now I sat here, a few hours before our flight, and wondered if I should cut the handle off my toothbrush, as some extreme adventurers are known to do to minimize weight, or ditch my deodorant to make room for Maya's favorite stuffed animal, a raggedy cat named Pelle, and still keep my backpack manageable for hiking. In the end, I do neither, instead choosing to leave behind my woolen long underwear and some other spare clothes for myself. Whether this is a wise decision or not remains to be seen.

I also pack my grandmother's favorite necklace, a simple silver chain with a heart pendant that she used to wear every day, which I've carefully tended since her death three years earlier. When she died, I'd wanted to spread some of her ashes in the mountains of Lapland, the place that she and Farfar had cherished and chosen to return to time after time, but was told by the funeral home that according to Swedish law it's not legal to split up the remains from a cremation. I decided instead to bury the necklace somewhere in Lapland—I would know the right place when I saw it—so that a part of Farmor would always remain in the mountains.

If we even make it there, that is. At six o'clock Friday evening, shortly after our first flight to Stockholm has taken off, negotiations over employment contracts between Scandinavian Airlines and the pilots' union break down and the pilots decide to call a strike. With this, most SAS flights, including the last leg of our trip, are canceled, leaving airports across the country crippled and teeming with frustrated travelers. After waiting in line for two hours to get help, all we have to show for it is a room for the night at a mediocre airport hotel, but no way of getting to Lapland in the near future. A sympathetic woman behind the SAS help desk books us on the first flight on Sunday but doesn't give me much hope that the strike will be over by then.

I swallow my disappointment, and after Maya falls asleep that night I fervently start searching for alternative ways of getting to our destination. All flights with other airlines are already booked up, but there's another way of getting there, one that my grandparents had always used—the night train. I'd initially opted against it to save time, but in light of the pilot strike, spending twenty-plus hours on a train seems like a bargain. The only seats available are in a car that allows pets, but at this point I don't care, as long as we get there.

Maya is not particularly upset over this turn of events—quite the opposite. To her, riding the train is much more exotic than flying, and the sleeping component only adds to the adventure. Each room in the sleeping car features six berths, and my hopes that we'll get one to ourselves are soon thwarted, as two female college students with big backpacks join us. Just before the train rolls out of the station, another young girl appears in the doorway. She's wearing hiking clothes and keeps her bangs, some of which are a faded blue color, tied up in a casual knot.

"I hope you're aware that pets are allowed here," she says slightly apprehensively before she lets her travel companion enter our suite. "This is Sandor." Sandor is an ocher-colored mix between a bull mastiff, a rottweiler, and a border collie, and he is approximately the size of a three-month-old calf. Nobody's exactly doing cartwheels at the thought of sleeping with this beast, but with his lovable demeanor, Sandor soon wins us over. His equally amicable mistress, Filippa, is fifteen years old and traveling up north by herself to go backpacking with friends. Since there's no Wi-Fi on the train and no screens to hide behind, everybody in the room actually talks to each other, and before too long Maya is teaching all three girls her favorite card game. "If I'd had Wi-Fi I would be on Snapchat right now," Filippa says. "This is much better."

The train takes us into ever more remote areas, eventually passing the Arctic Circle and chugging along northward. At two o'clock in the morning I wake up in my bottom bunk and immediately notice the soft light from the midnight sun filtering through the crack between the blackout curtain and the bottom of the window. Outside, an inaccessible world is passing by, pine tree by pine tree, bog by bog. If it hadn't been for the farting, overly affectionate canine panting down my neck, the moment would have been nothing short of magical.

The next morning, we finally reach our destination, Björkliden, population twenty-nine—of which twenty are retired, the lady who runs the town's only restaurant informs us. Aside from a group of Italian guest workers and a few older couples passing through in RVs, we seem to have the place to ourselves. The monumental silence is only broken a few times a day, when the heavy freight trains carrying precious iron ore from the mine in Kiruna roar through here on their way to a port on the Norwegian coast.

That night, we follow the characteristic cairns that mark the trails in the mountains and keep walking until we hit snow. Maya makes impromptu slides in some of the bigger snowfields. Even though it's cloudy and the midnight sun is elusive, we have a panoramic view over the lake and the famous pipe-shaped canyon in the distance. It's as if the scenery from my grandparents' slide projector had suddenly jumped out and come to life.

"Are you going to leave Farmor Anne-Marie's necklace here?" Maya asks as we reach another windswept peak and look out over a frothing stream that is crashing down from the mountains on our right.

"I don't know. What do you think?"

"I think you should keep it. Then you can carry a piece of her with you all the time. If you leave the necklace here, Farmor Anne-Marie will be all by herself."

"You know, that's true. I didn't think about that."

The following day we hike for seven miles in drizzling rain and arrive in another little town, Abisko, where I have booked a private room at a hostel. Although this is a bigger town, with a grocery store, approximately one hundred permanent residents, and at least seventy-five sled dogs, it's equally quiet. A sign on the hostel door notes that the reception is SOMETIMES OPEN, OTHERWISE CLOSED. Fortunately for us, we're greeted by Hassan, a thirty-year-old dogsled driver who doubles as the hostel's jack-of-all-trades. He shows us our room and the communal kitchen and bathroom and gives us a rundown of the procedures for the sauna, a staple in this part of the country.

"Just let me know if you have any questions," Hassan says, and gets ready to leave.

"What about our room key?"

Hassan smiles and shakes his head.

"There is none."

I stare at him, bewildered and pretty sure he's joking. He's not. However, he's visibly amused.

"We don't use keys here. Welcome to Lapland!"

Over the following three days, Maya and I get into a new rhythm—leaving for a hike in the morning, coming back for a nap in the afternoon, and then hiking some more in the late evening. We run into a sudden snowstorm on the top of a mountain and explore a camp built by the Sami, northern Scandinavia's seminomadic indigenous population who traditionally make a living raising reindeer. Twice, Hassan lets us have a private meet-and-greet with the sled dogs, who are resting all summer.

On our last day, Maya wants to hike all the way to the Lapporten canyon, a distance of at least fifteen miles out and back. I suspect that this is probably a little more than she can chew, but we have a go at it anyway. On the way out, she makes elaborate plans for the tree house she wants to build in the woods behind our house when we get back to the US.

"We'll need two bunk beds, one for me and Nora and one for when we have guests. And we need a TV and a kitchen to cook in, with white bags for trash and black bags for compost," she says, and adds, "We need a toilet too."

"Honey, this is starting to sound more like a fancy apartment than a tree house," I interject.

"So can we have a toilet?"

"No!"

"How about a port-a-potty?"

"No! You can have a hole in the ground. How about that?"

"Okay, that'll do."

After hiking for about four miles through a thick birch forest, we reach a clearing where a herd of reindeer are lingering on their way to new grazing grounds. As we eat our lunch on a flat rock, they raise their velvet antlers and watch curiously from a distance, wary but not scared. For a while we just sit there and take it all in, the semi-wild animals, the snowcapped, gently rolling mountains, the rugged meadows, the tiny, hardy wildflowers. I pull out the silver necklace from underneath my windbreaker and run the little heart back and forth on the chain, as I've been doing so many times in the past couple of weeks. Then I decide that it's time to let it go.

"This is for you," I tell Maya, and put the chain around her neck. "Thanks for coming with me to Lapland. You would've made Farmor Anne-Marie proud."

She fiddles with the silver heart and looks at me with an incredulous smile.

"Well, it's a good thing I came with you, so that I could save the necklace," she says assuredly.

"I know."

She is still wearing the necklace two days later as we're once again packing our bags, this time to fly back to the US.

My dad takes us to the airport in the old Saab, ironically while Jonas Blue's cover of "Fast Car" is playing on the radio. He looks healthy. The hollow face from last summer has filled out, and lazy days by the sea have given him a robust tan. Nobody would guess, just by looking at him, that he's just endured almost six months of preventive chemotherapy.

"See you on Skype" are his last words as we part ways and the girls and I head toward the security checkpoint.

We're going home.

9 TIPS FOR HIKING WITH YOUNG CHILDREN (WITHOUT GOING TOTALLY NUTS)

Hiking is often the first outdoor activity that people attempt after becoming parents, and with good reason. It doesn't require much equipment or planning, it's easy to do with a baby on your back, and it can often be done close to home. But once Baby has outgrown that carrier and you expect your young child to walk on his own, the situation changes. Although some kids are naturals and would gladly hike to the moon and back, others balk at the idea of walking more than a few hundred feet on their own. If your child belongs to the latter group, rest assured that there is hope. Start with these simple tips:

1. **Don't be in a hurry.** If you expect to power walk your way around the trail and make it back within a set time frame, your hike will surely turn into a miserable debacle. With a toddler, it may take you three hours to walk a mile, or it may take half an hour. But probably three, so be prepared.

2. **Start small.** If your child doesn't seem into the outdoorsy thing and you're not into carrying him around anymore, try shorter hikes more often instead of one really long one. That way, you have a greater chance of success, and in case of a meltdown, you're at least closer to the trailhead.

3. **Dress for the weather.** Clothing can make or break an outing. If your child has a different idea of what she should be wear-

ing (and typically, it will be considerably less than what you think is appropriate), don't fight it unless temperatures are dangerously low. Instead, bring extra clothes in a backpack so that you're prepared when your child starts to complain about having cold hands.

4. **Let your child be a leader.** Kids and dogs love to be ahead of the pack, so let them. Leading gives kids a sense of responsibility and will make them grow with the task; older children often enjoy reading maps too. If you have more than one child, have them take turns to avoid sibling power struggles.

5. **Find interesting things along the trail.** Where you may enjoy the view and the accomplishment of making it to the next mile marker, chances are your child is more interested in looking at an ant colony or playing with the pretty leaves on the ground. Pay attention to what piques your child's curiosity along the trail, and encourage it whenever you can.

6. **Choose kid-friendly trails.** Research in advance to find trails that have a lot of varying terrain that encourages adventure and imaginative play. Rock formations, ladders, fallen logs, bridges, and bodies of water are usually big hits with kids.

7. **Bring a picnic (and emergency snacks).** Food and the outdoors are like two peas in a pod. Stopping to eat breaks up the hike and gives everybody a chance to recharge their batteries. Reserve a special treat like hot chocolate to make hiking a special occasion in your child's mind. And be sure to pack some emergency snacks—if you occasionally have to resort to bribery to get back to the trailhead, nobody will judge you.

8. **Bring your furry friends.** If you have dogs, this is the time for them to make themselves useful. A game of fetch or hide-and-

seek with the dogs along the trail breaks up the walking for the kids, and the dogs love it too.

9. **Find your crew.** Hiking is much more fun—for kids and adults alike—when done with others. Groups like Hike It Baby get together to hike on a regular basis and have local chapters in many parts of the US. If there isn't a group in your area, why not start one?

Scandinavian Parenting Tip #7

There's no magic number of hours of screen time per day that works for everybody, so be sure to find the ideal level for your family. If you notice that electronic gadgets are stealing too much time from outdoor activities, active play with other children, or time spent doing things as a family, it's probably time to cut back. Creating screen-free zones in your home or establishing screen-free times of the day, as well as being mindful of your own electronic media use, can help.

Suggested reading: *Unplugged: 15 Steps to Disconnect from Technology and Reconnect with Nature, Yourself, Friends, and Family,* by Jason Runkel Sperling. Kindle Edition, 2016.

8

IT TAKES A VILLAGE

Nobody wants to be in the last generation
that remembers when it was considered normal
and expected for children to go outside and play. Nobody.
—RICHARD LOUV

It's midnight by the time we set foot in Indiana, but the June heat and humidity are as in-your-face as ever. As my husband pulls the car into our driveway I see a familiar display: hundreds, maybe even thousands, of lightning bugs bobbing up and down in straight columns over the grass behind our house. It's a recurring show I never get tired of watching.

Inside the house, it's as if no time at all has passed. The same Christmas cards and magnetic poetry are on the fridge, along with fast-food coupons that Maya and Nora had earned through their respective reading programs at school. In the girls' rooms, the rocks and shells that they had collected during various trips and vacations still sit in neat rows on their bookcases, along with a turtle shell, a raccoon skull, and a couple of jars full of shark teeth. Their stuffed animals are still arranged neatly on their beds.

Over the next couple of weeks, we gradually ease back into life in the US. For the girls, who are still on summer break, it's more or less a seamless transition. Meanwhile, I once again find myself reflecting over the differences in our lifestyle here versus in Sweden.

After spending six months living there after nearly fifteen years away, I realized that in some ways Scandinavia faces many of the same challenges as the US. Following a worldwide trend, more and more children are growing up in cities, where they are farther removed from nature. (Although, ironically, my friends in central Stockholm have access to bigger public green spaces within a ten-minute walk from their apartment than I have within a thirty-minute drive of our house in rural Indiana.) The Scandinavian tradition of risky play is still strong by American standards, but it's noticeably weaker than it was thirty years ago. Some schools no longer allow children to climb trees or have snowball fights, and due to regulations established by the European Union, safety surfaces around playground equipment are now a common sight. Simultaneously, a powerful trend known as "curling parenting," which seeks to make a child's life as smooth and free of adversity and emotional distress as possible, is competing with the tradition of fostering resilience. While young children still have a lot of time for unstructured play, the pressure is mounting on older children as some families almost seem to consider a busy schedule a fashion statement. Youth leaders are reporting that parents are putting more pressure on children in organized sports.

In education, a high PISA ranking has become somewhat of a holy grail in the Scandinavian countries, even though the test's many critics point out that it fails to measure students' creativity, imagination, and entrepreneurship, and is not a predictor of a country's future economic success. Some critics fear that the ever-increasing focus on the PISA rankings could hurt Scandinavia's educational tradition and lead to more high-stakes testing and, consequently, force educators to teach to the test. "Despite heavy skepticism from academics, PISA results have become a talisman, making headlines and sending low-scoring nations into a panic about falling standards," writes Carl Honoré in *Under Pressure: Rescuing Our Children from the Culture of*

Hyper-Parenting. In Denmark, he notes, "middling PISA scores have sparked fears that Danish schools place too much emphasis on the happiness of the pupils." Sure enough, in 2014 Denmark enacted a sweeping school reform designed to raise the country's PISA scores. The reform lengthened the school day and introduced mandatory "homework cafés" after school. Christine Antorini, Denmark's education secretary, said that the reform was inspired by China and other top PISA performers in Asia.

But one of the biggest challenges to connecting children with nature in Scandinavia today is probably their tendency to connect with digital devices instead. "The tradition of *friluftsliv* is still an important part of Scandinavian culture, but regardless of whether you live in Stockholm, Kyoto, Berlin, or Beijing, the problem is the same—children stay inside and play computer games, and they move around less," says Anders Szczepanski, director of the National Center for Outdoor Education at Linköping University.

In the US and in Scandinavia alike, it will take more than reminiscing over our own unplugged childhoods (cue images of drinking water straight out of the hose and building forts in the woods from sunup until sundown) to fix this one.

Rachel Carson, an American conservationist whose 1962 book *Silent Spring* inspired the start of the modern environmental movement, once wrote, "If a child is to keep alive his inborn sense of wonder, he needs the companionship of at least one adult who can share it, rediscovering with him the joy, excitement, and mystery of the world we live in." I agree with Carson, except for one thing. I don't think one adult is enough. If we want our children to fully engage in and draw the benefits from spending time in nature—and, just as importantly, if we think that them doing so is key to the future health of the planet—they need a village.

Scandinavia's advantage is that there is already a robust village in place to foster and protect children's connection with nature. I was lucky not only to have grown up right by a deep forest but also to be surrounded by people who all had their own way of connecting me with the natural world, whether they realized it or not. My dad, who would never call himself an outdoor enthusiast, taught me how to ski downhill and insisted on going camping every summer. My mom, who loved taking our dog for walks in the woods and always tinkered in her garden. My maternal grandparents, Mormor and Morfar, who had a small hobby farm where I would develop a lifelong love of rabbits and an equally deep fear of hissing geese. My paternal grandparents, Farmor and Farfar, who showed me that a simple cheese sandwich could taste like haute cuisine if only you ate it sitting on a blanket in the grass, listening to the bees humming in the distance. My community, where neighbors helped look out for each other's kids when we explored the woods and the town on our own. And yes, my preschool and elementary school teachers who took us to the forest and made us go outside for recess every day—rain, sleet, snow, or shine.

While we were in Sweden, the girls got a glimpse of that village as well. Not only were they surrounded by people who saw outdoor play and hands-on experiences in nature as a necessary part of a good childhood, but—thanks to *allemansrätten*—they experienced the meaning of playing in the woods as if it were their own, and both parks and wild places were plentiful, even in the big cities. At preschool, Nora played outside every day, regardless of the weather, and those of her classmates who didn't get out much at home were still able to forge a meaningful connection with nature through visits to the school forest and beyond. Maya was introduced to environmental education and got a taste of what it was like to get around on her own in a place where seeing unsupervised children on foot was still considered normal, and the cities were walkable and safe. Finally, keeping the nature connection alive at home was easy through the tradition of *friluftsliv*, a way of life that centers around exploring and enjoying nature.

In the US we need to build up our villages. While some states have a rich and strong outdoor culture comparable to Scandinavia's, others have a longer way to go. Even in states where the outdoors is a central part of life, children's access to nature often depends on the financial means and interest of the parents.

There are plenty of ideas for strengthening the connection between children and nature in the US, and as vast and diverse as this country is, we're more likely to see a patchwork of solutions than universal ones. Richard Louv, one of the most prominent visionaries for the children and nature movement in North America, thinks that embracing the "hybrid mind"—the result of marrying nature and technology, direct and digital experiences—will be key to this effort. The hybrid mind, he hypothesizes, will "increase our intelligence, creative thinking and productivity" and could lead to the creation of communities that aren't just sustainable but "nature-rich." In Louv's vision of a nature-rich community, schools reward teachers who get their students outside to learn on a regular basis, pediatricians prescribe outdoor exercise to combat obesity, and citizens, businesses, and local governments work together to increase green spaces and make neighborhoods more walkable.

For this to happen, and for the children-and-nature movement to prevail, he believes that the growing public awareness of the need for nature in children's lives must be paired with action at the individual, family, community, and government levels. "Government or large institutions alone cannot create a nature-rich civilization," he says. "A long-lived movement requires the rapid contagion of small actions taken daily by individuals, families, churches, schools, grandparents, and many others—actions encouraged by, but not dependent on, organizations, programs, public policies, and experts."

Louv is seeing many encouraging signs and calls 2015 a "banner year for the new nature movement." For example, he mentions that the controversial No Child Left Behind was replaced by the Every Student Succeeds Act, which, unlike NCLB, supports field studies and learning about the environment and conservation. Louv also notes that more physicians started prescribing nature time to get people outside and exercising, and that corporations and government agencies added millions of dollars in funding for initiatives that aim to connect children with nature. The same year, over 1.4 million people heeded outdoor retailer REI's call to #OptOutside on Black Friday instead of hitting the mall.

Forest schools, which were unheard-of when I moved to the US, and other nature-based education initiatives are starting to pop up not only where you would expect them to—in the outdoorsy Pacific Northwest—but in the rural Midwest and the South. Since Erin Kenny cofounded the US's first forest kindergarten in 2006, the number of nature-based preschools in North America grew to over two hundred by 2017, according to the Natural Start Alliance. That's still a long way from being available to everybody, and onerous government regulations, a litigious culture, and the fact that many new parents don't recognize the benefits of playing outside for hours on end remain major hurdles for the movement, in Kenny's opinion. Still, it's a move in the right direction. "There's definitely a backlash in this country against the intense academic expectations for three- and four-year-olds, and that's given rise to these forest programs," she says. "Many parents still feel pressured, but others are saying, 'This is not right; I can just feel it.'"

Several parts of the country have also seen a backlash against schools' poor recess policies and excessive use of high-stakes standardized testing. In Florida, parents picketed school district headquarters and lobbied the state government for their children's right to recess, and across the country the parents of nearly seven hundred thousand students chose to let them opt out of or boycott standardized tests in 2015, according to the advocacy group FairTest.

Meanwhile, dedicated educators are blazing a trail for nature-smart schools. In Vermont, public school teacher Eliza Minnucci started taking her kindergarten class to the forest all day every Monday, rain or shine. In Fort Worth, Texas, Eagle Mountain Elementary School was inspired by the Finnish model and tripled recess for kindergarten and first-grade students. Both teachers and parents immediately saw positive results. In Oregon, which has a long tradition of outdoor learning, lawmakers voted nearly unanimously to make a weeklong, overnight outdoor school available for every fifth- or sixth-grade student in the state. And south of Atlanta, at the Chattahoochee Hills Charter School, inspired by Louv's book *Last Child in the Woods*, 350 kindergarten through sixth-grade students from mostly low-income families learn outdoors for a third of the school day, which has so far resulted in fewer sick days and improved test scores. "Something magical happens when kids connect with nature. I think it allows them to think in a broader sense," the school's principal, Walter Buttler, told *CBS News*.

On the individual level, parents are fighting the fear of strangers that has crippled children's freedom to play outside by actively working to increase the social trust in their communities. In California, tech entrepreneur Mike Lanza wanted his three children to live in the same kind of play-friendly neighborhood in which he himself had grown up, and essentially created it by inviting the neighbor kids to his front yard. His book *Playborhood: Turn Your Neighborhood into a Place for Play* is helping others do the same thing.

Aimie Stilling, the American filmmaker, was so inspired after visiting the Danish junk playground Rainbow that she decided to create a miniature version for her daughter, Bella, in the family's backyard in Orlando, Florida. "I started to hang out in the front yard doing pop-up playground-type activities with loose parts to bait the neighborhood kids in. I left all kinds of crazy stuff for them to play with out on our front lawn, and that's when our kid tribe began," she says.

The friendships and the parents' trust grew, and eventually Aimie could transition the "tribe" to the backyard. Here, out of sight from the homeowners' association thanks to a green privacy screen, she gradually created a nature play area with trees, boulders, stumps, areas for digging, a mud kitchen, a water table, and an assortment of loose parts as well as some traditional playground equipment like swings, a zip line, and a geodesic climbing dome.

"When she turns nine, there will be saws, hammers, and nails," Aimie says. "By no means is our backyard a showpiece; it's an environment designed to meet the needs of our child, not our aesthetic. We've found that there is much more joy in watching the formation of a human."

Over the past year, I, too, had tried to think of ways that I could encourage outdoor play in my hometown in Indiana, and eventually I found some like-minded people. The summer before we left for Sweden, I had joined a community effort to revamp the old and deteriorating city playground where I often spent time with the girls after school. When we invited local children to design their dream playground, I was not surprised to see that what most of them wanted was a simple, timeless staple of childhood: a tree house. And so it was decided that the play-ground would have a tree-house theme. It will also be a place where children can get in touch with nature. In addition to traditional playground equipment like swings and slides, the final design features a sand and water play area, boulders to climb, a winding path through a butterfly garden featuring native plants, and a splash pad that is reminiscent of a creek bed. A new man-made mound that will double as a sledding hill will make the playground more appealing in the winter. Call us overly optimistic, but our hope is that if we build it, the kids will come.

It seems like the tide may finally be turning, not the least because more American parents seem to have noticed that their children don't play outside as they did, nor do they have the same freedom. And many of them are starting to recognize that it's a problem. I run into one of them at the local community pool one day, an acquaintance who has a young daughter. She works full-time and tells me that she's concerned about her daughter being too sedentary over the summer.

"Kids need to be outside and move around, not sit in front of a TV all day long. We didn't have cable when I was little; we were outside playing all the time," she laments. She proceeds to tell me about children whom she has encountered through her work as a speech-language pathologist, who have spent so much time watching TV that they lack the vocabulary and imagination to come up with a simple story. "You know, I saw this video on Facebook the other day. It was about these preschools in Europe where the kids are outside all day. I think they were called forest schools. Have you heard about them?"

I can't help but smile. I've known this mom for several years and never could have guessed that she was such a staunch fan of outdoor play.

"Yes, I have, actually. They do seem great, don't they?"

We spend many hours at the pool during that hot summer after we return from Sweden. But as one lazy day after the other rolls by, I notice that, without their posse of Swedish friends, Maya and Nora are less likely to stay out and play for longer than half an hour by themselves. That means I'm inevitably back in the role of cheerleader-in-chief for outdoor play and activities. It seems to do the trick. Within a couple of weeks of our return, they have spent countless hours wrestling each other in the hammock in our backyard; accompanied me on several bike rides; climbed a few trees; caught and released at least three toads; gone hiking and waterskiing; camped out and grilled s'mores over an open fire; baked several mud pies; cared for, buried, and mourned a mouse that fell victim to our dog; and purposely touched poison ivy just to see if they were susceptible to it (they were). We even find a couple of public nature areas across the state line, in Illinois, where the girls can play in the water without facing repercussions.

Inspired by some of their Swedish friends, both girls recently stopped eating refined sugar. Maya now polices the grocery cart with zeal, giving me little choice but to quit too. I even give up my favorite breakfast cereal and surprise myself by finding a recipe for a paleo chocolate tart that doesn't taste like cardboard. Apart from the poison ivy (and the unfortunate death of the mouse, bless its heart), it's shaping up to be a good summer.

For my own peace of mind, and to make sure there are no gaps that we need to fill over the summer, I take the school up on its offer to screen Maya in English and math before she heads into third grade. After all, she used a different math curriculum and had virtually no English for a whole semester. As I had expected, she is right where she needs to be. Nora, meanwhile, missed kindergarten screening while we were in Sweden. When I ask if Nora needs to do it before registering for school, one of the administrators says, "Let's not worry about it; I'm sure she's just fine." It's a refreshing response.

Maya still loves her tablet, but after our time in Sweden it seems as if we've been able to keep a better balance and fight less over screen time. Maya's interest in nature and compassion for animals seems to be stronger than ever. After successfully reuniting a fledgling baby bird with its parents when it fell out of its nest, she tells me that her dream is to become a veterinarian specializing in rescuing wildlife. She is currently working on her second book, which in an unconventional twist mixes a manifesto against eating candy and a guide for caring for your pets and nature. If being a wildlife vet doesn't work out, I bet a writing career will.

Nora doesn't know what she wants to be yet, but I can tell that her experience with the Swedish Scouts has made an impression. She still wants an iPhone for Christmas, but it's no longer at the top of her list: a whittling knife is. While waiting for Santa, she spends some of her birthday money on a Swiss Army knife, which she uses to saw through wood for our campfire with impressive precision and grit for a five-year-old. A week after our return to the US following six months of attending a preschool with no formal academics, she declares that she wants to learn how to read and starts spelling out her first Swedish words on some cards from a board game. Soon, she starts writing new words as well. Every night, she makes me read the short farewell note that the staff at her Swedish preschool gave her on her last day, until she knows it by heart.

As for myself, I'm still trying to navigate this mysterious thing called parenthood. The range of feelings that I go through on a daily basis now make my volatile teen years seem like pure Zen in comparison. Exhilarating and exasperating, emotional and exhausting—sometimes all at once—parenting is like no other experience I've ever had. Throughout this crazy journey, the outdoors have helped keep me sane, and not only because I sometimes (okay, often) send the kids outside to play on their own when I want to cook dinner without refereeing sibling quibbles, or simply because I need a moment to myself, but also because we often go outside together. Experiencing nature with my daughters—whether hiking and camping or just planting flowers and digging for earthworms together in the backyard—has brought us closer in a way nothing else has. It hasn't always been easy, and some of our outdoor adventures still end with faked injuries (theirs), crushed expectations (mine), and tears (could go either way). But those are the exceptions. No matter how lousy a day starts out, we can almost always turn it around by going outside and enjoying nature together. I still throw out the phrase "There's no such thing as bad weather, only bad clothes" on a regular basis, fully aware that the girls at some point likely will come to find it extremely annoying. That's okay. One day, I hope they'll understand that I didn't just do it because I find it incredibly catchy, but because I know how valuable spending time outdoors is to their physical and spiritual health and well-being. It's therapeutic to me too. I would go as far as calling it a primal need.

What will happen once summer is over and school is back in session? I don't know. With any luck, Nora will thrive in kindergarten, and Maya will be in high school before I hear "I hate school" again. Regardless, I believe that their experience abroad has affected them profoundly in more than one way. When they get older, maybe even have kids of their own, and they start reflecting on the places that made their childhoods special, I'm pretty sure a few of them will be in Sweden. Maybe they'll even carry these places in their hearts for the rest of their lives.

A few years ago, we sold our home in town and built a house

on a quiet hill with some acreage in the country. The very first evening that we spent in the new house, a herd of deer quietly made its way through the backyard as a pink sun was setting over the frost-covered stubble in the adjacent cornfields. I remember thinking to myself that this was a place I could call home.

After we moved, my walks around town became more and more uncommon. Getting both the kids, a good-size jogging stroller, and Barney and Ralphie, our black Labs, into my vehicle wasn't even possible. Instead, we mostly stayed on the country roads that meander through the area or explored the lush woods and open meadows behind our house, where a motley repertoire of wildlife—deer, coyotes, turtles, snakes, wild turkeys, vultures, rabbits, toads, owls, raccoons, possums—have continued to grace us with their presence.

More than a few people noticed that my curious entourage and I somehow had gone missing from the cityscape. But every once in a while, they can still catch a glimpse of us. Not too long ago, on an overcast but comfortable day, the girls and I put on our boots and rain gear and ventured into town for a walk. It had been storming off and on for days and we desperately needed to get out of the house, breathe the damp air, and watch the birds in the sky without the silencing filter of a window.

Barney and Ralphie had died a while ago, but Elsa—a decidedly worse-behaved yet somehow lovable hound mix that we ended up rescuing from a shelter when the house became too quiet—came with us. As we walked down tranquil, tree-lined streets with names reminiscent of American history—Washington, Jefferson, Harrison—a gentle rain started to fall. As it picked up strength, I stopped to zip up my jacket and tighten the girls' hoods. Suddenly, a woman stuck out her head from a small white house with a covered porch on our left. She was in her fifties or sixties, and she was looking our way.

"Would you like to get out of the rain, hon?" the woman shouted. "You can come onto my porch and wait it out here if you want."

"We're fine. We've got our rain gear on. Thank you, though!" I shouted back.

"Are you sure? That rain is really coming down."

"I'm positive."

Scandinavian Parenting Tip #8
Help build a village of support for outdoor play in your child's life by seeking out like-minded people—for example, by joining a local hiking group for parents with young children or by starting a nature-based homeschooling co-op. If homeschooling or forest schooling aren't an option, find ways to encourage your child's day care, preschool, or school to find more time for outdoor play and learning.

Suggested reading: *Vitamin N: The Essential Guide to a Nature-Rich Life*, by Richard Louv. Algonquin Books, 2016.

A SCANDINAVIAN MOTHER'S "GET UP AND GO OUTSIDE" MANIFESTO

1. There is no such thing as bad weather, only bad clothes.
One of the most useful semi-true parenting sayings to ever come out of Scandinavia, on par with "Fruit is candy." Use it liberally to get the kids used to playing outdoors in all kinds of weather* from an early age. (*Not to be taken too literally, of course! Thunderstorms, tornadoes, hurricanes, flash floods, life-threatening temperatures, or other types of crazy weather conditions are perfectly valid reasons for staying inside.)

2. Dress for the weather.
A must if you actually decide to enforce #1. If it rains, the kids wear rain gear. If it snows, they wear snowsuits. Pair with appropriate footwear, hat, and waterproof mittens. It's not rocket science.

3. Fresh air is good for you.
Yup, our parents were right when they told us that getting fresh air every day was good for us. Spending more time outside can reduce the risk for common infections, nearsightedness, vitamin D deficiency, and obesity, as well as lessen symptoms of ADHD, anxiety, and depression. Tip: It works wonders for adults too.

4. Just let them play.

No employer in his right mind will care if your child started reading at age four or seven. Let your preschooler bake mud pies and worry about academics later. Unstructured outdoor play has everything kids need for healthy physical, social, and cognitive development in the early years. Older kids need time to play too; busiest extracurricular schedule by third grade does NOT win.

5. A little dirt won't hurt.

Our modern indoor lifestyle has made kids too clean and likely triggered an epidemic of immunological disorders. To bring some beneficial germs back into your child's life, ditch that hand sanitizer and let him sink his hands deep down in dirt. Bonus points for not freaking out if Junior also happens to stick those dirty hands in his mouth.

6. Freedom with responsibility.

Kids need risky play to learn how to assess risk and prepare for adulthood. That doesn't mean they need to be juggling chain saws, just allowed to engage in some old-school outdoor fun like climbing trees, sliding on frozen puddles, using real tools, and walking to the park without an adult. If our parents could handle it, we can too.

7. Unplug to connect.

The internet is fantastic, and not only because it's full of funny cat videos and opportunities to play World of Warcraft with strangers. But if we want our kids to keep a foot in the natural world, we need to pry them away from their screens sometimes and do things outdoors as a family. Challenge yourself by leaving your own smartphone at home, or at least putting it in airplane mode.

8. It takes a village.
As a parent, being your child's only cheerleader for outdoor play can get old. Find some like-minded people and figure out how you can get kids back outside in your community, whether by starting a family nature club, protesting your school's no-recess policy, or fighting overzealous homeowners' association rules.

9. We are one with nature.
Children and nature make a really good fit. By immersing kids in the natural world early, we're increasing the chances of them wanting to take care of it later in life. With a little luck, they'll do a better job than their parents and grandparents.

ACKNOWLEDGMENTS

First of all, I would like to thank my agent, Brandi Bowles of Foundry Literary + Media, who saw the potential in my book and enthusiastically took me on as her client after Mollie Glick, who originally signed me, moved on to a new job. I'm also profoundly indebted to my editors at Touchstone/Simon & Schuster: Michelle Howry, who shepherded me through the first chapters, and Meredith Vilarello, who expertly helped me across the finish line. Without your unwavering support, encouragement, and thoughtful input, this book wouldn't be what it is today.

In addition, I feel extremely privileged to have had David Ebershoff Jr. as my mentor and personal cheerleader from the time I got the idea for this book until it sold. Your advice about the publishing industry as well as your edits of my book proposal were spot-on.

I'm incredibly grateful to my Swedish friends—new and old—and their families, who let me delve into their lives and ask all sorts of personal questions in my search for the heart and soul of the Scandinavian parenting tradition. You know who you are.

Thank you also to the wonderful residents of Äspered and the staff at the school for welcoming me into the community and sharing your thoughts on parenting and education in Sweden.

The same goes for the staff at Nora's preschool, who offered me valuable insights into early childhood education in Sweden. Thanks to you, Nora had the chance to spend her days baking mud pies while I was writing.

I'm indebted to my dedicated and fantastic test readers: Bob and Alinda Dickinson, Kay Hunter, Heather Dent, Linda Gustafsson, Amanda Strawser, and Vanessa Shaw, who gave me valuable feedback in various phases of this project, and Sue White and Jennifer Campbell, who meticulously critiqued the entire book. You all rock.

I would like to thank my mom, Margareta Åkeson, for passing on to me her profound love for this earth. I only wish I would have gotten a sliver of your green thumb as well. My sister, Susanne Lund, has supported me throughout the writing process and believed in this book long before I did so myself. Both of you, and your unwavering idealism, have inspired me beyond words. I'm equally grateful to my dad, Kjell Åkeson, for instilling in me his stellar work ethic and for advising me to follow my heart and pursue a career that I was passionate about. I did, and I have never looked back.

A profound thank-you also goes out to Kyle for letting me take our daughters to Sweden for nearly six months; I appreciate the sacrifices you had to make during the writing of this book.

Lastly, words cannot express the gratitude and love that I feel for my daughters, Maya and Nora. You are the reason why I embarked on this journey, and you continue to inspire me on a daily basis. May you never stop catching caterpillars and collecting random rocks in your pockets.

REFERENCES

Introduction

Juster, F. Thomas, Hiromi Ono, and Frank P. Stafford. "Changing Times of American Youth: 1981–2003." Research report, Institute for Social Research, University of Michigan, November 2004. http://ns.umich.edu/Releases/2004/Nov04/teen_time_report.pdf.

Tandon, Pooja S., Chuan Zhou, and Dimitri A. Christakis. "Frequency of Parent-Supervised Outdoor Play of US Preschool-Aged Children." *Archives of Pediatrics & Adolescent Medicine* 166, no. 8 (August 2012): 707–12. http://archpedi.jamanetwork.com/article.aspx?articleid=1149487.

Gomez, Jorge E., and Claire LeBlanc. "Active Healthy Living: Prevention of Childhood Obesity Through Increased Physical Activity." *Pediatrics* 117, no. 5 (May 2006): 7. http://pediatrics.aappublications.org/content/pediatrics/117/5/1834.full.pdf.

The Nature Conservancy. "Kids These Days. Why Is America's Youth Staying Indoors?" Accessed August 9, 2016. http://www.nature.org/newsfeatures/kids-in-nature/kids-in-nature-poll.xml.

Clements, Rhonda. "An Investigation of the Status of Outdoor Play." *Contemporary Issues in Early Childhood* 5, no. 1 (2004): 68–80.

http://www.imaginationplayground.com/images/content/2/9/2960/An-investigation-Of-The-Status-Of-Outdoor-Play.pdf.

Grossman, Samantha. "More Cities Are Banning Sledding Because Why Should We Get to Keep the One Good Thing About Winter."*Time*. January 5, 2015. http://time.com/3654671/us-cities-ban-sledding.

Zito, Julie M., et al. "A Three-Country Comparison of Psychotropic Medication Prevalence in Youth." *Child and Adolescent Psychiatry and Mental Health* 2, no. 26 (2008). doi:10.1186/1753-2000-2-26.

Chapter One

Pettersson, Ola. "Kaffechock efter nyår." *Aftonbladet*. December 22, 2007. http://www.aftonbladet.se/nyheter/article11315329.ab.

Gelter, Hans. "The Scandinavian Philosophy of Outdoor Life." *Canadian Journal of Environmental Education* 5 (2000): 77–90. http://www.natureandforesttherapy.org/uploads/8/1/4/4/8144400/friluftsliv_scandanavian_philosophy_of_outdoor_life.pdf.

Kronans Droghandel. "Tips för att hålla barnen friskare." Accessed April 9, 2013 (no longer available as of April 1, 2017). http://www.kronansdroghandel.se/Radgivning/barnklubb/Artiklar-oversikt/Aldre/Tips-for-att-halla-barnen-friskare.

Sobel, David. *Beyond Ecophobia: Reclaiming the Heart in Nature Education*. Great Barrington, MA: The Orion Society and The Myrin Institute, 2009.

af Sandeberg Andén, Jane. "Naturen tar över rollen som vår nya religion." *Svenska Dagbladet*. July 17, 2005. http://www.svd.se/nyheter/idagsidan/existentiellt/naturen-tar-over-rollen-som-var-nya-religion_439723.svd.

Uddenberg, Nils. *Det stora sammanhanget: Moderna svenskars syn på människans plats i naturen*. Nora, Sweden: Bokförlaget Nya Doxa, 1995.

Chawla, Louise. "Learning to Love the Natural World Enough to Protect It." *Barn* (Norsk senter for barneforskning), no. 2 (2006): 57–78. https://www.ntnu.no/documents/10458/19133135/Chawla1.pdf.

UNICEF. "A League Table of Child Deaths by Injury in Rich Nations." *Innocenti Report Card*, no. 2 (February 2001). https://www.unicef-irc.org/publications/pdf/repcard2e.pdf.

Nylander, Johan. "Sweden Among the Best Countries to Be Born." *The Swedish Wire.* January 15, 2013. http://www.swedishwire.com/politics/15856-sweden-among-best-countries-to-be-born.

The Swedish Wire. "Sweden's Mortality Rates World's Second Lowest." Accessed January 17, 2013. http://www.swedishwire.com/jobs/4256-swedens-mortality-rates-worlds-second-lowest.

Nordström, Åsa, and Barbro Dunér. "De flesta barn i förskola—oavsett bakgrund." Statistics Sweden. Accessed August 28, 2015. http://www.scb.se/sv_/Hitta-statistik/Artiklar/De-flesta-barn-i-forskola--oavsett-bakgrund.

Paguette, Danielle. "The Shocking Number of New Moms Who Return to Work Two Weeks After Childbirth." *Washington Post.* August 19, 2015. http://www.washingtonpost.com/news/wonkblog/wp/2015/08/19/the-shocking-number-of-new-moms-who-return-to-work-two-weeks-after-childbirth/?tid=sm_fb.

The Warsaw Voice. "Scandinavia: Excelling in Environmental Protection." October 27, 2011. http://www.warsawvoice.pl/WVpage/pages/article.php/24105/article.

Fredén, Jonas. "The Swedish Recycling Revolution." Sweden.se. Last modified March 29, 2017. https://sweden.se/nature/the-swedish-recycling-revolution.

Centers for Disease Control and Prevention. "Healthy Schools: Childhood Obesity Facts." Last modified January 25, 2017. http://www.cdc.gov/healthyyouth/obesity/facts.htm.

REFERENCES

US Department of Health and Human Services. "Physical Activity Guide for Americans." March 1, 2011. http://health.gov/paguidelines/blog/post/Playing-Outside-Could-Lead-to-Healthier-Children.aspx.

Dunckley, Victoria L. "Nature's Rx: Green-Time's Effects on ADHD." *Psychology Today*. June 20, 2013. https://www.psychologytoday.com/blog/mental-wealth/201306/natures-rx-green-times-effects-adhd.

Jarrett, Olga S. "A Research-Based Case for Recess." US Play Coalition. November 2013. http://www.playworks.org/sites/default/files/US-play-coalition_Research-based-case-for-recess.pdf.

World Health Organization. "Childhood Overweight and Obesity." Global Strategy on Diet, Physical Activity and Health. Accessed January 18, 2013. http://www.who.int/dietphysicalactivity/childhood/en.

Olds, T., et al. "Evidence That the Prevalence of Childhood Overweight Is Plateauing: Data from Nine Countries." *International Journal of Pediatric Obesity* 6 (2011): 342–360. doi: 10.3109/17477166.2011.605895.

Centers for Disease Control and Prevention. "Attention-Deficit/Hyperactivity Disorder (ADHD): Data and Statistics." Accessed November 23, 2014. http://www.cdc.gov/ncbddd/adhd/data.html.

Vårdguiden 1177. "ADHD." Accessed November 23, 2014. http://www.1177.se/Fakta-och-rad/Sjukdomar/Adhd.

Gíslason, Ingólfur V., and Guðný Björk Eydal, eds. *Föräldraledighet, omsorgspolitik och jämställdhet i Norden*. Copenhagen, Denmark: Nordic Council of Ministers, 2010.

Blumberg, Stephen J. "Trends in the Prevalence of Developmental Disabilities in US Children, 1997–2008." Centers for Disease Control and Prevention. *Pediatrics* 127 (June 2011):1034–42. https://www.cdc.gov/nchs/ppt/nchs2012/ss-22_blumberg.pdf.

Vitale, S., R. D. Sperduto, and F. L. Ferris 3rd. "Increased Prevalence of Myopia in the United States between 1971–1972 and 1999–2004." *Archives of Ophthalmology* 127, no. 12 (December 2009):1632–39. doi:10.1001/archophthalmol.2009.303.

Sveriges regering. "Statens stöd till friluftsliv och främjandeorganisationer." Ds 1999:78, January 1, 1999. Last modified May 2, 2015. http://www.regeringen.se/contentassets/6753 bc911e6e4cbfbfdeae3d59973aa2/statens-stod-till-friluftsliv -och-framjandeorganisationer.

The Nature Conservancy. "Indiana: Portland Arch." Accessed April 8, 2017. http://www.nature.org/ourinitiatives/regions /northamerica/unitedstates/indiana/placesweprotect/port land-arch-1.xml.

Louv, Richard. *Last Child in the Woods: Saving Our Children from Nature-Deficit Disorder*. Chapel Hill, NC: Algonquin Books, 2005.

Chapter Two

Swedish Forest Agency. "Sverige är ett skogsland." Accessed August 2, 2016. http://www.skogsstyrelsen.se/Upptack-skog en/Skog-i-Sverige/Fakta-om-skogen.

Ek, Bengt. "87 Miljarder Träd i Sverige." *Skogen*. June 8, 2009. http://skogsvardsforbundet.se/nyheter/87-miljarder-trad-i -sverige.

Nordlund, Christer. "Det naturälskande folket i norr." *Biodiverse* 7, no. 4 (2002): 3. http://www.biodiverse.se/app/up loads/2011/08/02_4.pdf#page=3.

Mårtensson, Fredrika, et. al. *Den nyttiga utevistelsen? Forskningsperspektiv på naturkontaktens betydelse för barns hälsa och miljöengagemang*. Naturvårdsverket rapport 6497. Stockholm: Naturvårdsverket, 2011.

Stenmyr, Hanna. "Från nytta till nöje: Allemansrätten i den svenska skogen." Thesis project, Fakulteten för Landskapsplanering, trädgårds- och jordbruksvetenskap, SLU Alnarp, 2010. http://stud.epsilon.slu.se/1396/1/stenmyr_h_100617.pdf.

Isaksson, Ulla, and Erik Hjalmar Linder. *Elin Wägner—en biografi*. Stockholm: Albert Bonniers Förlag, 2003.

Dunn, P. M. "Arvo Ylppö (1887–1992): Pioneer of Finnish Pediatrics." *Archives of Disease in Childhood. Fetal and Neonatal Edition* 92, no. 3 (May 2007): F230–32. doi:0.1136 /adc.2005.077552.

Tourula, M., A. Isola, and J. Hassi. "Children Sleeping Outdoors in Winter: Parents' Experiences of a Culturally Bound Childcare Practice." *International Journal of Circumpolar Health* 67, nos. 2–3 (June 2008): 269–78.

The World Bank. "Mortality Rate, Under-5 (per 1,000 Live Births)." Accessed January 19, 2016. http://data.worldbank .org/indicator/SH.DYN.MORT.

Söderström, Margareta, and Margareta Blennow. "Barn på utedagis hade lägre sjukfrånvaro." *Läkartidningen* 95, no. 15 (1998): 1670–72. http://ltarkiv.lakartidningen.se/1998/temp /pda17437.pdf.

Socialstyrelsen. *Smitta i förskolan—En kunskapsöversikt*. Stockholm: Socialstyrelsen, 2008.

Adams, Christy, et al. "The Importance of Outdoor Play and Its Impact on Brain Development in Children." University of Missouri, Kansas City, n.d. Accessed October 3, 2016. http://education .umkc.edu/download/berkley/The-Importance-of-Outdoor-Play -and-Its-Impact-on-Brain-Develpoment-in-Children.pdf.

Marcano, Tony. "Toddler, Left Outside Restaurant, Is Returned to Her Mother." *New York Times*. May 14, 1997. http://www.ny times.com/1997/05/14/nyregion/toddler-left-outside-restau rant-is-returned-to-her-mother.html?ref=annettesorensen.

Rohde, David. "Court Ruling Favors 2 Who Left Baby Out-

side." *New York Times*. July 23, 1999. http://www.nytimes
.com/1999/07/23/nyregion/court-ruling-favors-2-who-left
-baby-outside.html?ref=annettesorensen.

Svensson, Olof. "Lämnade bebis utanför krogen." *Aftonbladet*.
August 16, 2011. http://www.aftonbladet.se/wendela/barn
/article13479425.ab.

Niederer, Iris, et al. "Relationship of Aerobic Fitness and Motor
Skills with Memory and Attention in Preschoolers (Balla-
beina): A Cross-Sectional and Longitudinal Study." *BMC
Pediatrics* 11, no. 34 (2011). doi:10.1186/1471-2431-11-34.

Roach, Linda. "Myopia Risk Lowered When Children Play Outdoors." *Medscape*. May 7, 2013. http://www.medscape.com
/viewarticle/803783.

Jarrett, Olga S. "Recess in Elementary School: What Does the
Research Say?" EricDigests.org. Accessed January 26, 2016.
http://www.ericdigests.org/2003-2/recess.html.

Dalporto, Deva. "Finland's A+ Schools." We Are Teachers.
April 1, 2013. http://www.weareteachers.com/blogs/post/2015
/04/01/finland-s-a-schools.

Chakrabarti, Reeta. "South Korea's Schools: Long Days, High
Results." *BBC News*. December 2, 2013. http://www.bbc
.com/news/education-25187993.

Harper, Justin. "Asia's Teachers Say Copying Their School Hours
Won't Help Britain." *Telegraph*. May 21, 2013. http://www.tele
graph.co.uk/education/expateducation/10064798/Asias-teach
ers-say-copying-their-school-hours-wont-help-Britain.html.

NBC Nightly News with Brian Williams. "How Shanghai's Students Stunned the World." NBCNews.com. Last modified
November 2, 2011. http://www.nbcnews.com/id/44642475
/ns/nbc_nightly_news_with_brian_williams/t/how-shang
hais-students-stunned-world/#.V5icRDWgw-Y.

Tran, Irene, B. Ruth Clark, and Susan B. Racette. "Physical Activity During Recess Outdoors and Indoors Among Urban Public School Students, St. Louis, Missouri, 2010–2011." *Preventing Chronic Disease* 10 (November 2013). http://dx.doi.org/10.5888/pcd10.130135.

Lowen, Rebecca. "What Works for Kids? In Norway, It's a Less-Stressful Classroom Atmosphere." *StarTribune* (Minneapolis). November 7, 2013. http://www.startribune.com/in-norway-it-s-a-less-stressful-classroom-atmosphere/231064001.

Centers for Disease Control and Prevention. "Attention Deficit/Hyperactivity Disorder (ADHD): Data & Statistics." Accessed February 3, 2016. http://www.cdc.gov/ncbddd/adhd/data.html.

Eunjung Cha, Ariana. "CDC Warns That Americans May Be Overmedicating Youngest Children with ADHD." *Washington Post*. May 3, 2016. https://www.washingtonpost.com/news/to-your-health/wp/2016/05/03/cdc-warns-that-americans-may-be-overmedicating-two-to-five-year-olds-with-adhd.

Jakobsen, Hanne. "Girls Are Given Less ADHD Medication." *ScienceNordic*. September 11, 2012. http://sciencenordic.com/girls-are-given-less-adhd-medication.

Chapter Three

Skolverket. *Curriculum for the Preschool Lpfö 98. Revised 2010.* Stockholm: Skolverket, 2010. http://www.skolverket.se/publikationer?id=2704.

Skolverket. *Föräldrars val och inställning till förskola och fritidshem. Resultat från föräldraundersökningen 2012.* Stockholm: Skolverket, 2012. http://www.skolverket.se/publikationer?id=3067.

Ricci, Colleen. "Looking to Swedish Model of Childcare and Education." *Sydney Morning Herald*. May 15, 2015. http://www.smh.com.au/national/education/looking-to-swedish-model-of-childcare-and-education-20150518-gh48hj.html.

Carlsson-Paige, Nancy, Geralyn Bywater McLaughlin, and Joan

Wolfsheimer Almon. "Reading Instruction in Kindergarten: Little to Gain and Much to Lose." Alliance for Childhood. 2015. http://www.allianceforchildhood.org/sites/allianceforchild hood.org/files/file/Reading_Instruction_in_Kindergarten.pdf.

Walker, Tim. "The Joyful, Illiterate Kindergartners of Finland." *Atlantic*. October 1, 2015. http://www.theatlantic.com/edu cation/archive/2015/10/the-joyful-illiterate-kindergartners -of-finland/408325.

Whitebread, David. "School Starting Age: The Evidence." University of Cambridge. September 24, 2013. http://www.cam .ac.uk/research/discussion/school-starting-age-the-evidence.

Miller, John W., and Michael C. McKenna. *World Literacy: How Countries Rank and Why It Matters*. New York: Routledge, 2016.

Flood, Alison. "Finland Ranked World's Most Literate Nation." *Guardian*. March 11, 2016. https://www.theguardian.com/books /2016/mar/11/finland-ranked-worlds-most-literate-nation.

Lärarnas Historia. "Förskolan." Accessed August 4, 2016. http:// www.lararnashistoria.se/sites/www.lararnashistoria.se/files /attachments/F%C3%B6rskolan.pdf.

Froebel Australia. "Friedrich Froebel: The Inventor of Kindergarten." Accessed August 4, 2016. https://www.froebel.com .au/about-froebel/friedrich-froebel.

Play & Playground Encyclopedia. "Friedrich Froebel." Accessed August 4, 2016. http://www.pgpedia.com/f/friedrich-froebel.

McLeod, Saul. "Jean Piaget." SimplyPsychology. 2009. Last modified 2015. Accessed August 4, 2016. http://www.simply psychology.org/piaget.html.

———. "Lev Vygotsky." SimplyPsychology. 2007. Last modified 2014. Accessed August 4, 2016. http://www.simplypsycho logy.org/vygotsky.html.

Gopnik, Alison. "Why Preschool Shouldn't Be Like School: New Research Shows That Teaching Kids More and More, at Ever-Younger Ages, May Backfire." *Slate*. March 16, 2011. http://www.slate.com/articles/double_x/doublex/2011/03/why_preschool_shouldnt_be_like_school.html.

Wilson, Ruth. *Nature and Young Children: Encouraging Creative Play and Learning in Natural Environments*. New York: Routledge, 2012.

Hanscom, Angela J. *Balanced and Barefoot: How Unrestricted Outdoor Play Makes for Strong, Confident, and Capable Children*. Oakland, CA: New Harbinger Publications, Inc., 2016.

Clements, Rhonda. "An Investigation of the Status of Outdoor Play." *Contemporary Issues in Early Childhood* 5, no. 1 (2004): 68–80. http://www.imaginationplayground.com/images/content/2/9/2960/An-investigation-Of-The-Status-Of-Outdoor-Play.pdf.

Park, Alice. "Baby Einsteins—Not So Smart After All." *Time*. August 6, 2007. http://content.time.com/time/health/article/0,8599,1650352,00.html.

Schwarz, Joel. "Baby DVDs, Videos May Hinder, Not Help, Infants' Language Development." *UW Today*. August 7, 2007. http://www.washington.edu/news/2007/08/07/baby-dvds-videos-may-hinder-not-help-infants-language-development.

Nelson, Toben F., et al. "Do Youth Sports Prevent Pediatric Obesity? A Systematic Review and Commentary." *Current Sports Medicine Reports* 10, no. 6 (November/December 2011): 360–70. doi:10.1249/JSR.0b013e318237bf74.

Jayanthi, Neeru. "To Protect Against Injuries, Young Athletes May Need to Play More Just for Fun." Loyola University Health System. January 11, 2013. http://www.stritch.luc.edu/radiology/newswire/news/protect-against-injuries-young-athletes-may-need-play-more-just-fun.

Dagens Nyheter. "Zlatan Ibrahimovics karriär." August 28, 2010. http://www.dn.se/sport/fotboll/zlatan-ibrahimovics-karriar.

Bergdahl, Linda. "När idrotten blir till stress." *Upsala Nya Tid-*

REFERENCES

ning. February 19, 2014. http://www.unt.se/barnochforal drar/nar-idrotten-blir-till-stress-2912335.aspx.

Barker, Jane E., et al. (2014) "Less-Structured Time in Children's Daily Lives Predicts Self-Directed Executive Functioning." *Frontiers in Psychology* 5, no. 593 (June 17, 2014). doi:10.3389 /fpsyg.2014.00593.

Juul, Jesper. "Är det sunt att ha långtråkigt?" Family-Lab. Accessed March 22, 2016. http://www.family-lab.se/ar_det _sunt_att_ha_laangtraakigt.asp.

Nielsen, Glen. *Children's Daily Physical Activity: Patterns and the Influence of Socio-cultural Factors*. Copenhagen, Denmark: Copenhagen University, 2011.

Fjørtoft, Ingunn. "Landscape as Playscape: The Effects of Natural Environments on Children's Play and Motor Development." *Children, Youth and Environments* 14, no. 2 (2004): 21–44. http://www.jstor.org/stable/10.7721/chiloutenvi.14.2 .0021.

Chapter Four

Tamanini, Jeremy. *The Global Green Economy Index*. Washington, DC: Dual Citizen LLC, 2014. http://dualcitizeninc .com/GGEI-Report2014.pdf.

Fredén, Jonas. "The Swedish Recycling Revolution." Sweden .se. Last modified March 29, 2017. https://sweden.se/nature /the-swedish-recycling-revolution.

Kihlberg, Jannike. "Efterfrågan på ekologisk mat ökar i rekordtakt." *Dagens Nyheter*. January 29, 2015. http://www.dn.se /ekonomi/efterfragan-pa-ekologisk-mat-okar-i-rekordtakt.

———. "Så mycket mer kostar det att äta ekologiskt." *Dagens Nyheter*. January 11, 2014. http://www.dn.se/nyheter/sverige /sa-mycket-mer-kostar-det-att-ata-ekologiskt.

Uddenberg, Nils. *Det stora sammanhanget: Moderna svenskars syn på människans plats i naturen*. Nora, Sweden: Bokförlaget Nya Doxa, 1995.

Nebelong, Helle. *Vi leger at . . . Tanker om leg, læring og indretning af legepladser og sansehaver for barn*. Denmark: Dafolo, 2008.

Sobel, David. *Beyond Ecophobia: Reclaiming the Heart in Nature Education*. Great Barrington, MA: The Orion Society and The Myrin Institute, 2009.

Skogen i Skolan. "Skolskogen." Accessed April 9, 2016. http://www.skogeniskolan.se/sites/skogeniskolan.se/files/files/pages/skolskogen_3.pdf.

TV4. "Sveriges Historia." September 19, 2011. http://www.tv4.se/sveriges-historia/artiklar/mer-om-carl-von-linne-4fc009d704bf72519400ae4d.

Nordin, Torgny. "Linné lever!" *Populär Historia*. May 25, 2001. http://www.popularhistoria.se/artiklar/linne-lever.

Bentsen, Peter. "Udeskole in Scandinavia: Teaching and Learning in Natural Places." Children and Nature Network. February 12, 2013. https://www.childrenandnature.org/2013/02/12/udeskole-in-scandinavia-teaching-learning-in-natural-places.

Takami, Sachiko. "Vad Mulleborg betyder för Japan." Mulleborg.se. Accessed April 14, 2016 (no longer available as of April 3, 2017). http://www.mulleborg.se/home/verksamheten/japan.

Dimensions Educational Research Foundation. *Helping Children Learn to Love the Earth Before We Ask Them to Save It: Developmentally Appropriate Nature Education for Young Children*. Lincoln, NE: Dimensions Educational Research Foundation, 2005. https://wf-media.s3.amazonaws.com/nature/pdf/lovetheearth.pdf.

Leave No Trace. "Seven Principles Overview." Accessed May 29, 2016. https://lnt.org/learn/seven-principles-overview.

SVT Nyheter. "25 år sedan Tjernobylolyckan—Konsekvenserna för Sverige." April 21, 2011. http://www.svt.se/nyheter/nyhetstec ken/25-ar-sedan-tjernobylolyckan-konsekvenserna-for-sverige.

Carrington, Damian. "Eating Less Meat Essential to Curb Climate Change, Says Report." *Guardian.* December 3, 2014. Accessed April 12, 2016. http://www.theguardian.com /environment/2014/dec/03/eating-less-meat-curb-climate -change.

Food and Agriculture Organization of the United Nations. *Food Wastage Footprint: Impacts on Natural Resources.* Food and Agriculture Organization of the United Nations, 2013. www .fao.org/docrep/018/i3347e/i3347e.pdf.

Borås Stad. "Minst 25 procent av alla livsmedel är ekologiska." March 9, 2016. http://miljobarometern.boras.se/boras-stads -miljomal-2013-2016/mal-3-boras-ar-en-matsmart-kommun /3a-minst-25-procent-av-alla-livsmedel-ar-ekologiska/info1.

Borås Stad. "Matsmart." Last modified May 9, 2014. http://www .boras.se/kategorisidor/barnochutbildning/barnochutbildning /grundskola/matsmart.4.22527a05135e0697a87800013629.html.

Grahn, Patrik, et al. *Ute på Dagis: hur använder barn daghems-gården? : utformningen av daghemsgården och dess betydelse för lek, motorik och koncentrationsförmåga.* Alnarp: Movium, 1997.

Chapter Five

Rousseau. Jean-Jacques. *Emile, or on Education.* Basic Books, 1979.

Granberg, Ann. *Små barns lek—en livsnödvändighet.* Stockholm: Liber AB, 2003.

Friluftsfrämjandet. "History." Accessed April 22, 2016. http:// www.friluftsframjandet.se/detta-gor-vi/om-oss/historia.

Hansell, Bengt. "Här börjar Estelle förskolan." Sveriges Radio. August 25, 2014. http://sverigesradio.se/sida/artikel.aspx?pro gramid=83&artikel=5946175.

REFERENCES

Andréasson, Ulf. "När Lort-Sverige började bada—en berättelse om badrummets historia." *Populär Historia*. December 22, 2009. http://www.popularhistoria.se/artiklar/nar-lort-sverige-borjade-bada-en-berattelse-om-badrummets-historia.

Världens Historia. *Historiens tips och trick för föräldrar*. Malmö, Sweden: Världens Historia, 2011. https://white-album.s3.amazonaws.com/files/HI_SV_10_2469_Boerneopdragelse.indd.

Phone Soap. "Fun Facts." Accessed July 1, 2016. https://www.phonesoap.com.

No-Mess Indoor Portable Sandbox. Accessed July 1, 2016. http://indoorsandbox.com.

HomeAdvisor. "Playground Germs: How Dirty Are They?" Accessed July 1, 2016. http://www.homeadvisor.com/r/playground-germs/#.V3aRNTWgw-Z.

ABC News. "Playing with Danger: Germy Playgrounds." September 6, 2007. http://abcnews.go.com/GMA/OnCall/story?id=3565507&page=1.

Carter, Maria. "Children's Playgrounds Dirtier Than Toilets, Study Shows." *Woman's Day*. June 22, 2016. http://www.womansday.com/health-fitness/a55398/childrens-playgrounds-are-dirtier-than-toilets.

American Academy of Allergy, Asthma and Immunology. "Asthma Statistics." Accessed April 24, 2016. http://www.aaaai.org/about-aaaai/newsroom/asthma-statistics.

Asthma and Allergy Foundation of America. "Allergy Facts and Figures." Accessed April 24, 2016. http://www.aafa.org/page/allergy-facts.aspx.

Williams, Emma. "Därför ökar allergier: 'För lite bakterier i kroppen.'" *SVT Nyheter*. April 27, 2015. http://www.svt.se/nyheter/vetenskap/darfor-okar-allergier-for-lite-bakterier-i-kroppen.

Velasquez-Manoff, Moises. "A Cure for the Allergy Epidemic?" *New York Times*. November 9, 2013. http://www.nytimes .com/2013/11/10/opinion/sunday/a-cure-for-the-allergy-epi demic.html?pagewanted=1&_r=1&hp&rref=opinion&adxn nlx=1384126206-OrsHwzr2j9Hijr6rg4Z%208g.

BBC News. "Scientists Sniffing Out the Western Allergy Epidemic." August 27, 2014. http://www.bbc.com/news/health -28934415.

Sachs, Naomi. "It's in the Dirt! Bacteria in Soil May Make Us Happier, Smarter." *Therapeutic Landscapes Network* (blog). Accessed April 26, 2016. http://www.healinglandscapes.org/blog/2011/01 /its-in-the-dirt-bacteria-in-soil-makes-us-happier-smarter.

Shetreat-Klein, Maya. *The Dirt Cure: Growing Healthy Kids with Food Straight from Soil.* New York: Simon & Schuster, 2016.

American Society for Microbiology. "Can Bacteria Make You Smarter?" *ScienceDaily.* May 25, 2010. www.sciencedaily.com /releases/2010/05/100524143416.htm.

Johansson, Sandra, and IdaMaria Åkerberg. *Är regn och rusk den bästa pedagogiken? En studie av den pedagogiska verksamheten i en I Ur och Skur.* Halmstad, Sweden: Sektionen för lärarutbildningen, Högskolan i Halmstad, 2011.

Dellsle, Ralna. "Why You Should Delay Baby's First Bath." *Today's Parent.* March 23, 2016. http://www.todaysparent.com /baby/why-you-should-delay-babys-first-bath.

HuffPost Parents. "Household Bleach Linked to 'Increased Risk of Flu, Tonsillitis and Infection' Among Children." March 4, 2015. http://www.huffingtonpost.co.uk/2015/04/03/bleach-expo sure-children-health-infection_n_6998454.html.

Chapter Six

McCarren, Andrea A. "Free-Range Parenting: Controversial Method Explained." *WUSA* 9. Accessed April 19, 2016. http://

legacy.wusa9.com/story/news/local/maryland/2015/01/30 /free-range/22571221.

St. George, Donna. "Md. Officials: Letting 'Free Range' Kids Walk or Play Alone Is Not Neglect." *Washington Post*. June 11, 2015. https://www.washingtonpost.com/local/education/state -seeks-to-clarify-views-about-young-children-walking-alone /2015/06/11/423ce72c-0b99-11e5-95fd-d580f1c5d44e_story .html.

Kim, Eun Kyung. "Maryland 'Free Range' Parents Cleared of Neglect, Still Plan to Sue CPS, Police." *Today*. June 22, 2015. http://www.today.com/parents/maryland-free-range-parents -cleared-neglect-t27901.

Skenazy, Lenore. *Free-Range Kids: How to Raise Safe, Self-Reliant Children (Without Going Nuts with Worry)*. San Francisco: Jossey-Bass, 2009.

Alexander, Jessica Joelle, and Iben Dissing Sandahl. *The Danish Way of Parenting: What the Happiest People in the World Know About Raising Confident, Capable Kids*. New York: TarcherPerigee, 2016.

Mårtensson, Fredrika. "Children on Foot. Urban Landscapes and Sustainable Everyday Mobility." Research paper. Institutionen för landskapsarkitektur, planering och förvaltning. SLU Alnarp, 2006. http://proj.formas.se/detail.asp?arendeid=15497.

Eberhard, David. "I trygghetens Sverige ska det ofarliga förbjudas." *Dagens Nyheter*. September 9, 2005. http://www.dn.se /debatt/i-trygghetens-sverige-ska-det-ofarliga-forbjudas.

Pew Research Center. *Americans and Social Trust: Who, Where and Why*. Washington, DC: Pew Research Center, 2010. http://www.pewsocialtrends.org/files/2010/10/SocialTrust .pdf.

Höjer, Henrik. "Sveriges unika tillit sjunker: Kan man lita på folk?" *Forskning och Framsteg*. September 4, 2014. http://

fof.se/tidning/2014/8/artikel/sveriges-unika-tillit-sjunker-kan
-man-lita-pa-folk.

Centers for Disease Control and Prevention. *Childhood Patterns of Unintentional Injuries among 0–19 Year Olds in the United States, 2000–2006*. Atlanta: Centers for Disease Control and Prevention, 2008. http://www.cdc.gov/safechild/pdf/cdc-childhoodinjury.pdf.

UNICEF. "A League Table of Child Deaths by Injury in Rich Nations." *Innocenti Report Card*, no. 2 (February 2001). https://www.unicef-irc.org/publications/pdf/repcard2e.pdf.

Radford, Ben. "Child Abductions by Strangers Very Rare." *Seeker*. May 14, 2013. https://www.seeker.com/child-abductions-by-strangers-very-rare-1767508216.html.

Skenazy, Lenore. "Poll: Most Americans Want to Criminalize Pre-Teens Playing Unsupervised." *Reason*. August 20, 2014. http://reason.com/archives/2014/08/20/helicopter-parenting-run-amok-most-ameri.

Asthana, Anushka. "Kids Need the Adventure of 'Risky' Play." *Guardian*. August 2, 2008. http://www.theguardian.com/education/2008/aug/03/schools.children.

Thomas, Ashley J., P. Kyle Stanford, and Barbara W. Sarnecka. "No Child Left Alone: Moral Judgments About Parents Affect Estimates of Risk to Children." *Collabra* 2, no. 1 (2016): 1–14. http://doi.org/10.1525/collabra.33.

Lombrozo, Tania. "Why Do We Judge Parents for Putting Kids at Perceived—but Unreal—Risk?" NPR. August 22, 2016. http://www.npr.org/sections/13.7/2016/08/22/490847797/why-do-we-judge-parents-for-putting-kids-at-perceived-but-unreal-risk.

Sandseter, E. B. H. "Characteristics of Risky Play." *Journal of Adventure Education and Outdoor Learning* 9, no. 1 (2009): 3–21. http://dx.doi.org/10.1080/14729670802702762.

Brussoni, Mariana, et al. "What Is the Relationship Between Risky Outdoor Play and Health in Children? A Systematic Review." *International Journal of Environmental Research and Public Health* 12, no. 6 (2015): 6423–54. https://www.ncbi.nlm.nih.gov/pmc/articles/PMC4483710.

Brussoni, Mariana. "Risky Play and Children's Safety: Balancing Priorities for Optimal Child Development." *International Journal of Environmental Research and Public Health* 9, no. 9 (2012): 3134–48. http://www.ncbi.nlm.nih.gov/pmc/articles/PMC3499858/#B43-ijerph-09-03134.

Gray, Peter. "Risky Play: Why Children Love It and Need It." *Psychology Today*. April 7, 2014. https://www.psychologytoday.com/blog/freedom-learn/201404/risky-play-why-children-love-it-and-need-it.

De Baca, Christine. "Resiliency and Academic Success." Accessed May 3, 2016. Literature review. Williamsburg: ScholarCentric, 2010. http://www.scholarcentric.com/wp-content/uploads/2014/03/SC_Resiliency_Academic_Performance_WP.pdf.

Fleur, Calle. "Så farlig är älgen." *Fokus*. March 24, 2010. http://www.fokus.se/2010/03/sa-farlig-ar-algen.

Quinn, Calder, and Brad Rickman. "Selfies vs. Shark Attacks: Which Are More Deadly for Travelers?" *Condé Nast Traveler*. February 10, 2016. http://www.cntraveler.com/stories/2015-09-15/selfies-vs-shark-attacks-which-is-more-deadly-for-travelers.

Chapter Seven

Ny Teknik. "Fortsatt boom för svenska dataspel." August 11, 2014. Accessed August 2, 2016. http://www.nyteknik.se/digitalisering/fortsatt-boom-for-svenska-dataspel-6398541.

Findahl, Olle, and Pamela Davidsson. *Svenskarna och internet: 2015 års undersökning av svenska folkets internetvanor.* Stock-

REFERENCES

holm: Internetstiftelsen i Sverige, 2015. https://www.iis.se /docs/Svenskarna_och_internet_2015.pdf.

Statens Medieråd. *Småungar & medier 2015—Fakta om små barns användning och upplevelser av medier.* Stockholm: Statens Medieråd, 2015. http://statensmedierad.se/download /18.7a953dba14fef1148cf3a0e/1442841273052/Sma-ungar -och-medier-2015.pdf.

Lagerkrantz, Hugo. "Mycket tid framför skärm splittrar barns liv." *Läkartidningen.* January 8, 2013. http://www.lakartidnin gen.se/Functions/OldArticleView.aspx?articleId=19078.

Dunkels, Elza. "Skärmtid är ett förlegat begrepp." *SVT Nyheter Opinion.* March 31, 2015. http://www.svt.se/opinion/arti cle2805177.svt.

Reddy, Sumathi. "Pediatricians Rethink Screen Time Policy for Children." *Wall Street Journal.* October 12, 2015. http:// www.wsj.com/articles/pediatricians-rethink-screen-time-pol icy-for-children-1444671636.

Bresnahan, Samantha, and Will Worley. "When Video Games Become an Addiction." CNN. January 6, 2016. http://edition .cnn.com/2016/01/06/health/video-games-addiction-gentile -feat.

Kuss, Daria J. "Internet Gaming Addiction: Current Perspectives." *Journal of Psychological Research and Behavior Management* 6 (2013): 125–37. http://www.ncbi.nlm.nih.gov/pmc /articles/PMC3832462.

Kaiser Family Foundation. *Generation M2: Media in the Lives of 8–18-Year-Olds: A Kaiser Family Foundation Study.* Menlo Park, CA: Kaiser Family Foundation, 2010. https://kaiserfam ilyfoundation.files.wordpress.com/2013/01/8010.pdf.

Bergström, Malin. "Digitala medier." Rikshandboken Barnhälsovård. March 11, 2016. http://www.rikshandboken-bhv .se/Texter/Barn-och-media/Digitala-medier.

REFERENCES

Statistic Brain. "Television Watching Statistics." Statistic Brain. Accessed April 10, 2017. http://www.statisticbrain.com/tele vision-watching-statistics.

McDonough, Patricia. "TV-Watching Among Kids At an Eight-Year High." Nielsen. October 26, 2009. http://www.nielsen .com/us/en/insights/news/2009/tv-viewing-among-kids-at -an-eight-year-high.html.

Medline Plus. "Screen Time and Children." Last modified April 21, 2015. https://www.nlm.nih.gov/medlineplus/ency/patient instructions/000355.htm.

Harrie, Eva. "TV-tittande i Norden 2014." Nordicom. February 9, 2015. http://www.nordicom.gu.se/sv/mediefakta/nyheter /tv-tittande-i-norden-2014.

Thomsen, Dante. "Så mycket ser svenskarna på tv." *Dagens Media.* September 13, 2011. http://www.dagensmedia.se /medier/rorligt/sa-mycket-ser-svenskarna-pa-tv-6161513.

MMS. *Månadsrapport.* Stockholm: MMS, 2013. http://mms .se/wp-content/uploads/_dokument/rapporter/tv-tittande /manad/2013/M%C3%A5nadsrapport_2013-02.pdf.

Ferguson, Chris. "Parents, Calm Down About Infant Screen Time." *Time.* February 3, 2015. http://time.com/3693883 /parents-calm-down-about-infant-screen-time.

Rooney, Ben. "Women And Children First: Technology And Moral Panic." *Tech Europe* (blog), *Wall Street Journal.* July 11, 2011. http://blogs.wsj.com/tech-europe/2011/07/11/women -and-children-first-technology-and-moral-panic.

Farmer, Ben. "Parents' Smartphones Harming Children's Ability to Hold Conversation, Say Teachers." *Guardian.* May 9, 2016. http://www.telegraph.co.uk/education/2016/05/09/parents -smartphones-harming-childrens-ability-to-hold-conversati.

Li, Qing. "Effect of Forest Bathing Trips on Human Immune Function." *Environmental Health and Preventive Medicine*

15, no. 1 (January 2009): 9–17. https://www.ncbi.nlm.nih
.gov/pmc/articles/PMC2793341.

Chapter Eight

Becher Trier, Maria. "Antorini: Reformen bør hæve danske Pisa-
resultater." Folkeskolen.dk. December 3, 2013. https://www
.folkeskolen.dk/537423/antorini-reformen-boer-haeve-dan
ske-pisa-resultater.

Steinfeld, Thomas. "Pisa urholkar skolan i tävlandets namn."
Svenska Dagbladet. June 2, 2014. http://www.svd.se/pisa
-urholkar-skolan-i-tavlandets-namn.

Sjøberg, Svein. "Är Pisa något att luta sig mot?" *Pedagogiska
magasinet.* September 24, 2014. http://www.lararnasny
heter.se/pedagogiska-magasinet/2014/09/24/ar-pisa-nagot
-luta-mot.

Natural Start Alliance. "Nature Preschools." Accessed July 16,
2016. http://naturalstart.org/nature-preschool.

Honoré, Carl. *Under Pressure: Rescuing Our Children from the
Culture of Hyper-Parenting.* New York: HarperOne, 2009.

REI. "Opt Outside." Accessed July 25, 2016. https://www.rei
.com/opt-outside.

FairTest. "More Than 670,000 Refused Tests in 2015." December 12, 2015. http://www.fairtest.org/more-500000-refused
-tests-2015.

Cherney, Elyssa. "Lake County Parents Protest to Get Recess
for Kids." *Orlando Sentinel.* September 24, 2014. http://
www.orlandosentinel.com/features/education/os-school-re
cess-protest-20140922-story.html.

Postal, Leslie. "Parents Keep Up Fight for Required Daily Recess." *Orlando Sentinel.* February 19, 2016. http://www
.orlandosentinel.com/features/education/os-recess-schools
-moms-florida-legislature-20160218-story.html.

Hanford, Emily. "Out of the Classroom and into the Woods." NPR. May 26, 2015. http://www.npr.org/sections/ed/2015/05/26/407762253/out-of-the-classroom-and-into-the-woods.

Connelly, Christopher. "Turns Out Monkey Bars and Kick Ball Might Be Good for the Brain." NPR. January 3, 2016. http://www.npr.org/sections/ed/2016/01/03/460254858/turns-out-monkey-bars-and-kickball-are-good-for-the-brain.

Mongeau, Lillian. "What if Every Kid Got to Go to Summer Camp . . . During the School Year?" *Hechinger Report*. August 6, 2016. http://hechingerreport.org/what-if-every-kid-got-to-go-to-summer-camp-during-the-school-year.

CBS News. "Georgia School Ensures Kids Connect with Nature—and Go Home Dirty." April 13, 2016. http://www.cbsnews.com/news/georgia-chattahoochee-hills-charter-school-focuses-learning-outdoors.

Lanza, Mike. *Playborhood: Turn Your Neighborhood into a Place for Play*. Menlo Park, CA: Free Play Press, 2012.

About the Author

Linda McGurk is a Swedish American freelance journalist, author, and blogger. A nature lover and mother of two daughters, she believes that the best childhood memories are created outside, while jumping in puddles, digging in dirt, catching bugs, and climbing trees. McGurk is a regular contributor to *Outdoor Families Magazine*, and her writings about natural parenting, outdoor play, and green living have appeared in a wide range of publications and online outlets, including *Green Child Magazine*, *Mother Nature Network*, *The Green Mama*, *Childhood 101*, *Preschool Inspirations*, and *Children & Nature Network*. In 2013, she started the blog *Rain or Shine Mamma* to inspire outdoor play and adventure every day, regardless of the weather. *There's No Such Thing as Bad Weather* is her first book. Visit her at www.LindaMcGurk.com and www.RainOrShineMamma.com.